Promoting Social Justice for Young Children

EDUCATING THE YOUNG CHILD

VOLUME 3

This academic and scholarly book series will focus on the education and development of young children from infancy through eight years of age. The series will provide a synthesis of current theory and research on trends, issues, controversies, and challenges in the early childhood field and examine implications for practice. One hallmark of the series will be comprehensive reviews of research on a variety of topics with particular relevance for early childhood educators worldwide. The mission of the series is to enrich and enlarge early childhood educators' knowledge, enhance their professional development, and reassert the importance of early childhood education to the international community. The audience for the series includes college students, teachers of young children, college and university faculty, and professionals from fields other than education who are unified by their commitment to the care and education of young children. In many ways, the proposed series is an outgrowth of the success of *Early Childhood Education Journal* which has grown from a quarterly magazine to a respected and international professional journal that is published six times a year.

Beatrice S. Fennimore • A. Lin Goodwin
Editors

Promoting Social Justice for Young Children

Advances in Theory and Research, Implications for Practice

Springer

Editors
Dr. Beatrice S. Fennimore
Indiana University of Pennsylvania
Indiana Pennsylvania
USA
bzfennim@iup.edu

Dr. A. Lin Goodwin
Columbia University
Teachers College
New York
USA
goodwin@tc.columbia.edu

ISBN 978-94-007-0569-2 e-ISBN 978-94-007-0570-8
DOI 10.1007/978-94-007-0570-8
Springer Dordrecht Heidelberg London New York

Library of Congress Control Number: 2011921326

Cover Design: eStudio Calamar S.L.

Printed on acid-free paper

Springer is part of Springer Science+Business Media (www.springer.com)

Dedicated to the memory of my parents George Henry Schneller and Marjorie Cooney Schneller.

B.S.F.

Dedicated to the memory of my maternal grandmother Huang Gwan Mei.

A.L.G.

Preface

In 2009, it was my great honor to be named an "Equity Champion" by the Educational Equity Center of the Academy for Educational Development. I recall, in preparing my remarks for the gathering to celebrate this award, that I struggled with the term "equity" as a way to describe the work that people do, because it needs to be done, to create a just society and enact social justice. What is equity? What is the meaning of this word? What does it mean to achieve equity? I frequently discuss this term with my husband Peter and with friends. Yet, I cannot fully describe it nor translate it into just one word, as we do in English, for my mother in Colombia. I always have to use examples and tell many stories about certain actions or decisions; I describe it as way of thinking, of feeling, and of behaving. But if that is the case, then how does one grow into or learn this way of thinking and behaving? How did I learn these feelings? Why am I—and most members of my immediate and adopted family, as well as my closest colleagues and friends—so intolerant of inequity and exclusion—and how did we get that way? In preparing this preface, I was brought again to reflect on these questions, to ponder again deeply the meaning of equity and social justice.

In terms of equity in education—I believe that it holds (or should hold) a special meaning for all of us in this profession. We are in the education profession because we all choose/chose to do this equity work in one form or another. For some of us, equity and social justice are about excellent education, maximum opportunity for the largest and most possibly diverse group of learners. It is about preparation for having choices in life, access to work, housing, health, or the right to vote. It is also about participation, representation, and inclusion in important decisions and endeavors. It is about gender, about physical and mental health, about religion or language, and about freedom to choose our partners and life styles. Ultimately, I define equity and social justice as the infusion of whatever it takes to make things right and to make things fair, at a given time, in a particular place, and for the greater good.

Still, I realize the shortcomings or limitations of language for describing what a community of compassionate people needs to know, be, and act upon to make, to do, the right thing. Yet, in this collection of wisdom and knowledge from colleagues who have dedicated their life's work to minding the children and all that surrounds them or affects them in education and social policy, there are many ways of articulating, envisioning, and enacting social justice. Readers will either personally connect or intellectually identify with some of the perspectives offered by these authors; all will definitely find scholarly angles and definitions they had not considered before as a part of what they need to know to advance a just society.

Each section of the book is a point of entry for individuals with different passions and expertise, but each point of entry calls for compassion. Compassion is the prerequisite and foundation for appreciating and finding one's place of action in one or more of the perspectives presented in this volume. Why is compassion a requirement? Because in the absence of compassion, it often becomes too easy to rationalize ways to avoid what must be done, to turn away, or expect solutions to come from others. Compassion motivates us to act. We know it when we feel it or summon it at a random moment. It may be contained within a brief moment of recognition that someone needs our help and we are moved to intercede just because it is the right thing to do. But for educators, compassion cannot simply be collections of random moments. Compassion needs to be built into our policies, programs, and assessments. Informed compassion will help us question punitive teaching and policies, recognize oppression, and, when something seems dangerous or harmful, compassion will compel us to try to step in and stop it. These I believe are the imperatives behind this book.

Its audience should be anyone who feels that the challenge of difficult times renders us powerless to make the just decisions that affect other people in general and vulnerable people in particular. Yet, we are not powerless but sometimes have difficulty finding our way to positive action. The voices in this book speak of positive action and of hopefulness. As a whole, the book exemplifies foundations of education and a demonstration of the complex ecologies that must be considered to best meet the needs, find the strengths, and act on behalf of children, families, and the caregivers and schools educating vulnerable children placed in our care.

New York City Dr. Maritza B. Macdonald

Contents

About the Contributors

Jessica Bacon Doctoral Student, Syracuse University. Jessica Bacon received her master's from the Department of Cultural Foundations of Education at Syracuse University with a concentration in disability studies. Her research interests include inclusive education, self-advocacy, transition, and post-secondary education for adults with developmental disabilities, and the effects of high stakes testing and accountability systems on special education.

Liv Thorstensson Davila Ph.D. Candidate, School of Education at the University of North Carolina at Chapel Hill. Liv Thorstensson Davila is former English as a Second Language (ESL) and French teacher in the United States, Sweden, and Brazil, where she has also worked as a teacher trainer. Her research interests include issues in immigration and education, and ESL and foreign language pedagogy.

Anne Haas Dyson Professor of Education, University of Illinois at Urbana-Champaign. Dr. Anne Haas Dyson is a former teacher of young children. She was previously on the faculty of the University of Georgia, Michigan State University, and the University of California, Berkeley, where she was a recipient of the campus Distinguished Teaching Award. Dr. Dyson has studied and published widely in the areas of childhood cultures and literacy learning of young school children. Her book *Social Worlds of Children Learning to Write in an Urban Primary School* was awarded the David Russell Award for Distinguished Research by the National Council of Teachers of English.

Yvonne De Gaetano Associate Professor of Education, School of Education at Hunter College. Dr. Yvonne De Gaetano is the coauthor of *ALERTA,* one of the earliest early childhood bilingual programs in the United States. She currently coordinates the programs in bilingual education and advanced certificate in bilingual education at Hunter College in New York City. Dr. De Gaetano has published widely in the areas of children's language development, teacher development, multicultural education, and cultural competency. Her research interests focus on cultural and language diversity, and social justice in the classroom.

Beatrice S. Fennimore Professor of Education, Indiana University of Pennsylvania. Dr. Beatrice S. Fennimore is a teacher educator who began her career teaching young children in New York City. She is the author of multiple books, chapters, and articles in the areas of social policy, equity in public schooling, child advocacy, social justice, urban education, and multicultural education. Dr. Fennimore's current research interests are in the areas of human rights and social justice as the foundations of teacher education in a democratic society. She has been an active participant in public school equity initiatives and has also served as an Adjunct Professor at Teachers College, Columbia University for over 20 years.

Beth A. Ferri Associate Professor of Education, Syracuse University. Dr. Beth A. Ferri serves on the graduate faculty in Disability Studies and coordinates the Master's Program in Secondary Inclusive Special Education as well as the doctoral program in Special Education at Syracuse University. In her most recent book, she and coauthor David J. Connor examine archival newspaper sources to chronicle how problematic rhetorics of race and dis/ability were used to maintain and justify segregated education after the historic *Brown v. Board of Education* decision. Dr. Ferri was recognized in 2003 as an Outstanding Young Scholar in Disability Studies in Education.

Celia Genishi Professor of Education, Chairperson of the Department of Curriculum and Teaching, Teachers College, Columbia University. Dr. Celia Genishi has authored and coauthored many books, articles, and chapters about children's language, classroom observation and research, and assessment. A former preschool and high school Spanish teacher and formerly on the faculty of the University of Texas at Austin and The Ohio State University, Dr. Genishi is a recipient of the Distinguished Scholar Award from the Committee on the Status of Minorities in Education of the American Educational Research Association (AERA), and the Advocate for Justice Award, from the American Association for Colleges of Teacher Education (AACTE). She was recently named an AERA Fellow for her exceptional contribution to research and scholarship.

A. Lin Goodwin Professor of Education and Associate Dean for Teacher Education, Teachers College, Columbia University. Dr. A. Lin Goodwin is the author of numerous publications on the connections between teachers' identities and their development; between multicultural understandings and curriculum enactments; and on the issues facing Asian and Asian American teachers and students in U.S. schools. Her most recent articles examine the professionalization of teaching and the influence of globalization on the knowledge domains for teacher preparation. Dr. Goodwin has worked with educators throughout Europe and Asia around issues of diversity, educational equity, assessment, and teacher education. She is a recipient of the Distinguished Scholar Award from the Committee on the Status of Minorities in Education of the American Educational Research Association (AERA).

Jeremy Hilburn Doctoral Student, University of North Carolina at Chapel Hill. Jeremy Hilburn taught middle school social studies for seven years in the public schools of North Carolina. He currently teaches classes and supervises student teachers at UNC. His research interests include social studies education and immigration.

Min Hong Early Childhood Teacher, Department of Education, New York City. Dr. Min Hong has been an educator for 18 years and is a National Board Certified Teacher who also serves as an Adjunct Assistant Professor for the Department of Curriculum and Teaching at Teachers College, Columbia University. Dr. Hong is the author of numerous articles and books for early childhood teachers and has published children's books for young children. Her research interests include equitable schooling for English language learners, culturally responsive pedagogy, and professional development for early childhood teachers focusing on early literacy instruction and assessment.

Diane E. Levin Professor of Education, Wheelock College. Dr. Diane Levin leads a service-learning program at Wheelock College on the reconciliation process underway in schools in Northern Ireland. The author of eight books and numerous other publications, she is an internationally recognized expert on how sexualization and violence in media and commercial culture affect children and the wider society. Dr. Levin's most recent book focuses on the new sexualized childhood and what parents can do to protect their children. She is a cofounder of the Campaign for a Commercial-Free Childhood (www.commercialfreechildhood.org) and Teachers Resisting Unhealthy Children's Entertainment (www.truceteachers.org).

Maritza B. Macdonald Senior Director of Education and Policy at the American Museum of Natural History, Adjunct Professor, Teachers College, Columbia University and Lehman College (CUNY), New York City. A teacher of teachers, in particular, new and experienced teachers of science and the humanities, Dr. Maritza Macdonald's career path has been marked by a continuous search for equity through pedagogy that is driven by the needs and strengths of students and teachers. In her dissertation "An Urban Teacher's Quest for an Equity Pedagogy", she examined teacher knowledge possessed by excellent teachers and found, as with all strong teachers, they knew content, students, how to teach content, and why their knowledge was important. But what differentiated them from other excellent teachers was their boundless belief in the potential of education, and in their deep commitment to be the teachers who would work with students to achieve both their educational potential and happiness. From Migrant camps, to Head Start, schools, colleges, universities, and now the Museum, Maritza has found many colleagues who share these beliefs, and she considers herself a very happy museum teacher now.

Celia Oyler Associate Professor of Education, Teachers College, Columbia University. Dr. Celia Oyler directs the Elementary Inclusive Education Program in the Department of Curriculum and Teaching at Teachers College. She received her Ph.D. in curriculum from the University of Illinois-Chicago. Before becoming a university professor, Dr. Oyler worked as a special education teacher for 15 years in public schools in Chicago, Vermont, and Connecticut. Her research and teaching center on issues of democratic schooling, multilevel inclusive curriculum design, and anti-racist and critical multicultural teaching. Dr. Oyler's most recent publication is on classroom pedagogies for action and advocacy.

Valerie Polakow Professor of Educational Psychology and Early Childhood, Eastern Michigan University. Dr. Polakow has written extensively about women and children in poverty, homelessness, welfare, access to postsecondary education, and family and child care policies in national and international contexts. She is the author of seven books, the latest of which is an urgent call to action to address child poverty and the child care crisis in the nation. Her current research involves a cross-national study of poverty and children's rights. Dr. Polakow was a Fulbright scholar in Denmark and the recipient of the Distinguished Faculty Award for scholarship at Eastern Michigan University.

Paula G. Purnell Artist, Musician, and Adjunct Professor, Indiana University of Pennsylvania. Dr. Paula G. Purnell is an award-winning musician, specializing in historical and regional folk music. She is the cofounder of Sense of Place Learning, a partner affiliate of the Children's Museum of Pittsburgh, dedicated to raising the awareness, knowledge, and appreciation of the unique ecology, history, heritage, and artistic works intrinsic to specific locales through hands-on, interdisciplinary educational programs and materials.

Xue Lan Rong Professor of Education, University of North Carolina, Chapel Hill. Dr. Xue Lan Rong's research focuses on culture, race/ethnicity and education, and the impacts of immigration on K-12 students' schooling experiences and achievements. A prolific scholar and researcher, Dr. Rong's publications have appeared in major educational and sociological journals. She is also first author or coauthor of four books. Her most recent book, with coauthor J. Preissle, comprehensively outlines the demographic data, content knowledge, and culturally relevant strategies educators need to educate immigrant students in the twenty-first century.

Lindsey Russo State University of New York at New Paltz, Curriculum Consultant: Blue School, New York City. Dr. Russo is currently an assistant professor at SUNY New Paltz teaching courses in early childhood education. She received her doctoral degree from Teachers College, Columbia University. The Blue School, where she advises on the curriculum and conducts research, is a lab school for children from age 2 through second grade. Its mission is to place social/emotional learning, creativity and play at the center of child-directed, inquiry-based, and integrated curricula. Dr. Russo's research interests include the role of play in early childhood education, its relationship to learning within a climate of increased academic expectations and accountability in early childhood classrooms, the formation and role of peer culture in the classroom, and early childhood teacher education.

Mariana Souto-Manning Associate Professor of Early Childhood Education, Teachers College, Columbia University. Dr. Mariana Souto-Manning examines the sociocultural and historical foundations of early schooling, language development, and literacy practices from a critical perspective, studying how children, families, and teachers from diverse backgrounds shape and are shaped by discursive practices.

The author of multiple books and articles, her recent publications have focused on the role of culture circles and drama in supporting the multicultural understandings and practices of teachers. Dr. Souto-Manning was awarded the National Conference on Research in Language and Literacy Early Career Award in 2009, and the 2010 *Early Career Research Award* from *Kappa Delta Pi/AERA Division K (Teaching and Teacher Education).*

Joshua Sparrow, MD Assistant Professor in Psychiatry, Harvard Medical School, Director of Special Initiatives, Brazelton Touchpoints Center, Children's Hospital, Boston. Dr. Joshua Sparrow, in his role of Director of Special Initiatives at the Brazelton Touchpoints Center, consults on professional lifelong learning, cultural adaptations of child development and family support programs, and aligning systems of care with community strengths and priorities. He has worked with the Harlem Children's Zone, American Indian Early Head Start Programs, UNICEF, among other organizations, and has authored numerous scholarly papers and lectured extensively nationally and internationally on related topics. He has coauthored eight books with Dr. T. Berry Brazelton and also writes a weekly New York Times Syndicate column called "Families Today."

Judith Van Hoorn Professor Emerita, University of the Pacific. Dr. Van Hoorn worked for many years in programs serving young children and their families. Her research and writing focus on early childhood development and on adolescents' sociopolitical identity formation. She is coauthor of several books on topics such as play as central to curriculum and adolescent development in the context of rapid social change. She is a past president of the Society for the Study of Peace, Conflict, and Violence: Division 48 of the American Psychological Association.

Chapter 1
The Continuing Struggle for Social Justice for Children

Beatrice S. Fennimore

When I was around the age of seven, a visitor to my home gave me a book of short stories as a holiday gift. That night, before falling asleep in bed, I read the first story called *The Little Match Girl.* A poor, pathetic little girl, cold and freezing with no coat and bare feet on a wintry street, was trying to sell matches for money so her cruel father would not beat her when she returned home. Although she had been on the street for the entire day, not one person had purchased a match. Desperate and dying from the cold, too terrified to go home, she began to light the matches one by one to experience some semblance of warmth. Each match brought comforting visions of food and happiness and light; finally, a match burned so brightly that a vision of her beloved deceased grandmother came and swept her up and away in a loving embrace. The next morning, the body of the little girl lay frozen on the ground as people walked by.

How, I wondered sadly that night, could people have been so cruel? Why wouldn't they buy even one match? Why didn't someone save her? Over a half of a century later, I continue to ask myself the same kind of questions as millions of American children suffer and even die from social neglect in one of the richest and most powerful nations in the world. How and why do we continue to walk past these children—in homeless shelters, in juvenile detention centers, in adult prisons, in multiple foster placements, in segregated and impoverished communities, on dangerous street corners in a crossfire of drugs and violence, in underfunded schools characterized by hopelessness—why aren't we so alarmed at this betrayal of the American dream and fundamental human rights that we rise in a new revolution against the forces that allow such misery and wasted human potential to exist?

B. S. Fennimore (✉)
Indiana University of Pennsylvania, Indiana, PA, USA
e-mail: bzfennim@iup.edu

B. S. Fennimore, A. L. Goodwin (eds.), *Promoting Social Justice for Young Children,* Educating the Young Child 3, DOI 10.1007/978-94-007-0570-8_1,

Child Justice as an American Dilemma

Imagine children like the fictional little match girl fortunate enough to be born in a nation in which all children are entitled to high-quality child care, medical care, and nutrition maintenance programs. In spite of their desperate family circumstances, the children would be ensured of protections and services providing opportunities for safe and healthy development. In the absence of such entitlements, citizens do not seem to know quite what to do when they encounter children like the little match girl who suffer greatly. This uncertainty can lead to a host of misinformed or misdirected rationalizations. Why buy a match when it would do so little good for the well-being of this child? Why help this child when we are only supporting a lazy and abusive father? Is it our fault that the poor little child is out on the street without clothing or food? After all, we work and take care of our own families—we can't take care of everyone!

When I speak to groups of citizens about the needs of children in America, I frequently encounter comments quite similar to those above. I begin my presentations by asking who in the audience believes that all children in America should have enough to eat. Every hand appears to be raised. I continue in this line of questioning regarding home, safety, health care, and a high-quality education—all hands continue to be raised. Then I say, "If an unmarried teenager in a major city has two children and is living in extreme poverty, is it the responsibility of our society to be sure that all the above needs are met?" At that point, the concern previously shown for children unravels. "I support my own family, why should I support the families of irresponsible people?" "That teenager will just keep having babies and expect handouts instead of working." I listen silently for a few minutes. Then, I tell my audience that I am very glad we have not wasted a great deal of our time together talking in idealistic platitudes about what children *ought* to have. Since it can be easily demonstrated that many American children *do not have* access to essential resources, the dialog should focus instead on the need for a comprehensive paradigm shift on the way we think about child entitlements. Rather than consider government support of children and families to be "handouts," we in America might begin to envision basic entitlements for child care, health, and safety to be an irreducible national moral imperative. Within the shelter of such protections for all our children, we could begin to aggressively address the causes of poverty, joblessness, and other significant problems rooted more in the organization of a society than the presumed failings of individuals.

What Must America Do?

A nation grounded in liberty and justice for all—one that claims to stand as a model of democracy for the world—is a nation with the responsibility to articulate what is right and just for all its children. The alternative is to avoid democratic commitments by pretending that there is an even playing field where none exists; by attributing false blame to struggling parents who desperately want to help their families but cannot raise them out of poverty, and by withholding fundamental resources necessary for child survival and healthy development with specious rationalizations based on greed, prejudice, or false political premises.

To what should every child in America be entitled regardless of parental circumstances? Until our nation's leaders and concerned citizens create a public answer to that question, many will continue to oppose and resent child entitlements as "handouts" for adults who are presumed to be lacking in moral value, personal competence, and willingness to work. In resentment of the parents, we justify the inexcusable suffering of the children.

Certainly, parents must be held responsible to care for their children to the greatest possible degree. However, it is also the responsibility of a society to create the context in which parents can reasonably expect to gain employment adequate enough to care for their families, in which childcare makes that employment possible, in which children can grow up healthy and whole enough to become competent parents in the future, and in which children whose parents' personal or economic struggles are overwhelmingly severe will be protected by a threshold of social care under which no child in the nation will ever be permitted to fall (Howe 1994).

A Window of Opportunity for Social Justice

Now that a recent severe economic downturn has affected many Americans who have worked all their lives only to lose their jobs, homes, medical insurance, and retirement benefits, a window of opportunity may be opened. Those who have done what they believed was right only to find themselves betrayed by the greed and dishonesty of those in power may be more willing to examine the false assumptions about meritocracy in this country (we all have an equal chance and if you work hard enough you are rewarded). Indeed, it should be clear by now that anyone, no matter how hard they have worked, can experience severe hardship created by unanticipated losses. When that happens, they need help—just as American banks and businesses have needed bailouts. Perhaps we can now have more compassion as a nation for those whose poverty was so extreme or who faced discrimination that was so disabling that they really never had a fair chance at gaining cultural capital in the first place. Indeed, perhaps empathy and understanding for all who try to raise families in difficult economic circumstances might guide us to a better future.

Establishing Rights to Strengthen Social Justice

Without a consensus on what constitutes justice for children, many arguments against using social justice as a child-based concern arise. Certainly, this was clear in the recent decision of the National Council for Accreditation of Teacher Education

(NCATE) to eliminate social justice language from its documents (Wasley 2006). The challenge to NCATE's inclusion of the concept of social justice in teacher education accreditation materials came from groups claiming that social justice was a liberal and coercive term that could silence the political views and first amendment rights of students in education. I would argue that the challenge to the words *social justice* and the subsequent removal of those words from NCATE documents would have been highly unlikely in a nation with clearly articulated child entitlements. Once there is a consensus on the rights of child citizens, the continued protection of those rights can be argued to transcend government and current partisan politics (Ensalaco 2006). This would make social justice *everyone's* concern, over and above their rights to free speech and personal political points of view.

Building a New Consensus on the Rights of Children

Kenji Yoshino, the Chief Justice Earl Warren Professor of Constitutional Law at New York University, encourages those concerned with group rights to move toward a focus on universal rights of persons (Yoshino 2007). The Universal Declaration of Human Rights (1948) and the United Nations Convention on the Rights of the Child (1989) provide critical structures for those who seek greater protection of children in America. In a stronger context of rights and entitlements, the concept of social justice can be both simplified and strengthened as a politically empowered sense of fairness focused on those who have the least and those whose rights and entitlements are being ignored or violated (Rawls 1970, 2001). America is now the only nation in the world that has not ratified the Convention on the Rights of the Child. I would argue that this should be a matter of national concern and discourse. Hopefully, with the help of many advocates across professional and citizen groups, Americans can agree on child entitlements—thus preparing to take action and reduce child suffering while strengthening the present and future of this nation for all its people.

Organization of This Volume

Each of the authors in this book explores an issue or problem related to the promotion of social justice for children. We encouraged all the authors, many of whom are educators, to speak to a wide audience of readers who are professionally and personally concerned about children. It is important, we think, to reach across professions and citizen interests to support a stronger national dialog about children and social justice in America. Each author has viewed the selected topic through the lens of establishing the problem in its current form relating to young children, providing a conceptual background to the problem, proposing perspectives or solutions, and providing some vision for the future. While each chapter has a different focus, all the chapters are linked by recognition of harm to children and commitment to an America in which children can thrive and develop to their full potential.

Safeguarding Child Welfare and Protecting Children's Rights

In this first section, Valerie Polakow, Diane Levin, Joshua Sparrow, and Judith Van Hoorn and Diane Levin address issues regarding the fundamental needs of children as individuals who have the right to basic protections in the context of respect and regard for their safety, developmental needs, families, and communities. Valerie Polakow's chapter on child poverty, child care, and children's rights challenges us to see poverty not as inevitable but as a social phenomenon that undermines human rights, human potential, and the future of our nation. She further demonstrates that the creation of universal social citizenship rights, including the child care that is essential for the financial security of many parents, would allow all children to ultimately lay claim to the social heritage of a democratic nation. Diane Levin exposes the corporate greed reflected in child-directed media consumerism promoting interest in violence for boys and early sexiness in girls. She calls on families, educators, and policymakers to stop corporate profit from harmful early sexualization of children. Joshua Sparrow focuses on medically based interventions for children and argues that children's rights are inseparable from the rights of caregivers. He explains why intervention and educational programs that truly help parents to be competent must be developed with continuous input from the families being served. Judith Van Hoorn and Diane Levin's chapter on children and war at a distance gives insight into the stress experienced by children when parents are deployed and when images of war are viewed in the media. Furthermore, they warn of a perfect storm that may be created by the intersection of ongoing wars that siphon funds for services for children and families, the historic economic neglect of children and families, and the current economic crisis.

Relevance and Meaningfulness in Early Learning Experiences

In the second section, Celia Genishi, Anne Haas Dyson, Lindsey Russo, Yvonne DeGaetano, and Paula Purnell address important issues in learning experiences for young children. The prominence of educational issues in current federal policy and related media make it important for all citizens to understand problems and challenges below the surface of test scores indicating yearly annual progress. A critical issue in public understanding of fairness to children in early education is the developmental need to play and the relationship of meaningful play to real learning. Celia Genishi, Anne Haas Dyson, and Lindsey Russo emphasize the importance of early attainment of literacy in a social context that leaves space for children to balance academics with energetic and personalized play. They explain how such play reinforces learning through authentic and developmentally appropriate opportunities to rehearse and negotiate the meanings of the language and related skills learned in the classroom. Yvonne DeGaetano's chapter on the need for multicultural education for young children discusses the ways in which *No Child Left Behind* and a subsequent focus on early academics, increasing resentment of immigrants, and a lack of consensus on how multicultural education should be implemented in classrooms of young children have combined to obscure the increasing need of all American children to develop understandings of differences in a global context. She concludes with a clear description of how multicultural education can and should be implemented. Finally, Paula Purnell speaks from her experience as an artist-in-residence and an educator about the vulnerability of adequate exposure to the arts in the current test-driven climate of schools. She offers an alternative vision of interdisciplinary place-based education as an alternative to standardization.

Children of the World in Our Classrooms—Honoring Multiple Identities, Languages, and Knowledges

The third section of this book has a focus on immigration and social justice for children in America who have come from other nations speaking a variety of primary languages. Xue Lan Rong, Liv Thorstensson, and Jeremy Hilburn give insight into the needs of children from homes where there is a mix of documented and undocumented family members or where family members are undocumented. They establish the important consideration that must be given to the children of immigrants, who are the fastest growing segment of the American child population, and the difficulties encountered by children in undocumented families that are unable to access social services and may encounter problems such as the incarceration or deportation of parents. Mariana Souto-Manning gives insight into the importance of language and personhood in the context teachers or parents renaming children who come to school from different places of origin for the convenience of the teachers or out of parental fear of bias toward their child. She uses the work of Paolo Freire to illuminate a discussion of ways in which naming and using the names of children can lead to oppression, silencing, or affirmation of difference and identity. Min Hong takes the perspective of a classroom teacher and a parent while explaining the unnecessary vulnerabilities created for English Language Learners when schools create labels and placements that undermine their emergent language abilities. She challenges schools to create a context of respect in which children can discover themselves and their new language in the context of positive social interaction.

Educating Professionals for Social Justice Commitments

The last section of this book addresses the importance of including social justice concerns and commitments in the education of professionals who work with children. While Beth Ferri, Jessica Bacon, and Celia Oyler speak from the perspectives of teacher educators in the university, the underlying issues they address could be applied to professional preparation across a much wider spectrum of child-related careers. Beth Ferri and Jessica Bacon's chapter on inclusion and disability studies breaks through barriers of presumptions about normalcy and difference and suggest a new kind of Hippocratic Oath for educators—one that upholds the conviction that all children are competent. They argue the importance of seeing disability as a difference rather than a deficit and challenge readers to see every child as becoming, growing, and learning. Then, Celia Oyler explains the need for a carefully developed social justice orientation in teacher education that promotes a belief in the capacity, rather than the presumed deficits, of the diverse children in American classrooms. She explains how teacher educators must integrate studies in curriculum and pedagogy with empathy, analysis of student strength and need, and a keen eye for oppression and inequity.

In our opening and closing chapters, Lin Goodwin and I have attempted to capture the ongoing struggle for social justice for children in a way that can hopefully create optimism as well as the concern, courage, and determination that will be necessary to create a new America—one that is a world leader in humane and compassionate concern for all children. Our hope is that all of our readers will walk away from this volume with a commitment to the application of deep understanding of the complexities of social justice for children to personal and professional activism for the rights of all children.

References

Ensalaco, M. (2006). *Children's human rights: progress and challenges for children world wide.* Lanham: Rowman and Littlefield.

Howe, K. (1994). *Understanding equal educational opportunity.* New York: Teachers College Press.

Rawls, J. (1970). *A theory of justice.* Cambridge: Harvard University Press.

Rawls, J. (2001). *Justice as fairness: A restatement.* Cambridge: Harvard University Press.

United Nations Convention on the Rights of the Child (1989). http://www.unicef.org/crc/. Accessed 10 Feb 2010.

Universal Declaration of Human Rights (1948). http://www.un.org/en/documents/udhr/index.shtml. Accessed 2 May 2009.

Wasley, P. (2006). Accreditor of educational schools drops controversial "social justice" language. *Chronicle of Higher Education, 52*(41), A13.

Yoshino, K. (2007). *Covering: The hidden assault on our civil rights.* New York: Random House.

Part I
Safeguarding Child Welfare and Protecting Children's Rights

Chapter 2
Child Poverty, Child Care, and Children's Rights

Valerie Polakow

In this chapter, child poverty and the lack of fundamental rights accorded to young children in the United States are framed within a broader, international, human rights context. Persistent poverty and the lack of access to high-quality child care is a pervasive threat to young children's well-being and healthy development. In the following sections, brief narratives of homeless children and of mothers desperate for affordable, accessible, child care shadow the cold, statistical realities of poverty and inequality—in order to illuminate what it means for vulnerable children and their families when policy hits the ground. An instrumentalist cost-benefit discourse is juxtaposed against a rights discourse with a specific emphasis on child care as a human right—anchored in international human rights conventions; specifically the Convention on the Rights of the Child (CRC).

Michael's Story

> When Michael was eight years old, the school janitor discovered him in the basement of his elementary school, trying to climb into the furnace. A homeless child, Michael had attended several schools across two states as his destitute mother, fleeing from a violent partner, was unable to find safe, affordable housing and the family suffered chronic periods of homelessness. In the years that followed, Michael's troubled childhood was pierced by constant poverty, instability, violence, and recurring dislocations from school and community—culminating in expulsion from middle school followed by life on the streets. Twelve years later in March 2008, Michael was shot dead by a police officer, searching for a robbery suspect.[1]

Michael's tragic story is not unusual—poverty, daily dangers, chronic homelessness, lack of health care and child care, and the savage inequalities of education

[1] I interviewed Michael and his family during the late 1990s when they became homeless, and reported on their earlier experiences in Polakow (2003).

V. Polakow (✉)
Eastern Michigan University, Ypsilanti, MI, USA
e-mail: vpolakow@emich.edu

B. S. Fennimore, A. L. Goodwin (eds.), *Promoting Social Justice for Young Children*, Educating the Young Child 3, DOI 10.1007/978-94-007-0570-8_2,

continue to eviscerate young lives. Michael's youth is iconic of corrosive public policies and their consequences; consequences that lead to invisible daily tragedies that stamp the lives of children who matter little, and whose lives are cheap. What chance did Michael, a young African-American boy, have for a different life trajectory? He might have had one in another country perhaps—but certainly not here, not now, in the United States.

As foreclosures rise and unemployment spirals, the fundamental necessities that undergird social safety nets in other societies are simply not available to American families. How do children fare when their possibilities for healthy development are diminished and young capabilities are eroded by shameful living conditions that violate their human rights? Prior to the economic crisis of September 2008, families in poverty had already experienced dire threats to their family viability. With homelessness on the rise in both urban and rural America, families now comprise 30% of the homeless population and the number of children and youth experiencing episodic and chronic homelessness has risen to 1.35 million (National Coalition for the Homeless 2008).

Despite the provisions of the Mckinney–Vento Act of 1986 that require states to remove barriers and to protect their educational rights, homeless children experience multiple problems related to school access; and 23% of homeless children and youth do not attend school on a regular basis. Homelessness is a trauma and terror for children, disrupting their worlds, their friendship networks, their schooling, and their families. As significant numbers of single-mother families with young children enter shelters fleeing domestic violence, many homeless children also suffer from post-traumatic stress disorders (National Coalition for the Homeless 2008; National Law Center on Homelessness and Poverty 2008). Michael endured the terrors of both homelessness and domestic violence; yet he received *no* educational interventions to cope with his rapidly unraveling world until his attempted suicide in school. Such desperation illustrates how an accumulation of destabilizing life events coalesces to launch a young, impoverished child on a tragic life trajectory.

Poverty and Social Toxicity

Children living in impoverished communities are vulnerable not only to physical toxins in the environment such as lead paint, dilapidated and roach-infested living environments, toxic waste dumps that produce contaminated air and water—but also to the social toxins that infect their daily lives. Social toxicity (Garbarino 1995) is present in the daily dangers of street and family violence, the chronic threats of eviction and homelessness, the racial and ethnic discrimination, the isolation and the unremitting insecurity, and fear that characterize the early lives of millions of America's children. Toxic experiences are most potent in early childhood, when intense stress in the developing infant and toddler affects the wiring of the brain, radically reshapes the nervous system, impairs the immune system, and produces long-lasting damage to social, emotional, cognitive, and physiological health

(National Scientific Council on the Developing Child 2007). Paul Krugman, writing in the New York Times under a headline "Poverty is Poison," reports these and similar findings from a recent meeting of the American Association for the Advancement of Science, highlighting the damaging impact of acute early stress on the young child, particularly in relation to language and memory causing Krugman (2008) to comment:

> ...Now we have another, even more compelling reason to be ashamed about America's record of failing to fight poverty... To be poor in America today, even more than in the past, is to be an outcast in your own country. And that, the neuroscientists tell us, is what poisons a child's brain.

When the capacity for language and memory, the core of the developing child's human identity, is harmed at the very genesis of being, this constitutes a form of *state-sanctioned public violence.* In a wealthy, industrialized nation such as the United States, poverty is neither inevitable nor irresolvable, and should not be normalized as a "natural" phenomenon. Poverty is constructed and sustained by deep systemic inequalities, by political, social, racial, and gender injustices, by public policies that obstruct and damage children's human capabilities. Such policies can, and should be, undone. Yet, in the twenty-first century, the United States has still failed to implement public policies that address the elimination of child poverty.

Child Poverty in the United States

The United States has the highest child poverty rates among 19 wealthy industrialized countries (Innocenti Research Centre 2007)—13.3 million children live in poverty and 28 million live in low-income families.[2] The poorest of our children live in single-parent families that are predominantly female headed—57.1% of single parents with three children, and 33.8% of single parents with two children—live below the FPL. However, if more realistic family budget measures are used, the percentage of single-parent households in poverty is closer to 92% and 74.7%, respectively (Lin and Bernstein 2008). While children account for 26% of the US population, they represent 38% of all poor people. Between 2000 and 2006, child poverty increased dramatically by 1.2 million and almost a million of the newly poor children are under threes living in extreme poverty.

Children of color (African American, Latino, and American Indian) are also disproportionately poor, with 36% of African-American children living in poor fami-

[2] Families with incomes less than 50% of the federal poverty line (FPL). In 2008, the FPL is calculated to be US $21,200 for a family of four according to the Department of Health and Human Services. The US FPL is considered outdated, inaccurate, and out of step with the widely accepted international measure of relative poverty (less than 50% of the national median income). A low-income household is categorized as below 200% of the poverty line—about US $42,000 for a family of four. This measure is generally accepted as a more accurate indicator of actual child poverty in the United States.

lies, in contrast to 10% of white children. Employment in low-wage work is also no buffer against poverty; for 56% of children live in low-income families where a parent actually works full time (Douglas-Hall and Chau 2007; Fass and Cauthen 2008). As the public space shrinks, poor children receive less and less. With 9.4 million children lacking any form of health insurance (National Center for Children in Poverty 2008a) and 12.6 million estimated to be hungry or living on the edge of hunger (Food Research and Action Center 2007), children have become the most vulnerable subgroup in the United States, and persistent, deep poverty is a toxic threat to their well-being and healthy development.

The current economic crisis, which has led to a massive federal bailout of the financial industries, points to the vast inequality gulf in this country where gains are readily privatized, while losses are broadly socialized. During the past 8 years, there has been a dramatic increase in wealth inequality and in the most recent international report on inequality, the United States ranks near last (after Mexico and Turkey), with the poorest 10% of the US population subsisting on incomes of less than US $5,800 a year (OECD 2008). Despite the public outcry against the golden parachutes and the billions of dollars to bailout the banks and investment houses in what Greider describes as "Goldman Sachs Socialism" (Greider 2008, p. 5), there has been minimal redirection of government funds to help working poor families who have encountered years of losses in wages, health care benefits, and pensions (Lee 2008).

The grim economic conditions, following on the heels of "welfare reform" in 1996, have further shredded the already residual safety net, and exacerbated the acute need for child care for low-income parents, particularly single mothers.

In my recent study documenting the child care crisis of low-income single mothers (Polakow 2007), women tell their stories of loss and desperation as well as the diminished early lives of their children. As these women struggled alone to make it as parents and providers, they were affected not only by harmful public policies but by a gaping lack of available child care. The absence of appropriate levels of support violates both the rights of struggling parents and their children. Threaded through the women's narratives of struggle and determination to beat the odds stacked against them is the acute need for high-quality and affordable child care—frequently the tipping point between family viability and family disintegration.

Child Care: The Tipping Point

> Annette is a nineteen-year-old, white, single mother in Michigan with an eight-month-old baby, Nicholas, and a bleak future. Living in a homeless shelter with her baby son, Annette is working full-time at minimum wage; yet is unable to find affordable housing or quality, stable child care. In his short life, Nicholas has experienced four different placements—due to his mother's erratic work schedule and her decision to pull him out of dangerous and poor-quality child care settings. Annette has been unable to access state child care subsidies, and with nowhere to turn, she is on the verge of losing her baby to foster care.[3]

[3] I interviewed Annette in 2006. Part of her story is included in Polakow (2007).

As with most low-income mothers across the nation—good jobs with benefits and regular hours are hard to come by (Presser and Cox 1997; Cauthen and Dinan, 2008) and even more so in Michigan, with high unemployment, daily home foreclosures, and close to 420,000 children living below the poverty line (National Center for Children in Poverty 2008b). As a poor young woman who has not completed high school, working a minimum wage job with no benefits; desperate in her struggle to access child care subsidies, health care, and affordable housing, Annette's life and that of her young child is emblematic of what Martha Nussbaum terms "an acute failure of human capabilities" (Nussbaum 2000, p. 3). And Baby Nicholas is but one of almost half a million Michigan children whose lives are imperiled by poverty. His infancy has been disrupted by family homelessness and multiple placements in child care, and with no access to early intervention he is already suffering the consequences of poverty and the isolation from supportive networks that could protect and enrich his development. With denied fundamental human rights to housing, health care, and child care, Annette and her baby son constitute another discarded young family amid the rubble of American democracy gone awry. There are no exits without substantial public investment in their lives.

In contrast to the countries of Scandinavia and Western Europe, as well as Canada, Australia, and other industrialized wealthy democracies, the United States stands as an outlier nation, with no infrastructure of family support policies such as universal child care and paid parental leave. Such a care deficit takes a distinctively heavy toll on low-income families.

The Child Care Deficit

> Child care is a huge huge problem… What do you do? I mean you cannot leave your children at home, and you can't take a day off and you don't have child care… (Clara, a New York City immigrant mother, quoted in Polakow 2007, p. 2)

> It's the most frustrating thing in the world for me—I could yell and yell all day about daycare… You know, where people who have a lot of money—people like us get this ratty little building. (Hannah, a San Diego mother, quoted in Polakow 2007, p. 72)

Although a gaping care deficit exists for the children of working mothers, there are, nevertheless, large numbers of women with children in the labor force: 74.3% of mothers with children 6–17 years, 59.6% with children under 6 years, and 55.4% with children under 3 years (US Department of Labor 2008a, b). With 12 million children in some form of public or private child care, the crisis of affordable and good quality child care becomes particularly acute for single mothers with very young children. Children enter child care facilities as young as 6 weeks old and may be in care for 40 hours a week until they enter school. Only 14% of income-eligible families receive child care subsidies (Children's Defense Fund 2005) and even then subsidies do not pay the full cost of quality care, and there are thousands of children on waiting lists in the states—from 38,000 in New York City to 280,000 in the state of California (Carlson and Sharf 2004; Schulman and Blank 2005). Child care costs are so high that they often exceed the cost of college tuition at most public universities, ranging from US $4,542 to US $14,591 for full-time infant care, and from US $3,380 up to US $10,787 a year for a preschooler (National Association of Child Care Resources & Referral Agencies 2008). While costs are considerably cheaper in family daycare homes, many are unlicensed and lack of regulation and monitoring substantially increases the risks for young children.

Because there is no federal regulation of private child care, it is up to the states to set minimum standards for child care centers: but minimum translates to less than minimal in terms of regulating the quality of care. The National Association for the Education of Young Children (NAEYC) has developed accreditation standards for promoting program quality and best practices; yet with 12 million children under five in child care, there are less than 7,000 programs serving approximately 586,000 children, that have been accredited (NAEYC 2008). Low-income parents encounter greater hurdles obtaining licensed care as lack of resources diminishes choices, there is less access in poor neighborhoods to higher quality care, and unstable odd-hour work schedules make child care arrangements very difficult (Boushey and Wright 2004; Chaudry 2004; Presser and Cox 1997; Vandell and Wolfe 2000). Consequently, mothers must rely on makeshift and multiple care arrangements that create further instability in a young child's life. The fact that large numbers of poor children end up not just in bad licensed care but in the largely invisible underworld of unregulated care is alarming. Helburn and Bergmann (2002) estimate that about one third of children in child care from birth to five are in the unregulated sector.

The high numbers of infants and toddlers in child care are of particular concern because they are most susceptible to the harmful effects of bad care. Seventy-three percent of the infants and toddlers of employed mothers (about 6 million children under 3 years) spend much of their waking hours in child care. Under the 1996 Personal Responsibility and Work Opportunity Act, poor, single mothers were required to meet mandatory work requirements as a condition of receiving benefits. While federal law exempts mothers with infants under 12 months, several states (Massachusetts, Michigan, New York, Ohio, and Wisconsin) have increased the work requirements to include mothers with infants over 12 weeks. The escalating demand for child care has created desperate choices for single mothers, coerced into the low-wage workplace in order to avoid destitution (Kahn and Polakow 2000).

The developmentally damaging conditions that exist nationwide for millions of vulnerable young children in their most formative stages of development are a national disgrace. The severe child care crisis that exists has been documented for more than a decade: lack of regulation, lack of access, lack of affordability, poor quality, bad working conditions with low pay, high turnover, high ratios of children to staff, and substandard care that disproportionately impacts low-income children of color (Ebb 1994; Galinsky et al. 1994; Helburn 1995; Helburn and Bergmann 2002; Polakow 2007; Schulman 2000). While high-quality child care results in long-lasting social and educational impacts that are particularly significant for low-income children, they are also far more sensitive to the negative effects of bad child care (Klein and Knitzer 2007; Peisner-Feinberg et al. 1999).

Yet, despite the accumulating body of research that clearly points to what supports and enriches young children's lives and what *harms*, poor children have no entitlement to good-quality early care. In the absence of rights, their lives, like those of their parents, are largely expendable; and when poverty, low-wage work, and lack of child care coalesce to create an acute crisis of care, poor and often desperate parents must settle for *less, much less*.

Hobson and Lister (2002) argue that the lack of social and economic rights—the absence of any universal social citizenship rights that guarantee "a positive state" for women and their children—create fecund conditions for child poverty to flourish. Esping-Andersen (1990) characterizes social citizenship rights in advanced capitalist societies by their degrees of *decommodification*, the extent to which citizens are not dependent on the vicissitudes of the market—but rather are protected by stable and universal entitlements within their own societies. Such rights, argued British sociologist Marshall over half a century ago, are central to democracy, and the role of social policy is to ensure that all have "a claim to be admitted to a share in the social heritage" (Marshall 1963, p. 72). Yet, a young, poor, child in the United States has no such rights and no such claims. In contrast to the 27 countries that make up the European Union, the United States has no platform of social and economic rights for children or their working parents such as paid maternity and parental leave, a national child care system with targeted provisions for working parents, a national health care system, and a living wage that enables family sustainability. The dearth of such family policies and the crumbling public infrastructures that harm so many of our youngest and poorest have pushed vulnerable children and youth to the liminal edges of school and civic society. Lacking fundamental rights, children's lives in a "de-welfared" nation in the United States are no longer granted even the minimal protections associated with childhood in a modern democracy.

The Discourse of Cost-Benefits versus Rights

The dominant discourse in the United States about early childhood education is instrumentalist, constructing poor young children as "at-risk"—for educational failure, for later teen pregnancy, and/or criminality and violence, with ultimate costs to the nation. The prevailing arguments for early intervention are embedded in deficit, racialized assumptions about poor families and premised on a cost-benefit analysis of why investing now pays dividends in the future. Heckman and the Committee for Economic Development argue for a redirection of educational investments from public schools (which are already underfunded) to early childhood to redress the assumed "constellation of pathologies" in poor children's homes, calculating that early intervention provides better long-term returns (Heckman and Masterov 2004, p. 17).

However, this instrumentalist, "invest-now-or-pay-later" discourse obscures a language of rights, and constructs children as the sometime "deserving poor" focusing on the family as the dominant risk-inducing system; whereas poverty, itself, should be seen as a systemic pathology that corrodes family viability. Means-tested and segregated early childhood intervention programs construct poor, young children and their parents as post-modern beggars; such programs are also the first to be cut or eliminated when deficits loom large and when there is competition for scarce resources. Reframing persistent child poverty and the *absence* of child care in terms of human rights violations, and anchoring social policy in the frameworks of international conventions, creates another plane for the discourse about children's lives and their rights. If we view children as possessing fundamental rights to care and education that are grounded in international conventions, then it becomes an affirmative obligation of government to address child poverty alleviation and the provision of universal child care (Davis and Powell 2003; Polakow 2007).

Child Care as a Human Right

The International Convention on the Rights of the Child (CRC 1989) was adopted in 1989 and has been ratified by 194 countries; yet the United States has not joined the community of nations in affirming children's human rights. In the CRC children, for the first time, are recognized as "rights bearers," as citizens and as social actors (Kilbourne 1999). The CRC addresses children's rights to receive care and protection, and the promotion of their best interests for "full and harmonious development." Article 18 emphasizes that State Parties must provide "appropriate assistance to parents…" and take "all appropriate measures to ensure that children of working parents have the right to benefit from child-care services." Other key articles of the CRC affirm children's economic, social, and cultural rights (Article 4), the establishment of institutions, facilities, and social programs for support of children (Articles 18 and 19), rights and access to services for disabled children (Article 23), access to and quality of health care (Article 24), and rights to social insurance and social security (Article 26). The CRC in affirming children's inherent rights to social citizenship, and emphasizing the special interests and needs of children and their working parents closely aligns with Article 25 of the Universal Declaration of Human Rights which emphasizes that "Motherhood and childhood are entitled to special care and assistance. All children, whether born in or out of wedlock, shall enjoy the same social protection." (Universal Declaration of Human Rights 1948, Article 2). While Eleanor Roosevelt was a key figure in promoting the establishment of the Universal Declaration of Human Rights, we, in the United States, now routinely violate its key precepts in relation to the health, welfare, and child care of young children. Other international conventions such as the Convention on the Elimination of all Forms of Discriminations against Women (CEDAW), which has been ratified by 169 countries *excluding* the United States, affirm the rights of women to work, to maternity leave, and to child care.

The 27 countries of the European Union have not only committed to combating child poverty and social exclusion by expanding child care and paid maternity and parental provisions, but have also promoted wage guarantees and flexible working patterns (European Commission 2004). Child care is viewed as a human right and poverty and social exclusion are viewed as clear violations of children's human rights. European Commissioner Franco Frattini, speaking at the Second European Forum on the Rights of the Child, urged member countries to commit further resources to poverty alleviation and the care of children, stating "It is a violation of fundamental rights when children are denied food, or housing, or education" (Frattini 2008). Yet children's *rights* are not even part of the growing conversation about early childhood education in the United States, and, as Kamerman points out, the absence of paid parental leave and universal child care "exists in dramatic contrast to the policies that exist around the world and especially in our peer countries" (Kamerman 2000, p. 13). In Europe, the CRC forms the basis for social policy formation about children's welfare, well-being, education, and child care. Such rights are embedded in a notion of public care and public responsibility that supports children's human capabilities and makes possible the fundamental prerequisites for early growth and development and participation in child life in a modern democracy.

Recommendations for the Future—What Would It Take?

> In a rich, advanced economy like the United States, poverty should be viewed as an aberration. (Bernstein 2007, p. 1)

Ending child poverty and creating universal systems of child care and health care are national imperatives for children. The Center for American Progress (CAP) Task Force on Poverty (2007) proposes a national strategy to cut poverty by half in the next decade. Their recommendations are closely aligned with Britain's pledge, under Former Prime Minister Tony Blair to end child poverty by 2020 and to reduce child poverty by 50% by 2010. While that goal has not yet been met in Britain at the present time, some gains have occurred and it remains a national priority. Britain's 2003 Green Paper, *Every Child Matters* and the *Children's Act* of 2004, at the very least, created an explicit recognition and commitment to a policy agenda that calls for accountability in meeting those goals (HM Government 2003, 2004).

The CAP Task Force recommendations point to poverty as a critical social policy agenda for the incoming Obama administration. Their comprehensive recommendations include, but are not limited to, raising the minimum wage, expanding the Earned Income Tax Credit for low-income working parents, expanding child tax credits, guaranteeing child care subsidies to low-income families with incomes below US $40,000 a year, and developing a high-quality education system from early childhood to postsecondary that is universally available and accessible. If implemented, the key poverty reduction strategies are estimated to cost approximately US $90 billion a year. In contrast, the Bush tax cuts of 2001 and 2003 cost US $400 billion a year and in 2008, tax cuts to those with incomes above US $200,000 are estimated to be US $100 billion (CAP 2007, p. 5). Greenberg, the Task Force executive director, argues that a more equitable tax system with a partial redistribution of resources could dramatically cut poverty by half within a decade, with drops in child poverty of about 41%. The Task Force recommendations assume an even greater urgency in the current dire economic crisis which has pushed millions more families over the edge. The costs of such policy recommendations pale in comparison to the squandered resources, the Blackwater war profiteering, and the ongoing costs of the Iraq war, which are projected to reach US $3 trillion (Bilmes and Stiglitz 2008) and the US $700 billion federal bailout to financial institutions at the time of writing. The election of President Obama and the Democratic takeover of the Congress have created a window of possibility to begin the work necessary to transform such sordid inequalities; an opportunity to reframe the meaning of "public" to encompass social and economic justice for the common good.

The CAP task force recommendations address the acute child care needs of low-income parents by proposing that the current federal child care block grants be replaced by guaranteed subsidies to all working families with incomes below 200% of the FPL; and by creating a federal early care and education strategy fund. Such a fund would promote a comprehensive birth to school-age policy, double the current level of funding to states in order to coordinate and merge all public preschool programs such as Head Start and prekindergarten, thereby promoting quality upgrades and initiatives (CAP 2007, p. 33), and ensuring access to preschool for all three-year olds. While the child care proposals embody an ambitious agenda pointing to a dramatic and significant policy shift, they lack an in-depth understanding of the existential realities of child care on the ground—the all-pervasiveness of shoddy, inferior care meted out to poor children across the country.

Current child care subsidies are pegged at the 75th percentile of market rates in order to ensure "equal access" (US Department of Health and Human Services 2005), but actually fail to ensure this. In the unregulated free market of private child care, skyrocketing costs determine which toddlers play and which toddlers are confined to cribs in dirty basements; which preschool children attend centers that are NAEYC accredited with professional teachers, and which children attend "ratty little buildings" with untrained caregivers. The CAP proposals also significantly underestimate the problems in transforming both regulated and unregulated child care: Improving quality most certainly would require far more funding, extensive investment in staff training and education, comprehensive regulation and monitoring (including the tangled network of family daycare homes), and substantial wage increases for teachers and caregivers.

Helburn and Bergmann (2002) estimated in early 2000 that it would cost US $56 billion a year to create *affordable* quality care for every child, arguing that the federal government would need to finance such a system, building on existing public programs such as Head Start and preK. Their plan proposed creating affordable child care that would require parents to pay up to 20% of the portion of their income that exceeded the poverty line for child care costs. Families below the FPL would receive free child care. They, too, proposed investing in quality improvements using an incentive-based system of child care subsidies to licensed care settings, where centers that met and exceeded quality care standards would be rewarded by increased subsidies. But, as with the CAP proposal, there is a significant problem in building on a substandard foundation. More needs to be *undone* in terms of the pervasive segregation by class and race that currently exists for low-income children; and educational and training incentives are more likely to improve quality for those who already have, rather than for those who have not. Embedding child care in the free market, with its lack of regulation and corrosive profiteering, is not in the best interests of children.

Poor quality and lack of access exist in the public preschool sector as well. While the National Institute for Early Education Research (NIEER) reports that in 2006–2007 there were improvements in both spending and enrollment of children in 30 of the 38 states that offered public prekindergarten programs, quality and access issues remain severe. In those states that enroll the highest percentages of 4 year olds—Oklahoma, 68.4%, Florida, 56.7%, and Georgia, 53.3%—there are no programs for 3 year olds. Nationwide more than a million children now attend preK programs but, overall, that only accounts for 22% of 4 year olds and 3% of 3 year olds with 12 states providing no programs at all. Less than half of the 38 states require teachers to possess bachelor's degrees; and only 10 states actually meet 90% or more of NIEER benchmarks for quality standards (NIEER 2007). In addition, most programs are part-day, creating care gaps for working parents who must still juggle full-time child care needs.

Hence, the existing patchwork of stratified private and public early childhood programs and services provides neither a stable infrastructure nor a solid foundation on which to erect a comprehensive child care system. Unless child care is a *right*, it is subject to the exigencies of the free market and imperiled by federal and state social spending cuts during economic downturns. Universal child care does not come cheap. But once established as a right, the discourse about who deserves care and who does not, and the income and racial stratification embedded in current policies, can be transformed. Universal child care has a very successful history in Sweden, Denmark, and France and those countries have invested wisely in the well-being of children, integrating early care and pedagogy into national systems that are consistently rated as high quality, with Denmark and Sweden receiving international praise for "woman-friendly" work-family policies that promote social equality.

For those of us who advocate on behalf of families and young children in the interests of social and economic justice here at home, the election of President Obama introduces a new optimism and sense of possibility of what could be—perhaps the inception of "progressive universalism" (CAP 2007, p. 14) that may yet see the dawning of universal child care within the next decade? And there is much more to be said—about educational inequality, racial discrimination, juvenile injustice, lack of access to affordable housing and healthcare. It is certainly time to end an era of shame and appalling indifference to the lives of poor children and their parents. Violations of children's human rights should never be normalized. The urgent work that confronts progressives now is building a grassroots campaign to ratify the CRC, embed a language and consciousness of children's human rights in policy discourse, and mobilize to end child poverty and create universal child care. If not now, when?

References

Bernstein, J. (2007). Work, work supports and safety nets: reducing the burden of low-incomes in America (Briefing Paper no. 200). http://www.sharedprosperity.org/bp200/bp200.pdf. Accessed 10 Nov 2008.

Bilmes, L., & Siglitz, J. (2008). The Iraq war will cost US $3 trillion, and much more. http://www.washingtonpost.com/wpdyn/content/article/2008/03/07/AR2008030702846.html. Accessed 20 Nov 2008.

Boushey, H., & Wright, J. (2004). Working moms and child care (no. 3). http://www.cepr.net/index.php/publications/reports/working-moms-and-child-care/. Accessed 10 Sept 2008.

Carlson, B. C., & Scharf, R. (2004). Lost in the maze: reforming New York City's fragmented child care subsidy system. New York: Welfare Law Center.

Cauthen, N., & Dinan, K. (2008). *Making work supports work*. New York: National Center for Children in Poverty. http://www.nccp.org/publications/pub_824.html. Accessed 10 Nov 2008.

Center for American Progress (CAP). (2007). From poverty to prosperity: a national strategy to cut poverty in half. http://www.americanprogress.org/issues/2007/04/pdf/poverty_report.pdf. Accessed 1 Nov 2008.

Chaudry, A. (2004). Putting children first: how low-wage working mothers manage child care. New York: Russell Sage Foundation.

Children's Defense Fund. (2005). Child Care Basics 2005. http://www.childrensdefense.org/site/DocServer/child_care_basics_2005.pdf. Accessed 10 Nov 2008.

Convention on the Rights of the Child (CRC). (1989). United Nations Office of the High Commissioner for Human Rights. http://www.unhchr.ch/html/menu3/b/k2crc.htm. Accessed 10 Nov 2008.

Davis, M., & Powell, R. (2003). The international convention on the rights of the child: a catalyst for innovative child care policies. *Human Rights Quarterly, 25*(3), 689–719.

Douglas-Hall, A., & Chau, M. (2007). Most low-income parents are employed. http://www.nccp.org/publications/pub_784.html. Accessed 15 Sept 2008.

Ebb, N. (1994). *Child care tradeoffs: states make painful choices*. Washington: Children's Defense Fund.

Esping-Anderson, G. (1990). *The three worlds of welfare capitalism*. Cambridge: Polity Press.

European Commission. (2004). *Joint report on social exclusion*. Brussels: Employment and Social Affairs. http://ec.europa.eu/employment_social/publications/2005/keaq04001_en.pdf. Acessed 10 Nov 2008.

Fass, S., & Cauthen, N. (2008). Who are America's poor children? The official story. http://www.nccp.org/publications/pub_843.html. Accessed 20 Nov 2008.

Food Research and Action Center. (2007). Hunger in the U.S. http://www.frac.org/html/hunger_in_the_us/hunger_index.html. Accessed 15 Sept 2008.

Frattini, F. (2008). Second European forum on the rights of the child. http://europa.eu/rapid/pressReleasesAction.do?reference=SPEECH/08/124&format=HTML&aged=0&language=EN&guiLanguage=en. Accessed 10 Nov 2008.

Galinsky, E., Howes, C., Kontos, S., & Shinn, M. (1994). *The study of children in family care and relative care: Highlights of findings*. New York: Families and Work Institute.

Garbarino, J. (1995). *Raising children in a socially toxic environment*. San Francisco: Jossey-Bass.

Greider, W. (2008). Goldman Sachs socialism. *The Nation, 287*(11). http://www.thenation.com/article/goldman-sachs-socialism. Accessed 15 June 2010.

HM Government. (2004). Every child matters: change for children. http://www.infed.org/archives/gov_uk/every_child_matters.htm. Accessed 10 Sept 2008.

HM Government, Chief Secretary to the Treasury. (2003). Every child matters. http://www.everychildmatters.gov.uk/. Accessed 10 Sept 2008.

Heckman, J. J., & Masterov, D. V. (2004). *The productivity argument for investing in young children (no. 5)*. Washington: Committee for Economic Development.

Helburn, S. W. (Ed.). (1995). *Cost, quality and child outcomes in child care centers. Technical Report* (ED 386 297). Denver: Center for Research in Economic and Social Policy, University of Colorado.

Helburn, S. W., & Bergmann, B. (2002). *America's child care problem: The way out.* New York: Palgrave MacMillan.

Hobson, B., & Lister, R. (2002). Citizenship. In B. Hobson, J. Lewis, & B. Siim (Eds.), *Contested concepts in gender and social politics* (pp. 23–54). Cheltenham: Edward Elgar.

Innocenti Research Centre (2007). *Child poverty in perspective. An overview of child well-being in rich countries.* http://www.unicef-irc.org. Accessed 15 Sept 2008.

Kahn, P., & Polakow, V. (2000). Mothering denied: Commodification and caregiving under new US welfare laws. *SAGE Race Relations Abstracts, 25*(1), 7–25.

Kamerman, S. B. (2000). Parental leave policy: An essential ingredient of earlychildhood care policies. http:www.childpolicy.org/SocialPolicyReport-2000. vl4n2.pdf. Accessed 15 Sept 2008.

Kilbourne, S. (1999). Placing the convention on the rights of the child in an American context. *Human Rights, 28*(2), 27.

Klein, L., & Knitzer, J. (2007). Promoting effective early learning: what every policymaker and educator should know. http://www.nccp.org/publications/pub_695.html. Accessed 10 Nov 2008.

Krugman, P. (2008). Poverty is poison. http://www.nytimes.com/2008/02/18/opinion/18krugman.html. Accessed 20 Sept 2008.

Lee, T. M. (2008). Bail out working families. *The Nation, 287*(11), 6–7.

Lin, J. & Bernstein, J. (2008). What we need to get by. http://www.epi.org/content.cfm/bp224. Accessed 1 Nov 2008.

Marshall, T. H. (1963). *Sociology at the crossroads and other essays.* London: Heinemann.

National Association of Child Care Resources & Referral Agencies. (2008). Parents and the high price of child care: 2008 update. http://www.naccrra.org/. Accessed 21 Nov 2008.

National Association for the Development of Young Children (NAEYC). (2008). Summary of accredited programs for young children. http://www.naeyc.org/accreditation/center_summary.asp. Accessed 25 October 2008.

National Center for Children in Poverty. (2008a). '07 Issues portend continued hard times in '08 for low-income working Americans: Trends seen in housing, wages, health care, family leave. http://www.nccp.org/media/releases/release_37.html. Accessed 20 Nov 2000.

National Center for Children in Poverty. (2008b). Michigan: Demographics of poor children. http://www.nccp.org/profiles/state_profile.php?state=MI&id=7. Accessed 10 Nov 2008.

National Coalition for the Homeless. (2008). How many people experience homelessness? NCH Fact Sheet #2. http://www.nationalhomeless.org/publications/facts/How_Many.html. Accessed 20 Nov 2008.

National Institute for Early Education Research (NIEER). (2007). The state of preschool 2007. http://nieer.org/yearbook/pdf/yearbook.pdf. Accessed 21 Nov 2008.

National Law Center on Homelessness and Poverty. (2008). Some facts on homelessness, housing, and violence against women. http://www.nlchp.org/. Accessed 21 Nov 2008.

National Scientific Council on the Developing Child. (2007). The science of early childhood development: Closing the gap between what we know and what we do. http://www.developingchild.net/. Accessed 21 Nov 2008.

Nussbaum, M. (2000). *Women and human development: the capabilities approach.* Cambridge: Cambridge University Press.

Organisation for Economic Co-operation and Development (OECD). (2008). Growing unequal? Income distribution and poverty in OECD countries. http://www.oecd.org/els/social/inequality. Accessed 24 Oct 2008.

Peisner-Feinberg, E. S., Burchinal, M. R., Clifford, R. M., Culkin, M., Howes, C., Kagan, S. L., et al. (1999). *The children of the cost, quality, and outcomes study go to school: Executive summary.* Chapel Hill: University of North Carolina at Chapel Hill, Frank Porter Graham Child Development Center.

Polakow, V. (2007). *Who cares for our children? The child care crisis in the other America.* New York: Teachers College Press.

Presser, H., & Cox, A. G. (1997). The work schedules of low-educated American women and welfare reform. *Monthly Labor Review, 120*(4), 25–34.

Schulman, K. (2000). *The high cost of child care puts quality care out of reach for many families.* Washington: Children's Defense Fund.

Schulman, K., & Blank, H. (2005). Child care assistance policies 2005: States fail to make up lost ground, families continue to lack critical supports. http://www.nwlc.org/pdf/ChildCareSubsidyReport_September2005.pdf. Accessed 10 Nov 2008.

Universal Declaration of Human Rights (1948). http://www.un.org/en/documents/udhr/index.shtml. Accessed 2 May 2009.

US Department of Health and Human Services. (2005, May). State child care subsidies: trends in rate ceilings and family fees. http://www.nccic.acf.hhs.gov/pubs/issuebriefs/rateceilings.html. Accessed 20 Nov 2008.

US Department of Labor, Bureau of Labor Statistics. (2008a). Employment status of mothers with own children under 3 years old by single year of age of youngest child and marital status, 2006–07 annual averages. (Table 6). http://www.bls.gov/news.release/famee.t06.htm. Accessed 20 Nov 2008.

US Department of Labor, Bureau of Labor Statistics. (2008b). Employment status of the population by sex, marital status, and presence and age of own children under 18, 2006–07 annual averages. (Table 5). http://www.bls.gov/news.release/famee.t05.htm. Accessed 20 Nov 2008.

Vandell, D. L., & Wolfe, B. (2000, November). *Child care quality: does it matter and does it need to be improved?* (No. 78). Madison: Institute for Research on Poverty.

Chapter 3
Objectified Self, Objectified Relationships: The Sexualization of Childhood Promotes Social Injustice

Diane E. Levin

Popularity Equals Having the Right Clothes?

> On the first day of kindergarten in an urban public school, Jenna is sitting at a table in the cafeteria eating lunch with her teacher. She points to a table nearby and says to the teacher, "Those are the popular kids." Surprised, the teacher asks her how she knows this. Jenna responds that those children are wearing the 'right' clothes—with the right labels—the 'sexy' clothes. When the teacher asks how she knows this Jenna reports, "The Disney Channel." She adds, "My Mom won't buy them for me. She says they cost too much money". (Levin and Kilbourne 2008, pp. 84–85)

What does being popular mean to this 5 year old? What is Jenna seeing on the Disney Channel that is teaching her to equate popularity of peers with wearing "sexy" clothes that have the "right" labels? How does her mother *not* buying the right clothes for Jenna influence her popularity? How will this affect their mother–daughter relationship? How does what Jenna is learning affect her view of herself, her peers, and the nature of relationships and friendships?

Teasing and Bullying in First Grade?

> On the playground, Clara happily goes over to the jungle gym where several of her first grade classmates are playing. As she climbs on, a child calls out, "Yikes, get off, you're gonna break it!" Other children start loudly chanting, "You're gonna break it! You're gonna break it!" Clara, who is chubby, leaves in tears, as the chanters ignore her tears and continue playing.

What makes children be mean to another child based on her appearance? Where do children learn that being overweight is grounds for disdain? How can children see a classmate cry and show no signs of empathy or concern?

D. E. Levin (✉)
Wheelock College, Boston, MA, USA
e-mail: dlevin@wheelock.edu

B. S. Fennimore, A. L. Goodwin (eds.), *Promoting Social Justice for Young Children*, Educating the Young Child 3, DOI 10.1007/978-94-007-0570-8_3,

Sexual Harassment in Kindergarten?

> In April 2008, the Washington Post reported that during recess a 6 year old boy in Virginia hit a classmate's bottom. The girl told her teacher. The boy was sent to the principal. An incident report was filed for "sexual touching" which will remain on his student record permanently. Then, the police were called. (Schulte 2008)

This is not an isolated incident. The *Washington Post* reports that 255 elementary students were suspended in 2007 for offensive sexual touching. In Maryland, 166 elementary children were suspended for sexual harassment, including 3 preschoolers, 16 kindergartners, and 22 first graders.

Why are children as young as 4 years old being accused of sexual harassment? What's going on? Is it really sexual harassment? What does "sexual harassment" mean to a 4 year old child? Or a 6 year old? What is leading adults, supposedly trained to promote the wellbeing of children, to accuse children of being sexual harassers at age 6? What do they think the boy was trying to do to the girl? And why are police being called in? What does it mean for a 6 year old child to have a sexual harassment charge permanently on his school record? What meanings do other children make of situations like this when they hear about them, even if they are not directly accused?

What's Going On?

Children are growing up in a society that undermines many of the positive lessons we hope they will learn about social behavior, caring relationships, and social justice.

Media Madness

Increasingly, children's environments are influenced by the time they spend consuming electronic media. A 2003 Kaiser Family Foundation report found that children aged zero to six averaged approximately two hours of "screen time" a day. It also reports that 30% of children aged three and under and 43% of children aged four to six had a television set in their bedroom. According to the authors, "This study documented a potentially revolutionary phenomenon in American society: the immersion of our very youngest children, from a few months to a few years old, in the world of electronic and interactive media" (Kaiser Family Foundation 2003, p. 12).

As children are glued to the screen, they are exposed to an unprecedented amount of sex, violence, and other messages about social behavior and relationships. In 2005, a Kaiser Family Foundation survey reported that the number of sexual scenes on TV nearly doubled since 1998 (Kaiser Family Foundation 2005). In an earlier survey, 75% of traditional TV "family hour" programs were found to have sexual content, compared with 43% 20 years earlier (Kaiser Family Foundation 1996). No doubt, this content has played a role teaching Jenna the information she shared with her teacher the first day of school—that popularity is equated with having the right clothes and being sexy.

Consuming Kids

USA Today reports that corporations spend US $17 billion annually selling products to children (Horovitz 2006), up from a mere US $100,000 in 1983 (Schor 2005). As marketing to children increased, so did the sexual content in the media. Sexiness (especially designed for young girls) and violence (for young boys) are used to capture children's attention in order to sell them things (Ravitch and Viteritti 2003).

In addition to what children see on screens, most of the best-selling mass-market toys are highly gender divided—violence for boys and sexiness for girls (Carlsson-Paige and Levin 1990). These toys are usually linked to the television programs, movies, and other electronic media children watch. For instance, Bratz dolls and Disney princesses for girls and Spiderman, Transformer, and Star Wars toys for boys were among the best-selling toys in 2007 (U.S. toy industry 2008). When children play with highly structured toys like these, they are channeled into imitating the sexy and violent behavior they see on the screen (Levin and Carlsson-Paige 2006).

Finally, we need to look at the clothes marketed to children today. There are tee shirts for baby boys that say, "I'm a chick magnet" and "Jr. Pimp Squad" on the front. There are matching padded bra and bikini underpants for little girls as young as 4 years old. And many parents report that already in the preschool years, they have trouble finding basic, non-sexy clothes for their daughters. Furthermore, much of the sexiest clothing for girls is linked to popular media—such as Disney princesses, Hannah Montana and High School Musical (Levin and Kilbourne 2008).

Consuming by Marketers' Design

The media and consuming-saturated world in which children are growing up has not always been like this. In the 1980s under pressure from corporations to use media to market more aggressively to children, two major events occurred that has drastically changed childhood. First, the Federal Communications Commission deregulated children's television in the mid-eighties (Englehardt 1986). This is when the program-length commercial was born—i.e., it became possible to market whole-lines of products to children through television programming for the first time (Levin 1998). At about the same time, the Federal Trade Commission had its power to regulate marketing to children taken away by an act of Congress. Through these two events, marketing directly to children became big business and it has continued to expand ever since (Linn 2004; Media Education Foundation 2008; Schor 2005).

As marketing to children has been ratcheted up, the best interests of children have often been ignored. Marketers' job is to get children to want their products whether it is good for them or not—more and more, never enough, promising happiness, brand loyalty at younger and younger ages. And they also work hard to put the blame on parents when inappropriate products get into their children's hands, even though the marketers do everything they can to make it next to impossible for parents to say "no."

Why Does It Matter?

Children use their experience and what is going on in the society around them to build ideas about themselves and their social world: What it means to be a boy or a girl, how people treat each other, the nature of relationships, what to respect and ridicule, right and wrong, and fairness and injustice. In addition to family, the society plays a central role in teaching children these lessons (Carlsson-Paige 2009).

What children learn when they are young becomes the foundation onto which they build the ideas that will ultimately guide their thinking and behavior as adults (Ginsburg and Opper 1987). The three stories at the beginning of this article, while vastly different in many respects, are a reflection of the kinds of lessons today's media and commercial culture are teaching children. They seem to go against what most parents and educators would want their children to learn about social responsibility and justice.

In 2007, the *Report of the APA Task Force on the Sexualization of Girls* (American Psychological Association 2007) summarizes the growing body of research on the impact of sexualized childhood. For instance, the report found that sexualization contributed to eating disorders, low self-esteem, depression, and trouble having a healthy sexual self-image in preteen and adolescent girls. However, the report found little research on the impact of sexualization on young children. But based on what we know about the impact on older children and about children's overall social development and anecdotal reports like those at the beginning of the chapter, we can begin to postulate how the sexualization of childhood is affecting children's social development and sense of social responsibility and justice.

Extremely Limiting Gender Stereotypes

Beginning from a young age, children learn a gender label for themselves and then look to the world around them to try to figure out what the label means. Their ideas about gender, sex, and sexuality develop gradually and are greatly influenced by information that their environments provide (Kohlberg 1966; Maccoby 1998).

Today's media and commercial cultures are teaching children a very narrow view of what it means to be a boy or girl. It is also teaching harmful lessons about femaleness and sexuality—that girls need skinny bodies, and clothing, makeup, and accessories that make them look "pretty," "grown-up," and "sexy" (Lamb and Brown 2006). How well girls succeed with this determines their value. Masculinity doesn't fare much better as boys are taught they need to be tough like "He-man," ready to fight, and able to take care of themselves (Pollack 1998).

Both girls and boys are learning lessons that limit the development of their full potential. Already in first grade, Clara experiences the pain that comes from not meeting the glamorized ideal of being thin when her classmates chant that she will break the jungle gym. And the other children are learning that it's okay to be mean and unjust to another child who does not meet that ideal, with few concerns about the impact of their behavior on Clara.

Remote Control Childhood

While we tend to focus on the lessons children are learning from the content they see in media and commercial culture, we often fail to recognize how what's going on also affects *how children interact* with the world. When children are glued to a screen, they are having second-hand experiences based on someone else's agenda. They are not actively using their own imagination or creating their own unique ideas. Then, when children play, their media-linked, highly structured toys channel them into imitating what they saw on the screen, they are more like robots than creative players building their own ideas from and learning from play (Levin 1998).

When this happens, children are much more likely to become "remote controlled" and learn the "programs" related to the sexualization and violence in their media and toys. It is harder for them to come up with their own creative ideas or solutions to intellectual or social problems. I have often called this *problem solving deficit disorder* (PSDD) (Levin 2008a). In the long run, it can lead to remote controlled people, who exhibit conformist behavior, accept orders without questioning, and mimic the mean-spirited and unjust behavior they see on the screen.

Objectified Relationships

Children learn how to interact positively with others and take the needs of others into account through a slow process of construction. They use content from how they are treated, their interaction with others, and how they see people treating each other to build their own ideas about how to behave. They gradually learn what to say and do to work out problems and conflicts in a peaceful manner, and to have respectful give-and-take relationships. It is vital that children learn these skills when they are young, because research suggests that patterns of behavior at age eight are related to behavior in adulthood (Eron and Slaby 1994).

The time children spend glued to a screen takes time away from their having the opportunity to interact directly with others and see the effects of their actions. In addition, the sexualized and violent content they see can teach them to view and treat others as "objects" (Lamb and Brown 2006).

Girls are judged by how they look—by how skinny they are and the clothes they can buy, just as Jenna knew on the first day of kindergarten when she defines popularity based on appearance. Boys judge each other by how strong, independent, and ready to fight they are and to judge girls by their looks.

When children treat others as objects—in ways that make perfect sense given the lessons society is teaching about relationships—they may end up doing things that get them in serious trouble, as the boy did in the *Washington Post* story, when he touched a girl's bottom at school (Bowlby 1982; Green 2008).

Sexualized Childhood and Social Injustice

The objectification of relationships—in conjunction with a remote controlled childhood—is preventing children from developing the empathy they need to treat others in caring and just ways. Children are becoming desensitized to the painful effects their actions can have on others.

Many teachers tell me that they spend too much time trying to maintain the social and emotional safety of their classrooms. They say they resort to using more "time outs" and harsher "discipline techniques" than in the past. And there are even elementary schools that have abolished recess because children hurt each other on the playground and the schools are worried about lawsuits. At the same time, the demands of *No Child Left Behind* are putting teachers under pressure to focus on the academic curriculum, often at the expense of children's social–emotional learning needs (Lantieri and Golman 2008).

Today's sexualized childhood is violating children's right to become fully functioning social beings who can participate in caring and just relationships. We run the risk of creating a generation of children who have *compassion deficit disorder* (CDD), the inability to empathize with others or to relate to others with mutual care, affection, and a sense of fairness and justice (Levin 2008b). And, when we often end up punishing children, rather than trying to understand their point of view and working to teach them alternative lessons, we too are treating them as objects and further contributing to CDD and injustice (Levin 2009).

What Citizens, Parents and Teachers Can Do

All adults in America can play an important role in this problem.

Adults Can be Thoughtfully Involved with the Media in Children's Lives

This means trying to protect young children as much as possible from highly sexualized or violent content. It also involves helping children learn to self-regulate and make good viewing decisions, as they get older. This is often easier to do with young children. But even as children get older, parents and teachers can learn more about the media children are watching and want to watch, and help them learn to make good choices. Parents can establish rules and routines so that media is not a constantly escalating force in children's lives. But in setting limits, it's important to get beyond the "Just Saying 'No'" approach; instead, when limit setting is needed, it can provide an opportunity to talk about and work things out together. Coming up with win-win solutions, instead of imposing power over children helps them feel they have a voice in the decisions and take more responsibility for their own actions (Levin 2003).

Teachers can have class discussions during which children talk about the media rules in their lives and hear about the rules other children have. As parents are told about these discussions, it can help with rule making and limit setting at home. Schools can have meetings and talk to parents about appropriate use of media and help create communities of parents who can talk about these issues with each other (Levin 1998).

Take a Proactive Role in Helping Children Make Sense of What They See and Influencing What They Learn from It

Children need a safe place to process a sexualized environment to which they are exposed. Parents as well as educators in early childhood settings can help them with this. When situations, such as those at the beginning of this chapter, occur, let the children know you're interested in what they are doing. Try to find out about what they think and feel. For instance, in one kindergarten class when children pretended to go on dates, the teacher asked questions like, "What do you know about dates?"; "How do you decide who your date will be?"; "What do you do when you're on a date?"; "What happens if you don't have a date?" To open up to adults with what they really think and need, children have to know that whatever they bring up for discussion is okay, even if adults are not happy with what they hear!

From such conversations, children learn they can talk to the trusted adult without being embarrassed, ridiculed, or punished. Adults can answer questions and provide input that clears up misconceptions that worry and confuse children. They can also interject comments that *influence children's thinking*. This is especially important around helping children learn how to have positive relationships and to expand narrow gender stereotypes for both girls and boys—to get beyond today's narrow focus for girls on being pretty and sexy and attractive, and for boys on being tough and macho and ready to fight.

Try not to worry about giving "right answers" or if children have ideas that don't agree with the adults' understanding. The important thing is to *stay connected*—making sure that children know you are there as a resource to help them, not a punisher or critic (Levin and Kilbourne 2008).

Conclusion: Working for Change

We need to work at all levels of society to limit the power of corporations to market a sexualized childhood to children. Schools and community groups have a vital role to play in doing this and so do government legislation and policy. There are also organizations that have been successful at organizing the public to work for change. For instance, the Campaign for a Commercial-Free Childhood (CCFC—www.commercialfreechildhood.org), which this author co-founded in 2000, launched a successful letter-writing campaign that pressured Scholastic into removing Bratz doll products from its Book Club and Book Fairs. And with the inauguration of President Obama, CCFC began a lobbying campaign to get the new administration to take the lead reigning in corporate marketing practices that harm children.

The current situation is harming children, families, and ultimately all of society. There is much that needs to be done to create a society that supports children's healthy gender and sexual development, and positive relationships with others—a society that cares more about children than profits. The more we work together to stop the corporate exploitation of children, the more social justice we will succeed in reclaiming for them.

References

American Psychological Association. (2007). *Report of the APA task force on the sexualization of girls.* Washington: American Psychological Association.

Bowlby, J. (1982). *Attachment and loss. Vol. 1: Attachment* (2nd ed.). New York: Basic.

Carlsson-Paige, N. (2009). *Taking back childhood: A proven roadmap for raising confident, creative and compassionate kids.* New York: Plume.

Carlsson-Paige, N., & Levin, D. (1990). *Who's calling the shots? How to respond effectively to children's fascination with war play and war toys (and violent TV).* Gabriola Island: New Society.

Englehardt, T. (1986). Saturday morning fever: The hard sell takeover of kids' TV. *Mother Jones, 11*(6), 38–48, 54.

Eron, L., & Slaby, R. (1994). Introduction. In L. Eron, J. Gentry, & P. Schlegel (Eds.), *Reason to hope: A psychological perspective on youth and violence* (pp. 1–22). Washington: American Psychological Association.

Ginsburg, H., & Opper, S. (1987). *Piaget's theory of intellectual development* (3rd ed.). Englewood Cliffs: Prentice Hall.

Green, M. (Ed.). (2008). *Risking human security: Attachment and public life.* London: Karnac.

Horovitz, B. (2006, November 22). Six strategies marketers use to make kids want things bad. *USA Today,* p. 1b.

Kaiser Family Foundation. (1996). *Sex, kids and the family hour: A three-part study of sexual content on television.* Menlo Park: Kaiser Family Foundation.

Kaiser Family Foundation. (2003). *Zero to six: Electronic media in the lives of infants, toddlers and preschoolers.* Menlo Park: Kaiser Family Foundation (Fall).

Kaiser Family Foundation. (2005). *Sex on TV 4: Executive summary.* Menlo Park: Kaiser Family Foundation (November).

Kohlberg, L. (1966). A cognitive-developmental analysis of children's sex-role concepts and attitudes. In E. Maccoby (Ed.), *The development of sex-differences* (pp. 82–173). Stanford: Stanford University Press.

Lamb, S., & Brown, L. (2006). *Packaging girlhood: Rescuing our daughters from marketers' schemes.* New York: Norton.

Lantieri, L., & Golman, D. (2008). *Building emotional intelligence.* Louisville: Sounds True.

Levin, D. (1998). *Remote control childhood? Combating the hazards of media culture.* Washington: National Association for the Education of Young Children.

Levin, D. (2003). *Teaching young children in violent times: Building a peaceable classroom* (2nd ed.). Cambridge: Educators for Social Responsibility and Washington: National Association for the Education of Young Children.

Levin, D. (2008a). Compassion deficit disorder? The impact of consuming culture on children's relationships. In M. Green (Ed.), *Risking human security: Attachment and public life* (pp. 87–102). London: Karnac.

Levin, D. (2008b). Problem solving deficit disorder: Creative versus programmed play in Korea and the United States. In E. Goodenough (Ed.), *Where do children play?* (pp. 137–141). Detroit: Wayne University Press.

Levin, D. (2009). Too young to be a consumer: The toll of commercial culture on the rights of childhood. *Exchange Magazine, 31*(3), 49–52.

Levin, D., & Carlsson-Paige, N. (2006). *The war play dilemma: What every parent and teacher needs to know.* New York: Teachers College Press.

Levin, D., & Kilbourne, J. (2008). *So sexy so soon: The new sexualized childhood and what parents can do to protect their kids.* New York: Ballantine.

Linn, S. (2004). *Consuming kids: The hostile takeover of childhood.* New York: New Press.

Maccoby, E. (1998). *The two sexes: Growing up apart, coming together.* Cambridge: Belknap.

Media Education Foundation. (2008). Consuming kids: The commercialization of childhood. DVD available at: www.mediaed.org.

Pollack, W. (1998). *Real boys: Rescuing our sons from the myths of boyhood.* New York: Random House.

Ravitch, D., & Viteritti, J. (2003). *Kids stuff: Marketing sex and violence to America's children.* Baltimore: Johns Hopkins University Press.

Schor, J. (2005). *Born to buy: The commercialized child and the new consumer culture.* New York: Scribner.

Schulte, B. (2008, April 3). For little children, grown-up labels as sexual harassers. Washington Post. http://www.washingtonpost.com/wp-dyn/content/article/2008/04/02/AR2008040203463.html. Accessed 5 Apr 2008.

U.S. toy industry sales generate $22 billion in 2007. (2008, February 12). *Business Wire.*

Chapter 4
Child Justice, Caregiver Empowerment, and Community Self-Determination

Joshua D. Sparrow

Child Justice Means Justice for Caregivers and Communities

For several decades, international bodies have sought intercultural consensus on children's rights (U.N. General Assembly, Convention on the Rights of the Child 1989), many of which correspond to biological requirements for survival and health. The biological construct has served as a basis for appeals to "universality," while child development has often been conceptually separated from survival, narrowly construed as dependent on water, food, shelter, and basic healthcare. Yet children's survival also depends on the fulfillment of basic developmental needs, for example, undisrupted attachments to primary caregivers (Ainsworth 1962; Bowlby 1988a, b; Bronfenbrenner 2004; Winnicott 1964/1987). When children lose critical attachment figures in the first years of life, they may stop eating and die from starvation and the associated stress can also suppress their immune systems, leading to life threatening infections (Spitz 1945; Soulé et al. 1995).

The continuity of children's early attachments depends on the health and well-being of their caregivers. In order to survive, grow, and thrive, children need caregivers whose own survival, development, and ability to nurture their young are not endangered. Development-promoting early interactions must be nested within strong communities where broader social relationships protect and reinforce these primary ones. Yet the inseparability of children's rights from those of their caregivers sometimes goes unrecognized, as does the critical role of the community context for child survival and development.

J. D. Sparrow (✉)
Harvard Medical School, Boston, USA
e-mail: joshua.sparrow@childrens.harvard.edu

B. S. Fennimore, A. L. Goodwin (eds.), *Promoting Social Justice for Young Children*, Educating the Young Child 3, DOI 10.1007/978-94-007-0570-8_4,

Despite the powerful effects of resilience, poverty can weaken communities, jeopardize caregiver functioning and survival, and impede child development. Anti-poverty programs can support caregiver functioning if initiated, designed, and implemented with full and continuous input from the families and communities that they are intended to serve. Otherwise, despite the best of intentions, they risk disempowering caregivers. Caregivers' active participation in development-promoting relationships with their children, in the fulfillment of their children's rights, depends in part on ongoing experiences of being able to positively influence their children's lives.

The Intergenerational Transmission of Poverty and the Educational Achievement Gap

Poverty is not perpetuated by educational disadvantage alone, but by a host of factors impinging on children's development and on caregivers' capacity to promote it. These include disparities in access to healthcare and nutrition, and exposure to environmental toxins (Dietrich et al. 2005) that may first begin to affect a child's brain development before birth. They also include social and economic policies that perpetuate these and other disparities (Commission on the Social Determinants of Health 2008), while impinging on parents' sense that they can make a difference in their children's lives. Damaging disparities in access are often based on race, ethnicity, religion, class, and other pretexts for discrimination, oppression, and exploitation—experiences that also have direct effects on child development and caregiver functioning.

Anti-poverty interventions aimed at improving academic performance must address factors such as these. Those that provide purely educational services alone run the risk of locating the "cause" of poverty within the child (e.g., "who does not try to learn or does not care"), the parents (e.g., "who do not read to the child"), or group (e.g., "which does not value education"). Inadvertently, such interventions may reproduce and reinforce the experience of disenfranchisement that is both a result of poverty and a factor in its perpetuation.

Yet intergenerational poverty is in part structurally determined in wealthy industrialized democracies such as the United States by the educational achievement gap that opens before kindergarten. Skills and capacities necessary for school readiness and later productive employment—including self-regulation, self-agency, and self-esteem—nurtured in early adult caregiver–child interactions are critical to closing this gap and breaking the cycle of poverty (Bardige 2005; Dawson et al. 2003; Henderson and Berla 1994; Shonkoff and Phillips 2000; Sroufe 1983; Zigler et al. 2002). Caregivers play a central role in laying these foundations for children's future development-dependent survival. Anti-poverty interventions targeting higher educational attainment expand their effectiveness when they ensure caregivers' capacity to function effectively in this role.

Brain Development Depends on the Social Determinants of Health and Parental Emotional Availability

Brain development critical to learning readiness unfolds most extensively in the fetus and earliest years (Huttenlocher and Dabholkar 1997; Nelson 2000; Nelson and Bloom 1997) when it is most vulnerable to malnutrition, traumatic stress, poor health, environmental toxins (Adibi et al. 2003; Choi et al. 2006), and other social determinants of health. It also depends on early relationships with caregivers whose ability to engage in interactions with their infants may also be compromised by the multiple stresses of poverty.

Human interactions are the most complex source of brain stimulation. They are also the locus for the regulation of arousal, attention, affect, and sensory processing necessary for external stimulation to positively influence brain structure and function (Bigelow 1999; Bornstein and Bornstein 1995; Bornstein and Tamis-Lemonda 1997; Bush et al. 2000; Campos et al. 2004; Cassidy 1994; Kirsch et al. 1995; Spangler et al. 1994). Emotional availability, on which these processes depend, in turn depends in part on the ability to put aside distractions and shift attention to the interaction. This allows the adult to sensitively register and respond to the infant or young child's subtle behavioral cues. Adult caregivers' emotional availability is essential to the arousal and attention of the infant or young child, to the modulation of stimulation so that it can be taken in and processed meaningfully, and to effective responses to signs of readiness for stimulation and overload (Bigelow 1999; Tronick et al. 1986; Tronick and Weinberg 1997). It also supports the infant's emerging emotional availability necessary for participation in these earliest relationships and for eliciting nurturance from adult caregivers.

Parental Emotional Availability Depends on Relationships to Community Supports

Emotional availability of adult caregivers is impeded by numerous factors that may be associated with poverty, for example, social isolation, political disenfranchisement, hopelessness about one's family's future, mental illness, and overwhelming stress (Dawson et al. 2003; Guterman 2001; Hans 2000; Murray et al. 2003; Scheper-Hughes 1992; Sparrow 2007; Tronick et al. 1986; Tronick and Weinberg 1997; Yellow Horse Brave Heart and Debruyn 1998). Normal, predictable developmental crises of a child may add to such stress (Brazelton 1999; Brazelton 2006). Emotional availability is promoted by a host of other factors, for example, parental sense of competence and efficacy, hope for the child's future, as well as social connectedness and sense of empowerment—that can be derived from community-based supports. Social isolation and disempowerment are also risk factors for child abuse and neglect—extreme forms of parental emotional unavailability (Daro et al. 1993; Guterman 2001).

Characteristics of Programs that Promote Caregivers' Emotional Availability

Programs that increase caregivers' emotional availability to infants and young children by addressing these factors improve brain development and learning readiness (Schorr and Schorr 1989; Shonkoff and Phillips 2000). However, many programs targeting improved child-development outcomes do not promote emotional availability (caregiver sensitivity, contingent responsiveness, and attunement) and the factors such as social connectedness and empowerment that affect it. Instead they focus on providing information and "teaching" parenting skills that may be useful, but insufficient for optimal child development, and may inadvertently undermine parents' confidence in their own abilities.

In recent years, a number of parent support programs have recognized the need to go beyond the unilateral transmission of parenting 'skills' and child development 'knowledge' and have incorporated developmental, relational and strengths-based strategies, including those derived from the Touchpoints Approach, based on the work of T. B. Brazelton and co-workers (Brazelton 1999; Brazelton 2006; Brazelton and Sparrow 2008). In this approach, parents and care providers share observation and discovery of child behaviors and parent–child interactions so that emotional availability is experienced and reinforced. Parents and professional providers establish and build understanding and mutual support through the co-construction of the meanings of a child's behavior, decreasing social isolation, increasing parents' understanding of their child, and promoting parental sense of competence. This approach stabilizes mounting parental stress (Copeman et al. 2007; Easterbrooks et al. 2007) and increases emotional availability by offering anticipatory guidance on predictable developmental crises. When temporary regressions in a child's behavior are understood as normative, parents are encouraged to interpret them as positive signs of a child's healthy development that they can take credit for and continue to nurture.

Parent Engagement in Programs Offering Social Connectedness and Empowerment

Many parents feel threatened by and thus avoid basic educational, social, and preventive healthcare services for their children and themselves. Many do not engage in parent-education programs that offer information and skills without also offering respectful, trusting, and inspiring relationships (Adelman 1996; Arnett 1989; Copeman et al. 2007; Edelwich and Brodsky 1980; Fagan 1994; Galinsky 1990; Platt and Olsen 1990; Shpancer 1999; Zigler and Turner 1982). When parents do attend, they may "just go through the motions," even providing the desired responses on "fact"-based questionnaires, without increased emotional availability to their children and without a greater sense of their own competence as parents or of connection to other parents that might enhance their effectiveness.

Why? In part, because the unstated message of these programs may seem to them to be that they lack information and skills and, as a result, the competence and efficacy to influence their children's lives. The unintended consequence is to further undermine parental self-confidence and reinforce disenfranchisement. In turn, this interferes with parents' ability to engage deeply with their children in the present moment and to invest emotionally in hope for their futures. It also may have a damaging effect on their readiness to engage in systems of care that they may associate with unhelpful and even negative experiences.

Strengths-based and collaborative approaches, rather than those that are more didactic, can be inherently empowering because the locus of expertise is understood to reside in parents and their communities. Relationship-building strategies can be used to help parents connect to each other and other social supports, and also to create safety, trust, and hope in their relationships with providers. When parents receive their relationships with professional caregivers (e.g., their children's childcare providers) as positive and supportive, they experience less stress than their peers without such supports, and emotional availability increases as a result (Copeman et al. 2007; Easterbrooks et al. 2007).

Professional Caregivers' Emotional Availability to Children and Families

Within the child-focused professions, formal preparation for work with parents is often limited. Rarely is specific training offered on parent behavior and development. Most professionals working with families of young children are unprepared to engage parents in systems of care, to help them dare to hope and discover their motivation to participate, and to promote the qualities of parent–child interactions critical to brain development and early learning. Few have been systematically encouraged to actively welcome and respect parents' views and wisdom, nor have they been taught other strategies for re-equilibrating the parent–professional power imbalance. Yet stances that sustain this imbalance stress both parents and providers, and diminish the potential positive effects of their relationships on children's development (Baker and Manfredi-Pettit 2004; Owen et al. 2000; Shpancer 1999).

The emotional availability of professional caregivers (Copeman et al. 2007; Shonkoff and Phillips 2000) allows them to model, understand, and sensitively interact with families in which emotional availability and the developmental processes that depend on it are threatened by overwhelming stress. Yet service providers to children and parents in pain or poverty are *at risk* for compassion fatigue, vicarious trauma, demoralization, and the loss of their own emotional availability (Edelwich and Brodsky 1980; Platt and Olsen 1990). Professionals are rarely taught to protect themselves from these endemic outcomes, and the institutions that employ them rarely address these predictable challenges (Beardslee and Demaso 1982; Beardslee and Gladstone in Press). Ineffective service delivery is the widespread result—including insensitive interactions with children and judgmental and punitive interactions with parents. Strategies based on established principles of adult education, group process, and reflective practice can be incorporated into professional training as well as ongoing institutional operations (Adelman 1996; Arnett 1989; Bernstein et al. 1994; Fenichel 1992) to protect the emotional availability of "at risk" professional caregivers. When these are successfully employed, providers often find that they are less stressed, feel more rewarded by their work, and discover mutual support from parents as they exercise their professional role in supporting children's development (Jacobs et al. 2010; Singer and Hornstein 2010).

Collaboration Among Systems of Care

Systems of care and service providers are generally not coordinated to address the full range of challenges that families confront (Schorr and Schorr 1989). Most families with limited material resources face not one but multiple challenges. Parents must navigate several different systems of care in order to meet their children's needs, and are likely to encounter a confusing range of approaches and underlying perspectives in the professionals and agencies that intend to serve them.

The obstacles to effective cross-sector coordination and collaboration are substantial, including client confidentiality and eligibility requirements, increasing specialization, separate funding streams, and conflicting institutional and professional cultures. Service providers are rarely trained nor have they had significant experience in effective cross-sector collaboration and coordination. Approaches that provide a set of over-arching principles, and a common language across healthcare, early care and education, early intervention, and social services sectors can help multi-disciplinary providers to build relationships, identify common ground and shared goals, while mobilizing them to resolve conflicts. In communities where a common language among agencies is adopted that reflects the strengths and hopes of families, a coherent and seamless array of services can result (Tough 2008). Participating parents are more likely to arrive at a sense of mastery and inclusion, rather than isolation.

Realigning Professional Caregivers and Their Institutions with the Strengths and Needs of the Families They Serve

Most systems of care arise from professional cultures rather than the cultures of those they serve, and often devolve into policies, procedures, and practices that are out-of-sync with family needs and strengths (Schorr and Schorr 1989). An alternative is to build on the inherent strengths that most adults can discover in themselves through the process of becoming parents—regardless of culture or circumstance—as well as on the parallel processes within professionals who devote their work to children. This approach rekindles providers' dedication to their mission and realigns their dedication with that of the parents themselves. A focus on providers' strengths and positive intent prepares them to re-examine their own deficit-focused practices and the negative assumptions that they are based on, as well as the biases that may prevent them from understanding and integrating the perspectives of the families they serve (Sparrow and Brazelton 2008).

Culturally Adapted Programs

Family engagement in systems of care depends on culturally informed professional practices (Osofsky 2004), since culture is a central context in which families and communities promote children's development. Service providers require continuing training and professional development in order to sustain the ongoing process of understanding other cultures and their own, and to confront their reluctance to give up power in order to empower those who live with poverty. Approaches that are collaborative rather than prescriptive emphasize the strengths of those they serve rather than deficits, and rely on strategies designed to re-equilibrate the traditional provider-program participant power imbalances. These approaches may be readily transformed by the cultures of the families and communities they are intended for, when offered with the invitation to do so (Sparrow and Brazelton 2008).

Child-rearing practices are largely cultural, and no one culture can claim superiority in its approach or impose its beliefs on another without risking undermining essential effective practices (LeVine et al. 1994; LeVine 2004). Parent "education" can be a culturally presumptuous undertaking. The cultural origins of what is being "taught" must be carefully examined, as should the consequences of positioning parents as "students." While useful information may be provided in parent-education programs, these must take care not to invalidate culturally derived practices that may be equally safe and effective while also conferring a greater sense of personal connection to sources of experience and wisdom. The process of becoming a parent depends on a larger set of experiences, conditions, and contexts that contribute to parents' sense of competence and efficacy in protecting and nurturing their young. More recently, some parent-support programs have begun to strive also to promote and reinforce these.

The Touchpoints Approach—An Example

The Touchpoints Approach, for example, builds on parents' experiential learning through observation of their own children's behavior. Parents actively engage in discovering their own child's development from the perspective of their own culture. They watch as their infants generate behaviors that draw them in and lead them to respond. Interventions that incorporate careful observation of individual infant behavior and its contribution to parenting responses are more meaningful and compelling to parents, and more supportive of parental mastery than didactic, one-size-fits all informational ones. In addition, the human infant brain has evolved to be attuned to and stimulated by parent behaviors that sensitively respond to the infant's cues (Posner and Rothbart 2000; Shonkoff and Phillips 2000), and such parental responses can be promoted through careful observation of infant behavior.

Bolstering the Power of Attachment to Optimize Parent–Child Interactions

The Touchpoints Approach aims at mobilizing parents' motivation and hope, in support of their children's health and development, when adversity risks disempowering them. Such motivation arises from the pervasive biological processes of attachment—evolved for the human species' survival. Yet attachment may be diminished or absent in settings where parent or child survival is threatened (Bowlby 1988a, b; Scheper-Hughes 1992). Threats to children's development such as disruption of primary caregiver attachments can jeopardize their survival. Threats to parents' survival can jeopardize children's survival and development. Threats to children's survival jeopardize not only children's development but also their parents' capacity to invest in them emotionally. In such dire circumstances, programs aimed at promoting parental emotional availability must also, of course, address urgent survival needs. Such efforts may be implemented so as to offer experiences of social connectedness and empowerment, but they must also provide realistic hope for survival and the family's future.

Integrating Developmental, Relational, Strengths-based, Collaborative, Culturally Adapted Approaches

In some settings, parent education programs are offered in lieu of other services addressing families' basic survival needs, without recognizing the critical role of the conditions and contexts in which childrearing occurs. Approaches that promote parental engagement, empowerment, social connectedness, and emotional availability are additive to but not a replacement for services that address the wide range of health, educational, nutritional, housing, legal, and other material needs of materially impoverished families (Tough 2008). Yet such approaches can expand the effectiveness of these services when integrated into programs for families from minoritized cultures living with poverty that have traditionally been considered "hard-to-reach," unlikely to engage, and have good reason to be skeptical and even suspicious of healthcare, educational, and social services.

Used in urban and rural settings, with peoples from a wide range of cultural and ethnic backgrounds, the Touchpoints Approach is appropriate for programs serving families of young children in early care and education, early intervention, healthcare, child welfare, and social services sectors. Respectful, strengths-based, collaborative approaches reposition service providers on the same playing field as families (Sparrow and Brazelton 2008). Providers find new self-understanding, humility, courage, and commitment needed to learn from the families they serve, and to align their goals, strengths, and needs with them.

Challenges and Opportunities for Child Justice

Children's survival, like their development, depends on relationships with parents and other caregivers. Caregivers engage most effectively in these development-promoting relationships when they feel competent about their caregiving abilities, connected to a community that supports them in this function, to a culture that provides guidance in childrearing practices, and to a future for themselves and their children that they feel empowered to influence (Guterman 2001). Future opportunities to uphold and widely disseminate justice for children will arise through the design and implementation of services and supports for children, families, and communities that are comprehensive enough to ensure survival and health yet are also developmental, relational, strengths-based, and culturally transformed. The challenge is to do so via processes driven by communities themselves and by the empowering principles of self-determination.

References

Adelman, H. S. (1996). *Restructuring education support services: Toward the concept of the enabling component.* Kent: American School Health Association.

Adibi, J., Perera, F. P., Jedrychowski, W., Camaan, D., Barr, D., & Whyatt, R. M. (2003). Prenatal exposures to phthalates in New York City and Krakow, Poland. *Environmental Health Perspectives, 111*(14), 1719–1722.

Ainsworth, M. D. (1962). The effects of maternal deprivation: A review of findings and controversy in the context of research strategy. In M. D. Ainsworth, & R. G. Andry (Eds.), *Deprivation of maternal care.* Geneva: World Health Organization.

Arnett, J. (1989). Caregivers in day care centers: Does training matter? *Journal of Applied Developmental Psychology, 10,* 541–552.

Baker, A. C., & Manfredi-Pettit, L. A. (2004). *Relationships, the heart of quality care: Creating community among adults in early care settings.* Washington: NAEYC.

Bardige, B. (2005). *At a loss for words: How America's failing our children and what we can do about it.* Philadelphia: Temple University Press.

Beardslee, W. R., & DeMaso, D. R. (1982). Staff groups in a pediatric hospital: Content and coping. *American Journal of Orthopsychiatry, 52*(4), 712–718. (Reprinted from *Coping with physical illness: New directions*, by R. H. Moos, Ed., 1984, New York: Plenum)

Beardslee W. R., & Gladstone T. R. G. (in Press). Health prevention and promotion. In R. C. Talley, G. L. Fricchione, B. G. Druss, & R. Martinez (Eds.), *Caregiving and mental health.* New York: Oxford University Press.

Bernstein, V., Percansky, C., & Wechsler, N. (1994). Strengthening families through strengthening relationships: The ounce of prevention fund developmental training and support program. In M. Roberts (Ed.), *Model programs in service delivery in child and family mental health.* Hillsdale: Erlbaum.

Bigelow, A. E. (1999). Infants' sensitivity to imperfect contingency in social interaction. In P. Rochat (Ed.), *Early social cognition: Understanding others in the first months of life* (pp. 137–154). Mahwah: Erlbaum.

Bornstein, M., & Bornstein, H. (1995). Caregivers' responsiveness and cognitive development in infants and toddlers: Theory and research. In P. L. Mangione (Ed.), *Infant-toddler caregiving: A guide to cognitive development and learning.* Sacramento: CDE Press.

Bornstein, M. H., & Tamis-LeMonda, C. S. (1997). Maternal responsiveness and infant mental abilities: Specific predictive relations. *Infant Behavior and Development, 20*(3), 283–296.

Bowlby, J. (1988a). *Attachment & loss. Vol. III. Loss, sadness and depression.* London: Hogarth and The Institute of Psychoanalysis.

Bowlby, J. (1988b). *A secure base.* New York: Basic Books.

Brazelton, T. B. (1999). How to help parents of young children: The Touchpoints model. *Journal of Perinatology Supplement, 19,* 6–8.

Brazelton, T. B., & Sparrow, J. D. (2006). *Touchpoints: Birth to three: Your child's emotional and behavioral development.* (2nd ed.). Cambridge: Da Capo.

Bronfenbrenner, U. (Ed.). (2004). Making human beings human: Bioecological perspectives on human development. *The SAGE Program on Applied Developmental Science.* Thousand Oaks: Sage.

Bush, G., Luu, P., & Posner, M. I. (2000). Cognitive and emotional influences in the anterior cingulated cortex. *Trends in Cognitive Science, 4,* 215–222.

Campos, J. J., Frankel, C. B., & Camras, L. (2004). On the nature of emotion regulation. *Child Development, 75,* 377–394.

Cassidy, J. (1994). Emotion regulation: Influences of attachment relationships. In N. A. Fox (Ed.), *Monographs of the Society for Research in Child Development,* 59(2–3), 228–249 (Serial no. 240).

Choi, H., Jedrychowski, W., Spengler, J., Camann, D. E., Whyatt, R. M., & Rauh, V. (2006). International studies of prenatal exposure to polycyclic aromatic hydrocarbons and fetal growth. *Environmental Health Perspectives, 114,* 1744–1750.

Commission on Social Determinants of Health. (2008). Closing the gap in a generation: Health equity through action on the social determinants of health. *Final Report of the Commission on Social Determinants of Health.* Geneva: World Health Organization.

Copeman, A., Miranda-Julian, C., Goldberg, J., Davis, C. R., Brady, M., Adams, L., et al. (2007). *Associations among childcare provider characteristics, parent-provider relationships, and parent anxiety. Poster session.* Boston: Society for Research in Child Development.

Daro, D., Jones, E., & McCurdy, K. (1993). *Preventing child abuse: An evaluation of services to high-risk families.* A report for the William Penn Foundation. Philadelphia: William Penn Foundation.

Dawson, G., Ashman, S. B., Panagiotides, H., Hessl, D., Self, J., & Yamada, E. (2003). Preschool outcomes of children of depressed mothers: Role of maternal behavior, contextual risk, and children's brain activity. *Child Development, 74,* 1158–1175.

Dietrich, K. N., Eskenazi, B., Schantz, S., Yolton, K., Rauh, V. A., & Johnson, C. B. (2005). Principles and practices of neurodevelopmental assessment in children: Lessons learned from the Centers for Children's Environmental Health and Disease Prevention research. *Environmental Health Perspectives, 113,* 1437–1446.

Easterbrooks, A., Copeman, A., Goldberg, J., Miranda-Julian, C., & Swartz, M. (2007). *Supporting parent–child relationships in early care and education.* The Society for Research in Child Development Biennial Conference, Boston, MA.

Edelwich, J., & Brodsky, A. (1980). *Burn-out: Stages of disillusionment in the helping professions.* New York: Human Sciences Press.

Fagan, J. (1994). Correlates of maternal involvement in on-site and off-site day care centers. *Child and Youth Care Forum, 23,* 275–290.
Fenichel, E. S. (Ed.). (1992). *Learning through supervision and mentorship to support the development of infants, toddlers and their families: A source book.* Arlington: Zero to Three, National Center for Clinical Infant Programs.
Galinsky, E. (1990). Why are some parent-teacher partnerships clouded with difficulties? *Young Children, 45,* 2–39.
Guterman, N. B. (2001). *Stopping child maltreatment before it starts: Emerging horizons in early home visitation services.* Thousand Oaks: Sage.
Hans, S. L. (2000). Parenting and parent–child relationships in families affected by substance abuse. In H. E. Fitzgerald, B. M. Lester, & B. S. Zuckerman (Eds.), *Children of addiction: Research, health and policy issues* (pp. 45–68). New York: Taylor & Francis.
Henderson, A. T., & Berla, N. (Eds.). (1994). *A new generation of evidence: The family is critical to.* Washington: Center for Law & Education.
Huttenlocher, P. R., & Dabholkar, A. S. (1997). Regional differences in synaptogenesis in human cerebral cortex. *Journal of Comparative Neurology, 387,* 167–178.
Jacobs, F., Swartz, M. I., Bartlett, J. D., & Easterbrooks, M. A. (2010). Placing relationships at the core of early care and education programs. In B. Lester & J. D. Sparrow (Eds.), *Nurturing children and families: Building on the legacy of T. Berry Brazelton.* Hoboken: Blackwell (in press).
Kirsch, S. J., Crnic, K. A., & Greenberg, M. T. (1995). Relations between parent–child affect and synchrony and cognitive outcome at 5 years of age. *Personal Relationships, 2,* 187–198.
LeVine, R. (2004). Challenging expert knowledge: Findings from an African study of infant care and development. In U. P. Gielen, & J. L. Roopnarine (Eds.), *Childhood and adolescence: Cross-cultural perspective and applications* (pp. 149–165). Westport: Praeger.
LeVine, R., Dixon, S., LeVine, S., Richman, A., Leiderman, P. H., & Keefer, C. H. (1994). *Child care and culture: Lessons from Africa.* Cambridge: Cambridge University Press.
Murray, L., Cooper, P., & Hipwell, A. (2003). Mental health of parents caring for infants. *Archives of Women's Mental Health, 6,* 71–77.
Osofsky, J. D. (Ed.). (2004). *Young children and trauma: Intervention and treatment.* New York: Guilford Press.
Owen, M. T., Ware, A. M., & Barfoot, B. (2000). Caregiver–mother partnership behavior and the quality of caregiver–child and mother–child interactions. *Early Childhood Research Quarterly, 15*(3), 413–428.
Nelson, C. A. (2000). Neural plasticity and human development: The role of early experience in sculpting memory systems. *Developmental Science, 3,* 115–136.
Nelson, C. A., & Bloom, F. E. (1997). Child development and neuroscience. *Child Development, 68*(5), 983.
Platt, J. M., & Olsen, J. (1990). Why teachers are leaving special education. *Teacher Education and Special Education, 13,* 192–196.
Posner, M. I., & Rothbart, M. K. (2000). Developing mechanisms of self-regulation. *Development and Psychopathology, 12,* 427–441.
Scheper-Hughes, N. (1992). *Death without weeping: The violence of everyday violence in Brazil.* Berkeley: University of California Press.
Schorr, L., & Schorr, D. (1989). *Within our reach: Breaking the cycle of disadvantage.* New York: Anchor Books Doubleday.
Shonkoff, J., & Phillips, D. (Eds.). (2000). *From neurons to neighborhoods: The science of early childhood development.* Washington: National Academy Press.
Shpancer, N. (1999). Caregiver–parent relations in daycare: Testing the buffer hypothesis. *Early Child Development and Care, 156,* 1–14.
Singer, J., & Hornstein, J. (2010). The Touchpoints Approach for early care and education providers. In B. Lester, & J. D. Sparrow (Eds.), *Nurturing children and families: Building on the legacy of T. Berry Brazelton.* Hoboken: Blackwell (in press).

Soulé, M., Lauzanne, K., & Leblanc, N. (1995). La carence de soins maternels. In S. Lebovici, R. Diatkine, & M. Soulé (Eds.), *Nouveau traité de psychiatrie de l'enfant et de l'adolescent* (Vol. 4, pp. 2529–2545). Paris: Presses Universitaires de France.

Spangler, G., Schieche, M., Ilg, U., Maier, U., & Ackermann, C. (1994). Maternal sensitivity as an external organizer for biobehavioral regulation in infancy. *Developmental Psychobiology, 27,* 425–437.

Sparrow, J. D. (2007). Understanding stress in children. *Pediatric Annals, 36*(4), 187–194.

Sparrow J. D, & Brazelton, T. B. (2008). A developmental approach to the prevention of common behavioral problems. In T. K. McInerny, H. M. Adam, D. E. Campbell, D. M. Kamat, & K. J. Kelleher (Eds.), *American Academy of Pediatrics textbook of pediatric care* (1st ed., pp. 1156–1163). Elk Grove Village: American Academy of Pediatrics.

Spitz, R. A. (1945). Hospitalism: An inquiry into the genesis of psychiatric conditions in early childhood. *Psychoanalytic Study of the Child, 1,* 53–74.

Sroufe, L. A. (1983). Infant–caregiver attachment and patterns of adaptation in preschool: The roots of maladaptation and competence. In M. Perlmutter (Ed.), *Minnesota symposium in child psychology, 16* (pp. 41–81). Hillsdale: Erlbaum.

Tough, P. (2008). *Whatever it takes—Geoffrey Canada's quest to change Harlem and America.* Boston: Houghton Mifflin Harcourt.

Tronick, E. Z., Cohn, J., & Shea, E. (1986). The transfer of affect between mothers and infants: In T. B. Brazelton & M. W. Yogman (Eds.), *Affective development in infancy* (pp. 11–25). Norwood: Ablex.

Tronick, E. Z., & Weinberg, M. K. (1997). Depressed mothers and infants: Failure to form dyadic states of consciousness. In L. Murray & P. Cooper (Eds.), *Post partum depression and child development* (pp. 54–81). New York: Guilford.

U.N. General Assembly, Convention on the Rights of the Child (1989), United Nations. http://www2.ohchr.org/english/law/crc.htm. Accessed 15 June 2009.

Winnicott, D. W. (1964/1987). *The child, the family, and the outside world.* Reading: Addison-Wesley.

Yellow Horse Brave Heart, M., & Debruyn, L. M. (1998). The American Indian holocaust: Healing historical unresolved grief. *American Indian & Alaska Native Mental Health Research, 8*(2), 60–82.

Zigler, E. F., & Turner, P. (1982). Parents and day care workers: A failed partnership? In E. F. Zigler & E. W. Gordon (Eds.), *Day care: Scientific and social policy issues* (pp. 174–182). Boston: Auburn House.

Zigler, E. F., Finn-Stevenson, M., & Hall, N. W. (2002). *The first three years and beyond: Brain and development and social policy.* New Haven: Yale University Press.

Chapter 5
Not in Harm's Way. Or are They? War, Social Justice, and Young Children in the United States

Judith Van Hoorn and Diane E. Levin

In this chapter we use a peace and social justice framework to examine the impact of war on children in the United States. Why would we focus on social justice and the effects of war on children living in the United States? We argue that when war occurs, children and families on all sides are "in harm's way" even when the wars are in faraway lands.

The inextricable relationship between peace and social justice is obvious when we see photos of Afghan and Iraqi children living at war's epicenter. Tens of thousands have been killed or injured, millions more left traumatized, destitute, and displaced. Beyond these tragic *direct effects*, armed conflict and the special stressors created by deployment lead inevitably to *structural* violence that impacts children—the collapse of systems that support such basic needs as food and shelter, medical services and education. Then there are all the *lessons learned* about how countries use violence to solve their conflicts with each other.

Much has been written about the effects of war on children who live in areas of armed conflict but not about children, like those in the United States, who live far away from *their country's war*. The growing literature on young children and social justice seldom considers the impact of the current wars in Afghanistan and Iraq on children here.

We use a peace and social justice framework as a lens for understanding and responding to the effects of war on young children in the United States. First, we look at children with parents in the US military who have been deployed in Afghanistan and Iraq as well as all young children as they hear accounts from media, parents, and peers about the war their country is waging. We then consider the toll of the insidious structural violence of war resulting from macrolevel societal policies and practices, in this case, the tradeoff between financing war on the one hand and insufficient spending on domestic programs that undermines children's wellbeing. Finally, we suggest how early childhood educators can respond at multiple levels, from children in classrooms to the level of national policy.

J. Van Hoorn (✉)
University of the Pacific, Stockton CA 95211, USA
e-mail: jvanhoorn@pacific.edu

B. S. Fennimore, A. L. Goodwin (eds.), *Promoting Social Justice for Young Children*, Educating the Young Child 3, DOI 10.1007/978-94-007-0570-8_5,

A Peace and Social Justice Framework

Numerous UN declarations and conventions integrate peace and social justice, as shown in the UNESCO definition of peace:

> There can be no genuine peace when the most elementary human rights are violated, or while situations of injustice continue to exist; conversely, human rights for all cannot take root and achieve full growth while latent or open conflicts are rife. (UNESCO 1983, p. 259)

During the past decade, Christie et al. (2008) have refined a framework for peace psychology and related disciplines, including education, that is consistent with UNESCO's definition and makes explicit the relationships between peace and social justice. The framework is international and multicultural, based upon multidisciplinary work, and informed by many writers.

Christie et al. (2008) propose a model in which *systems of violence* include both direct violence and structural violence; and *systems of peace* include both peacemaking and peacebuilding. This comprehensive framework is particularly useful to educators because it distinguishes between nonviolent conflict that is integral to children's development and systems of violence that are destructive and assault children's wellbeing. The concept, *systems of peace* helps us distinguish between stopping violent conflict (peacemaking) and eliminating the underlying inequities (peacebuilding). For educators committed to social justice, this framework illuminates the often hidden relationships between peace and social justice at multiple levels, e.g., family, school, community, nation, and across multiple systems, e.g., social, cultural, economic, political.

In this chapter on young US children, war, and social justice, we elaborate this model to emphasize the connection between peace and social justice, thereby explicitly joining two areas of early childhood literature. The framework develops the following four-part model (Christie et al. 2008).

Direct violence is observable and includes intentional threats and violent behavior causing assaults on personal wellbeing, e.g., bodily injury, death, and psychological trauma. There is substantial educational literature that discusses direct violence in schools, families, and communities.

Structural violence results in social injustice: social, cultural, economic, and political inequities. Though structural violence may also result in assaults on personal wellbeing including death and psychological trauma, such assaults may not be clearly visible. The vast educational literature on structural violence is multilevel (school, family, community, etc.) and includes work on destructive processes such as poverty, racism, sexism, unequal access to education, housing, and medical services as well as constructive processes that promote children's healthy development, e.g., play and recreation.

Peacemaking encompasses nonviolent approaches to stop, reduce, and prevent direct violence. Work in this field ranges from international negotiations to stop interstate wars, to community efforts to reduce gang violence. Peacemaking in educational settings encompasses school-based conflict management and conflict resolution programs, for students of all ages, preschool through college. When direct violence is addressed and eliminated, the result is a *negative peace*, that is, the absence of violence. However, unless the underlying inequities are addressed, episodes of direct violence are likely to reoccur.

Peacebuilding aims to create a comprehensive peace: social justice. Peacebuilding is a useful term for educators because it describes the proactive process, our ongoing efforts. Christie and his colleagues explain that:

> ...a comprehensive peace would not only eliminate overt forms of violence (negative peace) but also create a more equitable social order that meets the basic needs and rights of all people (positive peace)..."positive peace" (refers to) transformations within and across institutions that rectify structural inequalities...(Christie et al. 2008, pp. 11, 18)

As we discuss throughout this chapter, a meaningful peace requires not only the cessation of armed conflict, but also a society characterized by increasing social equity and opportunities, whether in Afghanistan, Iraq, or the United States.

The Effects of War on Young Children in the United States with Parents Deployed in Military Combat

More than 800,000 US parents have been deployed in Iraq and Afghanistan since 2001 (Glod 2008). More than 5,000 US combatants, many with young children, have been killed. A large number of combat veterans are returning with severe and often permanent injuries, physical and psychological. About 30% of the approximately 1.6 million US military combatants deployed in Iraq and Afghanistan are now in need of mental health services (Sammons and Batten 2008). These huge numbers translate into serious real-life effects on these soldiers' children.

The psychological impact on children is evident prior to a parent's departure and can continue well beyond a parent's return. In *The Emotional Cycle of Deployment: A Military Family Perspective,* Pincus et al. (2005) delineate a five-stage model: predeployment; deployment (first month); sustainment (second to last month); redeployment (last month); and postdeployment (often called reunion). A second-grade teacher shared the following vignette in a conversation with Levin:

> Hannah's second-grade teacher reports to the school counselor that Hannah is having mood swings, from being withdrawn and bursting into tears, to becoming easily angered and lashing out to her peers and teacher. The school counselor meets with Hannah's mother who tells her that she has just come back from being deployed in Iraq.[1]

Hannah's response underscores how important it is for adults to be aware of what is happening in a child's life during all stages of parental deployment and the effects each stage can have.

[1] The examples in the chapter are true though the names have been changed.

Each family member's sense of family connectedness and relationships remains whether or not a parent is present (Huebner et al. 2007). These researchers explain that during the entire deployment cycle, "…a family member may be physically absent but psychologically present, or a family member may be physically present but psychologically absent…" (p. 112).

Importantly, there are no current studies of the impact of parental deployment on young children's patterns of attachment across the cycle of deployment. But when Huebner et al. (2007) interviewed adolescents with deployed parents, they found many had powerful feelings of uncertainty and loss: "…we just didn't know like how long we would have to go without our parent" (p. 116); "The worst time is when the phone rings because you don't know who is calling. They could be calling, telling you that he got shot or something" (p. 117).

Of the few studies of parental deployment in the current wars, only one examines the effects of deployment on young children. Chartrand et al. (2008) found that preschoolers 3–5 year old with a deployed parent were more apt to be aggressive or act out than their peers. In a second study, young children were included in a comprehensive study of child maltreatment in Army families (Gibbs et al. 2007). Alarmingly, among children 2–5 years old the rates of moderate to severe maltreatment rose significantly. Possible relationships between these findings (i.e., increases in parents' maltreatment and increases in children's aggressive behaviors) have not been examined.

A peace and social justice framework alerts us to additional ways structural violence takes a toll on children. Children with a parent in the Reserves or National Guard face different and often greater challenges than those with parents in the regular enlisted forces (Levin et al. 2008). Because these children do not live on military bases, they often do not have the programs and support available on bases, such as affordable housing, health care, or childcare. They may have no peers who understand or share their experiences. Their teachers or caregivers may not even know that the child has a parent deployed in combat, never mind know how to support them.

The policies that lead to large numbers of successive deployments are clearly taking a major toll on young children and families. Military families themselves are speaking out about the complex struggles they face when dealing with multiple deployments in rapid succession. In her New York Times op-ed, "One husband, two kids, three deployments" Melissa Seligman writes:

> Amelia would beg for days to see her daddy on the computer and then, when he appeared on the screen, ignore him. David pleaded with his eyes, but she walked away, defiantly—as only a toddler can do. (Seligman 2009, A19)

Glod (2008) points out that more than 20% of deployed parents have experienced two deployments, with about half of these experiencing three or more. The five-stage emotional cycle of deployment may be inadequate to describe what we have called the "yo-yo" effects caused by multiple deployments on children and families (Levin and Van Hoorn 2009).

While more research is needed, enough now exists for us to conclude that the stressors created for young children by their parents' multiple deployments is taking a toll on their healthy development, learning, and behavior. And this situation is undermining these children's right to develop fully—thereby creating societally-imposed injustice for these children.

The Impact of the Wars on All Young Children in the United States

The United States has been waging a war in Afghanistan since 2001, longer than any war fought in recent decades. Consequently, all young children in the United States have lived their entire lives in a nation at war fought at a distance. At the same time that adults teach young children to "use words" to settle disputes with peers, children regularly hear how adults resort to wars to solve their conflicts, on a scale of violence young children cannot fully comprehend.

Even when children and their families are physically out of harm's way, they see that the wider world is a violent and dangerous place despite the lessons adults try to teach. For instance, here we see a 7 year old child struggling to deal with what he sees depicted in the newspaper.

> Michael asks about the photo of a man running with an injured child as they flee from bombed buildings. Though Daniel's parents monitor media access carefully, his grandmother inadvertently left a newspaper on the table. That night Daniel awakens, disturbed and asking about the "dead" child.

Whether their parents are deployed or not, all young children's emotional reactions and the meanings they make of the violence they see differ from those of adults and are based on their level of development and prior experience.

> Natasha's mother reports that their family was in a car accident near an airport just as a low-flying plane went over the car. Six-year-old Natasha got hysterical, screaming that their car had been bombed because, "planes drop bombs when there's a war." Her parents realized that the night before, when the TV news was on at dinner, Natasha was paying particular attention to the war report.

Natasha's terrified reaction and her certainty that the plane dropped a bomb on her car reflect what she learned from TV. Her parents' calm, reassuring, and logical explanation that the war is "taking place far away" does not seem to change her understandings (Levin 2003). While older children and adults comprehend that the images of war they view is broadcast from "far away," because of how they think, younger children relate the violence they see and hear on the media to their lives and, therefore, as personally threatening to themselves and their families.

Consider the power of war images when young children watch a screen where adults fire missiles and drop bombs. Images of war relate to major themes of young children's development: life and death; power and powerlessness; love and hate. Photos of the direct violence of war lead to indirect violence in the lives of children. Early childhood educator and advocate John Surr hypothesizes that, "any child witnessing other children being targeted for destruction can be much more compelling as a terrorizer than to witness adult soldiers as casualties" (J. Surr, May 20, 2009, Concerned Educators Allied for a Safe Environment, personal communication).

We found no research on the effects of media coverage of the real violence of these wars on children despite all of the extensive research on the effects of "entertainment" violence. The 2000 *Joint Statement on the Impact of Entertainment Violence on Children* (American Academy of Pediatrics 2000) emphasizes the long-term effects of media violence on children and points to research findings that children who regularly watch TV violence are more apt to display more real-life violence and see the world as a dangerous place.

What happens when pretend violence mirrors and magnifies real violence as in *GI JOE: The Rise of Cobra,* a PG 13 movie with nonstop bombs and bullets, released in the summer of 2009? It is an example of a movie marketing dozens of realistic toys targeted at young children which channel them into imitating what they see on the screen in their play (Levin and Carlsson-Paige 2006).

While we can extrapolate on the effects on young children based on what we already know, research is needed to explicate the effects on today's young children who have now seen pretend and real violence and war coverage throughout their lifetimes. Are they more likely to behave aggressively or glorify violence as the way to solve conflicts? Are they more likely to develop lasting stereotypes about who are the good guys and bad guys? Are they more likely to see violence as the way to solve problems rather than as a problem that must be solved in ways that promote social justice?

The Structural Violence of War: Budget Priorities have Consequences for Young Children

A 2007 UNICEF report ranks the United States 20th out of 21 industrialized nations on a multifactor index of children's wellbeing that includes such variables as levels of poverty, infant mortality, and amount of money spent on education (United Nations Children's Fund 2007). In 2009, indicators and observations show that children in the United States are faring even worse than in the 2007 report, and that societal policies and funding remain woefully inadequate.

> Official statistics are not readily available, but there is little doubt that poverty and family homelessness are rising, that the quality of public education in many communities is deteriorating and that legions of children are losing access to health care as their parents join the vastly expanding ranks of the unemployed. (Herbert 2009, p. A25)

The great toll on children resulting from woefully low levels of funding is clear to early childhood educators. It contributes to structural violence as across the country schools are closing, the number of teachers is being reduced, and vital school programs are being axed. The most vulnerable children are often in schools that are most affected. While the economic downturn is playing a key role in budget cuts for children, we see few similar budget cuts for war spending. The Congressional Research Service (CRS) estimates that war funding since 2001 will soon total over

US $1 trillion, including about US $642 billion to the war in Iraq and US $189 billion to the war in Afghanistan (CRS Report for Congress 2009) and defense spending continues to increase as we write.

We emphasize that the relationship between funding for these wars and funding for programs that support children's wellbeing is complex. It is not a simple calculation of "X dollars" spent on the wars in Iraq and Afghanistan being subtracted from "Y" funds for programs for children and families. The point is that national policies and budgets reflect competing priorities and interests. The priority of funding these wars is one major variable that is interacting with others. From a peace and social justice perspective, these variables include the United States' historical neglect of social programs that support families with young children, to which was added eight years of heightened neglect by the Bush administration, and the still incalculable impact of the current economic crisis. These factors are creating what we consider "a perfect storm" that is taking a toll on all children (Levin and Van Hoorn 2009).

A peace and social justice perspective leads us to ask why children's welfare ranks so low in the United States compared to children in comparable nations. Across nations, what relationships exist between military expenditures and children's wellbeing? What other factors contribute or interact? To promote a positive peace, it is vital to go beyond analysis of the variables that contribute to the dismal rank of American children's wellbeing and learn which policies work when children are a priority.

Transformations: Promoting Social Justice

> The preparation of the child for responsible life in a free society, in the sprit of understanding, peace, tolerance, equality of sexes, and friendship among all peoples, ethnic, national and religious groups and persons of indigenous origin…. (United Nations Convention on the Rights of the Child 1990)

A meaningful positive peace is fundamental to all young children's healthy development and to what they will learn about social justice. In war, children on all sides learn harmful lessons about peace and social justice. US children with deployed parents experience risk of developing a deep sense of social injustice. But all US children are learning disturbing lessons about justice as they see how adults use violence to solve their disputes. Even when the United States conducts war at a great distance, it is inevitable that children pay a high price as their right to social justice in their own lives is endangered when budget priorities compete with meeting children's needs.

The peace and social justice framework discussed throughout this chapter leads not only to an understanding of the complexities of the problem but to multilevel approaches to solutions with family wellness and resilience as their cornerstone and childhood professionals working actively. Promoting a positive, genuine peace entails addressing the structural goals of creating "a more equitable social order that meets the basic needs and rights of all people…transformations within and across institutions that rectify structural inequalities" (Christie et al. 2008, pp. 11, 18).

Counteracting the Impact of War on Children

A peace and social justice framework requires responses at multiple levels: child, family, school, community, state, and national.

- Parents and teachers can respond to children's questions about war by finding out what they want to know, and providing appropriate information and reassurance. They can try to maintain children's routines and sense that their needs, including their need for safety, will continue to be met. Adults can also create an atmosphere that helps children maintain emotional equilibrium through play and the creative arts.
- At the school level we can learn to recognize the effects of the multiple stressors that can result from the deployment of a parent. For instance, building strong relationships and responding as a team is critical when we see evidence of possible changes in children's or parents' behaviors (Kim and Yeary 2008).
- Parents and teachers can be partners, sharing observations and concerns, as we saw in the example of Hannah. Teachers and parents can work together to protect young children from being overwhelmed by what they see, hear, and learn about the violence of war.
- At the community level, effective liaisons among schools, medical offices, and community organizations are essential in order to connect families, particularly families in crisis, with developmentally and culturally appropriate resources for children and families.
- At the research level, current, detailed information is necessary so all adults can better meet the needs of young children and influence the lessons they learn. Research can provide policymakers and legislators with a stronger case for supporting children when they make decisions on funding priorities. We need to use the growing number of resources to create the policies and practices that support the wellbeing of young children.

Advocating for Social Justice on Behalf of Young Children

Advocating calls for a multidisciplinary, social justice approach that brings economists, historians, and others to the same table. We can begin by moving to a coordinated service approach—with educators promoting educational services, psychologists providing mental health services, and social workers promoting community programs. Commitment to children's wellbeing must be the common priority as we work together to promote peace and social justice for children at multiple levels.

A peace and social justice perspective keeps us focused on major structural inequities with the goal of transformation. This perspective requires boldness in posing fundamental critical questions: "When we wage wars, do we as a nation take into account the ways war puts young children in harm's way?" "Why should parents of young children be deployed?" "What does it take for the US budget to support and foster children's wellbeing?" And, the most basic question of all in a social justice paradigm: "Why war?"

References

American Academy of Pediatrics (2000). Joint statement on the impact of entertainment violence on children. Congressional Public Health Summit. http://www.aap.org/advocacy/releases/jstmtevc.htm. Accessed 27 May 2009.

Chartrand, M. M., Frank, D. A., White, L. F., & Shope, T. R. (2008). Effect of parents' wartime deployment on the behavior of young children in military families. *Archives of Pediatric and Adolescent Medicine, 162,* 1009–1014.

Christie, D. J., Tint, B. S., Wagner, R. V., & Winter, D. D. (2008). Peace psychology for a peaceful world. *American Psychologist, 63*(6), 540–552.

CRS Report for Congress (May 15, 2009). The cost of Iraq, Afghanistan, and other global wars on terror operations since 9/11. http://assets.opencrs.com/rpts/RL33110_20090515.pdf. Accessed 12 Oct 2009.

Gibbs, D. A., Martin, S. L., Kupper, L. L., & Johnson, R. E. (2007). Childmaltreatment in enlisted soldiers' families during combat-related deployments. *Journal of the American Medical Association, 298*(5), 528–535.

Glod, M. (2008). Coping with their parents' war: Multiple deployments compound strain for children of service members. http://www.washingtonpost.com/wpdyn/content/article/2008/07/16/AR2008071602878_pf.html. Accessed 11 July 2009.

Herbert, B. (2009). *Children in peril.* http://www.nytimes.com/2009/04/21/opinion/21herbert.html. Accessed 15 May 2009.

Huebner, A. J., Mancini, J. A., Wilcox, R. M., Grass, S. R., & Grass G. A. (2007). Parental deployment and youth in military families: Exploring uncertainty and ambiguous loss. *Family Relations, 56,* 112–122.

Kim, A. M., & Yeary, J. (2008). Making long-term separations easier for children and families. *Young Children, 63*(5), 32–36.

Levin, D. E. (2003). *Teaching young children in violent times: Building a peaceable classroom* (2nd ed.). Cambridge: Educators for Social Responsibility & Washington: National Association for the Education of Young Children.

Levin, D. E., & Carlsson-Paige, N. (2006). *The war play dilemma* (2nd ed.). New York: Teachers College Press.

Levin, D. E., & Van Hoorn, J. (2009). Out of sight, out of mind, or is it? The impact of the war on children in the United States. *Childhood Education, 86*(6), 342–346.

Levin, D. E., Daynard, C., & Dexter, B. (2008). *The "So Far" guide for helping children and youth cope with the deployment and return of a parent in the National Guard.* http://www.sofarusa.org/downloads/SOFAR_2008_Final.pdf. Accessed 14 Nov 2008.

Pincus, S. H., House, R., Christensen, J., & Adler, L. E. (2005). *The emotional cycle of deployment: a military family perspective.* http://www.hooah4health.com/deployment/familymatters/emotionalcycle.htm. Accessed 30 May 2009.

Sammons, M. T., & Batten, S. V. (2008). Psychological service for returning veterans and their families: Evolving conceptualizations of the sequelae of war-zone experiences. *Journal of Clinical Psychology in Session, 64*(8), 921–927.

Seligman, M. (May 4, 2009). One husband, two kids, three deployments. *New York Times*, A19.

UNESCO (1983). *Second medium-term plan, 1984–1989. Paris: United Nations Educational, Scientific and Cultural Organization.* http://unesdoc.unesco.org/images/0005/000546/054611eb.pdf. Accessed 19 Mar 2010.

United Nations Children's Fund (2007). *Child poverty in perspective: an overview of child well-being in rich countries*. Florence: UNICEF Innocenti Research Centre.

United Nations Convention on Rights of the Child (1990). Article 29d, http://www.unhchr.ch/html/menu3/b/k2crc.htm. Accessed 26 July 2009.

Part II
Relevance and Meaningfulness in Early Learning Experiences

Chapter 6
Playful Learning: Early Education that Makes Sense to Children

Celia Genishi, Anne Haas Dyson and Lindsey Russo

Introduction

In their everyday lives many children in English-speaking countries become familiar with this iconic example of environmental print: STOP. They may soon recreate it with marker and paper to accompany a block construction or tell someone to STOP annoying them when their teacher urges them to "use your words." As we consider what it means to promote social justice in settings for children from infancy through grade 2, we wonder how these settings have become so filled with academic lessons—to which children may want to say STOP! We wonder if the grown-ups in charge are responding to a mandate to "stop making sense," an emphatic command (and movie title [Goetzman & Kurfirst 1984]), instead of offering choices that make sense to children.

In this chapter we address the question of what early education consists of when it makes sense to children. We begin, though, with a brief description of lessons that may *not* make sense to large numbers of children because of their predetermined structure and narrow objectives. We then focus on contrasting child-structured examples that foreground language and literacy in classrooms where children from prekindergarten (preK) and kindergarten engage in diverse kinds of play. Finally, we reflect on how we might change the prevailing curricular mandate from "stop making sense" to "make sense with children," as they have opportunities to choose among child-sensible and child-worthy options.

The Problem: Sense-Making Is Hard to Find

Try to make sense of the following lesson called "Say it fast." An adult, who could be the child's parent, reads from a published script, as follows:

C. Genishi (✉)
Department of Curriculum and Teaching, Teachers College, Columbia University, New York, NY, USA
e-mail: genishi@tc.columbia.edu

B. S. Fennimore, A. L. Goodwin (eds.), *Promoting Social Justice for Young Children,* Educating the Young Child 3, DOI 10.1007/978-94-007-0570-8_6,

1. Let's play say-it-fast. My turn: **lawn** (pause) **mower** (pause). Say it fast. **Lawnmower**.
2. Your turn. Wait until I tell you to say it fast. **Lawn** (pause) **mower** (pause). Say it fast. [child says:] "**lawnmower**." (Repeat step 2 until firm.)
   (Engelmann et al. 1983, p. 33)

These are the first two steps of a nine-step lesson, which includes instructions on how adults can teach children to "say it fast." They are aiming to reach a particular learning objective—so that the behavior of saying words fast is "firm" within the child's repertoire. In short they are playing a word game as a warm-up to saying sounds. After a few more game-like, scripted lessons, a number of the sounds will be linked to letters, and according to the authors of the book *Teach Your Child to Read in 100 Easy Lessons*, children will be transformed into beginning readers and writers within months. Further, because the "input" to the children is scripted and shouldn't vary from lesson to lesson or child to child, the "output" or learning what's in the lessons, is considered to be an accurate measure of how well the lessons teach reading.

There are a string of questions that come to our minds in the context of this claim: for example, what does saying *lawnmower* fast have to do with reading? Is it sensible to expect children to learn to read in 100 lessons, easy or hard? Is a tidy "input-output" model key to children's learning of literacy? And who are the children in these lessons? As if anticipating our question, Engelmann et al. (1983, p. 8) state that the 100-lesson program is appropriate for preschoolers, specifically "bright 3.5 year olds, average 4 and 5 year olds."

As we seek sense-making in settings for all young children, we challenge the claim that lessons like this one are appropriate for "average" learners. (At the same time, we acknowledge that some children will happily and successfully complete the program with their parents or teachers.) Our challenge is based on knowledge of how children are cultural and linguistic beings who learn in diverse and divergent ways. Visitors in public school classrooms in many locales see—or hear—in a few minutes that "average" children are hard to find, if by average we mean a 4 or 5 year old whose parent has time and leisure to teach a daily lesson with very particular aims in textbook or "standard" English.

Today visitors to early childhood classrooms are likely to see children who are racially and ethnically different from each other, speaking English and other languages. This cultural and linguistic diversity is corroborated by data from the 2000 US census: 20% of all children in the United States have at least one parent who is an immigrant or newcomer. Since about 1990, immigration has peaked; 57% of immigrants in the United States entered the country during the last two decades (US Census Bureau 2009). Although the census does not document the number of English learners (ELs), educators recognize that their number in classrooms is and will be increasing. Thus "average" children speaking "standard" English are indeed hard to identify and challenging to teach with narrowly structured lessons.

Moreover there are multiple variants of English. As with any language, American English is an abstraction; the ways in which it is spoken vary across regions of the country, all of which have their own "standard," determined by a region's most powerful people. Similarly social variants of English exist too, shaped by the different sociocultural histories and geographies of groups of people, as in "Chicano English" or "African American Language." Whether regional or social, "dialects" involve differences in the ways speech sounds are combined and pronounced (phonology), the ways words are combined to form grammatical sentences (syntax), the meanings of words (semantics), and the ways speech varies among situations (pragmatics), how, for example, one speaks respectfully with elders, talks appropriately with babies, or teases one's peers.

For example, 6 year old Mandisa accuses a peer: "You dippin' in the kool aid and don't even know what flavor it is." She is not in need of "frequent opportunities to repeat (correctly formed) sentences" with subject/verb agreement (California State Department of Education 2007, p. 39). In fact, she is not speaking an "incorrect" form of English but displaying her linguistic acumen, her social playfulness, and her sociocultural heritage, as she has learned from her grandmother a popular African American idiom about "dippin' in the kool aid" (Dyson & Smitherman 2009). So too all our children's voices carry echoes of their sociocultural histories, their family circumstances, their own timetables for learning language, and their reading of the current situation (Genishi & Dyson 2009). And all our children too need to expand their control of language to negotiate a range of communicative situations, including, as they progress through school, those requiring the Language of Wider Communication (i.e., a standardized English). Our goals as teachers are to make school welcoming and accessible to young children with different language repertoires and to provide communicative situations and social supports that will allow them to participate in an ever-widening world. Chief among our pedagogical tools for broadening language is a cross-cultural predilection of the young: play.

Start Making Sense: Multiple Contexts for Children's Play

In N. Scott Momaday's book, *In the Bear's House* (1999, p. 40), Bear asks Yahweh how language began: "How did it happen?" Yahweh explains that the children "went out and played together," and when they came home, they had this miraculous tool of language. Bear then understands: "Language is child's play."

And so it is. Play is an ancient, cross-cultural tool for language learning. When children engage in social and imaginative play, they build on what is perhaps our most defining characteristic as human beings: our attunement to others and our capacity for reciprocity (Kenneally 2007). We do not simply imitate what others do; we reciprocate, complement, and collaborate. We do this first with our caregivers when we are very small. For example, mom verbalizes and baby gurgles back; or, to borrow an example from Tomasello (cited in Kenneally 2007), mom blows a raspberry on her baby's arm and the baby does one in return (not on himself). We learn first to negotiate shared worlds with others, and, within those worlds, language emerges (Nelson 2007).

In young children's classrooms, child players have to attune themselves to one another and to their evolving action if they are to get a fantasy going and to sustain it. Through their play, they enact an analysis of their experiences; they adopt relevant social roles, and guided but not limited by those experiences, they improvise dramatic moves. In doing so, children manipulate not only words and gestures but their very voices—their intonation, volume, rhythm, and pitch. They thus become a mommy, a baby, a police officer, a bad guy, or a superhero who saves the day. They are adrift in a boat, huddled in a house away from the rain, cooking in a restaurant or maybe a kitchen, taking dinner orders or putting babies to bed. To carry out their actions, children stretch their language and, together, enact a world. To illustrate we next present examples from three varied early childhood contexts where children who speak different home languages and dialects construct through talk their multiple yet shared worlds.

Luisa in a Multilingual Head Start

In the growing number of preK classrooms where children speak a language other than English, children and their families hope for a curriculum that is expansive enough to include their home language and a schedule that stretches to accommodate the time individual children need to learn the language(s) and culture of the classroom, including English, the Language of Wider Communication, in the United States. Luisa is a child whose first out-of-home experience happens in a Head Start room for 3 year olds. At her center the teachers follow the *High/Scope* program (Hohmann et al. 1979) with its plan-do-review format, at the same time that they are committed to a play-based curriculum with child choice. So the activities children like Luisa are asked to plan and do include play in the family or block area, art, table toys, and using the class computer. Outdoor play occurs as regularly as the weather allows.

Luisa enters this curricular context with 15 other girls and boys, most of whom speak Spanish at home and a few of whom speak English. Her home language is Mixteco, an indigenous language of southern and southwestern Mexico, which adults at the center do not hear her or other Mixteco-heritage children speak. During the 3's year, Luisa is notably quiet, saying very little in either Spanish or English, the languages that the children and teachers speak, until the spring of the year. Indeed it is a year later in the spring of the 4's year when she demonstrates her eagerness to be verbal within the activity contexts of preK. Having followed her own gradual timeline to become a talker, Luisa declares that she is ready to be a player:

(Luisa has found a button and brought it to the sand table.)

Luisa:	Lookit, I found it.
Josué:	*Dame, dame.* (Translation from Spanish: Give me, give me.)
Luisa:	I want to play.
Josué:	You want to play? (sounding surprised) Someone stop. Luisa wants to play.
Josué and Sarine:	Miguel is done.
Luisa:	I play, I play! (said with animation and some adamance). (Genishi and Dyson 2009, p. 35)

In order to play at the table, Luisa needs a smock; and checking out the children in the group, Josué and Sarine decide Miguel is ready to move on. In fact Luisa assertively steps up to play without the required smock.

Later in the 4's year, Luisa's language—and play—become more complex, and her knowledge of Spanish and English grows. Listen in as she and her friend Rebeca declare that it is raining outside their pretend house. Although they usually speak Spanish to each other, Luisa appears to direct the play as she instigates play with languages themselves:

Luisa: *Está mucho* raining!
Rebeca: It's raining.
Together: *Mucho* raining! *Mucho* raining!

The two girls shriek "*mucho* raining," which becomes "*mucha* raining," as they chant for several minutes. Later they take out the eensy weensy spider puzzle, which does have "*mucho*" rain washing the spider out, as readers probably recall.

Luisa: *Está mucha* raining.
Rebeca (sings): The eensy weensy spider went up ....
(Genishi and Dyson 2009, p. 63)

A few months earlier, Luisa's spoken language did not seem to be extensive enough for her to participate in an imaginary drama or in bilingual word play. But in the above example, Luisa uses talk to engage her friend not only in her imagined rainstorm, but also in a sustained duet filled with fun and playful code switching. Luisa and her peers illustrate the cultural universality of play as a means for entering into a shared social life with other children. Note that Luisa needed more than a year of engagement with the preschool world before she was able to enter into the kinds of play that spoken language enables. Indeed all children require time, space, interactional partners, engaging objects, and observant teachers who further the communicative strengths revealed and nurtured by play. In the next section we present playful examples from a preK classroom with a more academic focus than the curriculum at Luisa's Head Start.

Milesky and Her Friends in a Pressured PreK

In early childhood settings where most children speak English, the verbal buzz sounds different from that in Luisa's Head Start, though you will see that play continues to be the children's context of choice. Every year from April through October many migrant families make a small farming community in upstate New York home when they arrive to work on the local farms. The children are assimilated into the local schools during these months but then leave late in the fall to return to their native Mexico. Milesky, however, a child in the 4 year old class of the village preschool, remains in the area with her family when her father obtains a permanent job. While the children in her class come from diverse backgrounds, they and their teachers all speak English as their first language. Milesky began the school year speaking very little English. By the beginning of November, although some of the children find her difficult to understand, her comprehension and conversational skills have improved a great deal. Thus she can respond to all verbal communications in English as you see in the following example.

Milesky has been working on a puzzle but becomes bored and walks over to the table where Sabrina and Bella are playing. They are engaged in a play activity where each holds an animal figure and walks it across the tabletop. The animals are going to school. Sabrina has a gorilla, Bella a giraffe, and Milesky a rhinoceros.

Sabrina: I'm taking my gorilla to school.
Bella: I'm taking my giraffe to school too.
Milesky: I'm taking my scrunchy pig to school.

Milesky does not know the word for *rhinoceros* but is able to describe the animal in her own words:

Savanna: That's a funny name! It's a rhino, silly.
Milesky: Rhino?! I'm taking my scrunchy pig rhino to school.

Bella and Sabrina giggle, and Milesky joins in laughing.

Sabrina: Scrunchy pig, scrunchy pig!!
Bella: Scrunchy pig, scrunchy pig!!
Ms. Kathy: Use your inside voices please, girls.
(Russo 2009, p. 129)

Thinking that the girls are on the edge of being disruptive and speaking from a distance, Ms. Kathy, the teacher, splits them up. She sends Sabrina and Bella to the kitchen and Milesky to the Lego table. Teachers in this room are often not available to closely observe how play develops because they are at stationary positions at a project table where they work one-on-one with children on their pre-reading and writing skills. From this vantage point, teachers can intervene in play episodes. In the example above Ms. Kathy is unaware of the content of the girls' talk and identifies playful behavior as undesirable and possibly disruptive. As a result a productive play episode is prematurely dissolved. In the months that follow Sabrina and Bella nonetheless continue to provide social support for Milesky through play as she develops her English vocabulary and language skills.

Bella has another friend, Grace, in the same classroom. In the following episode they are sitting at a small table playing with wooden puzzles that have pictures of objects with spaces underneath for the letters that spell out the corresponding word. Bella at first finds the activity difficult, but Grace scaffolds Bella so that she remains motivated, on task—as defined by the two friends—and engaged in the fun. Grace loves to sing, and she sings the letters repeatedly as she attempts to identify them. Both she and Bella name letters and articulate their sounds:

Grace: That's a song *N-N-N-N-N* (she hums).
Bella: Now I need an *L*.

Grace: I found one. Here you can have it. See it goes here.
Bella: Wow, that's a good one!
Grace: There's an *E* over there. An *E-E-E-E*.
Grace: *E* for elephant.
Bella: Now I need an *I*.
Grace: Hey. I need an *I* too. There has to be another one. There's lots of *I's* in words....
Grace: No, I need an *N*.
Bella: *N-N-N-N-N-N*.
Grace: We're going on an *N* hunt (singing).
Bella: Maybe all the *N's* got lost.
Grace: Yeah, kids throw them on the floor.
(Russo 2009, pp. 157–158)

Grace gets under the table to look for more letters. She finds some and puts them back on the table. Here is an excerpt of what follows:

Bella: I need an *F*.
Grace: *F-F-F-F-F-F-F-F*. We learned *F* today. Fish. I fed the fffffffish.
Bella: *F-F-F-F* is fish.
Grace: This is fun. Ffffffun.
Bella: It's too hard. Can you help me?
Grace: Yeah, I'll help. It's tricky.
Grace: (Makes and repeats the sound of L.) I llllove the llllletter *L-L-L-L-L-L*.
Bella: *L-L-L-L-L*. I love it. Lllllllllove.
Bella: Is this an *L-L-L-L-L-L-L*?
Grace: No it's an *I-I-I-I-I-I-I-I-I I I*!
(Russo 2009, p. 158)

The literally fun-filled letter-and-sound play episode ends because the girls are called over to the rug for rug time. Playful learning has again conceded to the teacher's schedule.

Children's play with letters and their sounds originates in their desire and ability to play with and manipulate symbolic materials (Dyson 1990); and in this preK classroom, playful talk is embedded in a curriculum that explicitly incorporates academic skills. For example, since the beginning of the school year the children have spent most Fridays concentrating on a different letter of the alphabet. Every activity, from the books that they read to snack, is focused upon the letter of the day, whereas on other days it is the focal point of rug time and the daily project only. The last Friday of data collection at the site was *P* day or "pajama day." The children and teachers all came to school dressed in their pajamas. As usual at rug time the teacher modeled the way to write upper case and lower case *P* to initiate the activity. They made and cooked a pizza in the kitchen and popped popcorn in a hot-air machine. They then sat in the hall, pulled down the movie screen, watched a Winnie the Pooh movie, ate their pizza and popcorn, and drank purple grape juice. The children were engaged all afternoon; and, as they left with their parents, they were excitedly telling stories about all the "*P* things" they had done that day (Russo 2009, p. 114).

Interestingly the weekly focus on a single letter demonstrates how children can be playfully learning with their teachers, as children act upon the letter *P*, by dressing in their pajamas or eating popcorn. Thus, although the preK teachers in this school feel pressured to teach directly things like alphabet letters, numbers, and colors (and were observed to cut off opportunities for play revolving around language and literacy), children are still able to find their own time and space for playful learning. Looking back at the example of Milesky's "scrunchy pig rhino," we wonder whether in the course of *P* day Sabrina, Bella, or Milesky remember their unique *P* phrase, one collaboratively constructed around a *P* word, well before *P* was introduced to the class as the letter of the week.

Alicia and Mrs. Bee's Kindergarteners

The academic focus evident in the preK room of Milesky and her peers only increases as children proceed into the early grades, where opportunities for playful invention decrease dramatically. Under the influence of state and federal mandates, scripted literacy teaching has become dominant and is viewed as the means for closing racialized and classed achievement "gaps," despite contrary evidence (see Miller and Almon 2009). Teachers, like Mrs. Bee, who work in urban neighborhoods and schools with low-income populations, are under particular pressure to meet benchmarked standards.

As a kindergarten teacher, Mrs. Bee had to get her children reading and writing in conventional ways. There was no official time for play. The mandated curriculum (Calkins et al. 2003) stressed personal narratives and actively discouraged social and imaginative play during writing. Still the children did play. In doing so, they made writing relevant to their lives together. That notion of "relevance" is basic to child writing: A teacher cannot compel a child to have an intention, a felt need to write (Vygotsky 1978); that social intention comes from a desire to join in, to participate.

Consider, for example, 5 year old Alicia. She had not had any formal schooling before she entered Mrs. Bee's kindergarten. A speaker of African American Language (AAL), she was oriented to playing with the external features of written language—its symbols, their arrangement on a line, their distribution on a page. She would read her writing, and, in that way, she used it as a means of connecting with her peers, especially her best friend Willo.

In fact, the only word, other than her own name, Alicia wrote conventionally in her first kindergarten year was Willo's name; Willo had taught her how to spell her name right. Sometimes Alicia walked around the room asking other children to write their names and telephone numbers on her paper, especially if those others were talking about an anticipated birthday party. Alicia was always up for a potential party!

One day Mrs. Bee asked the children to write letters to their mothers for Mother's Day. When Alicia sat down at her table, she began to draw her mother and, then, the rest of her family, all in a line holding hands, with hearts on their heads. Sitting across from Alicia was Willo, who was attentive to her friend and found a way to make a place for herself in Alicia's production:

Alicia: I'm gonna write [draw] my mommy and my dada.
Willo: I'm your sister.
Alicia: I can put you here with my mama and my dada.

Alicia did just that, and when I asked her to tell me about her picture, Willo piped up and explained, "We're playing sisters, on paper." (transcript excerpt first presented in Genishi and Dyson 2009, p. 95)

On Alicia's paper, Willo's name was a repeated and steady anchor in a river of letters. When Mrs. Bee asked her to read her writing, Alicia did so, framing her text as directed to her mother, just as was assigned:

Mom, you is me and Willo mommy.
I see Willo in my dreams.
Her is my best sister.

"Hey," Willo objected. "There's no two 'Willo.' 'Willo, Willo Willo'," she said, reading her name in Alicia's text. That is, you should have read *Willo* more than twice (because there are more *Willo*'s in your text).

Alicia's intense interest in others and their names was potentially a means for Mrs. Bee to take a dictation and to play with voice/print match with Willo and Alicia, even having them collect other children's names to put in their family, for example. But the curriculum was a lens that kept Mrs. Bee focused on the mandated personal writing and the benchmarked skills, especially stretching out one's words orally, listening to sounds, and transcribing those sounds into letters—a task for which Alicia, still adrift in letters, needed much social assistance. Mrs. Bee herself knew that the curriculum was too rigid for a classroom of children with diverse experiences in literacy, a range of interests, and varied dispositions. But she felt trapped, as the assessment days rolled around periodically to see how children were progressing on those skills.

As for Alicia, she repeated kindergarten. The second time around, her peers continued to provide Alicia with reasons to write. Willo had gone on to first grade, but, in time, Alicia found new friends. They put each other in their drawings and eventually in their writing. Of course, Mrs. Bee's efforts to guide her writing were important (e.g., see Genishi and Dyson 2009). But, when Mrs. Bee moved on to another child, it was Alicia's peers whose interest in and talk about her efforts continued to scaffold her social pathway into writing.

In this last example, Alicia and her friends Ella and Denise are supposed to be writing "poems" on individual topics. Ella's topic is her cat; Alicia's is Tinker Bell. The girls, though, are interested in each other's efforts. Moreover, their talk leads to more formalized written speech. In their talk, all of the girls speak AAL and frequently exercise the grammatical option to delete the *be* verb (e.g., "My Tinker Bell cute"). But in the slow, orally articulated process of announcing their efforts, the *be* verb appears:

Ella: (to Alicia) What are you writing about?
Alicia: Tinker Bell. (reading) "My Tinker Bell [says but has not written] cute."
Ella: It's supposed to be "My Tinker Bell is" whatever color your Tinker Bell is.
Alicia: Her gonna be pink. Don't Tinker Bell have dresses?
Ella: Yes, 'cause I watched the movie.
Denise: Me too. I watched the mo-vie.
Alicia: Ella, no Tinker Bell has no pants on, girl.
Ella: I know that. But they fly. So you might wanta draw fly. And you might wanta do dots.
Denise: Tinker Bell don't have no dots.
Ella: Yeah she do.
Alicia: On their dresses they do. Sometimes on their nails they do. Sometimes they don't.
Ella: "My cat is white" (rereading).
Alicia: (rereading)… "My Tinker Bell is" cute. I forgot to write *cute*!
Ella: And you said *pretty* too!
Alicia: How you spell *pretty*?
Ella: "My cat is" pretty. How you spell *pretty*?
Alicia: P-E.
Ella: Pre *ty*, Pretty

And together the girls come up with *prety*.

…

Alicia: Oh, you, me, and Denise lost 2 teeth.

We girls share our work with each other and our words…and even the experience of losing teeth. Our writing, rather than being a matter of independent personal expression, is a means of social participation, of being included in the goings on.

Toward a Playful Future

In this chapter you have met a number of children in varied classroom contexts who have made sense of their educational settings through the universal medium of play. Luisa, Milesky, Alicia, and their friends differ in their home languages or dialects and differ in their experiences of classroom time and space; yet their need to make sense of their own learning leads irresistibly to play. We met Luisa as a 3 year old in a Head Start center where teachers are firm in their commitment to play as the basis of the curriculum and willing to allow children their own time lines, no matter how gradual. Milesky and her friends are in a preschool where teachers allow talk and play but feel pressured to include explicit instruction about literacy and math skills. The sound and word play that weaves through academically related talk in Milesky's classroom suggests that despite the pressures, teachers allow quite a lot of space for children to make sense of potentially decontextualized and dry letters and sounds in fun-filled ways. Alicia is in a kindergarten where the literacy program is mandated, but she too amply demonstrates her ability to draw on her own linguistic and cultural knowledge within the narrow spaces of primary-grade writing lessons.

So, although present-day curricula in language and literacy, unmediated by play, often make no sense to young children, we conclude, first, that we can rely on children to persist in their own ways of making sense. The children in this chapter assert through their own takes on letters, words, and language itself that their playfulness is unstoppable. With the help of peers and adults, each young learner draws a child-sensible path toward learning. In short, part of a socially just curriculum for young children is just that, providing multiple pathways for children to participate in school in ways that respect their need for time to learn, space to play, and for socially and pedagogically responsive adults. Those adults themselves experience pressures to deviate from paths that make sense to them. They too need curricular time and space so that they can observe, know, and interact with their children.

Finally, we conclude that curricular moves toward social justice require new mandates: first, to STOP requiring children to engage in repetitiously constraining activities and, second, to start expanding curricular spaces to incorporate the many forms of play that children embrace without instruction. In this way, we are more apt to learn of the communicative strengths, cognitive puzzles, and social desires that energize the intellectual and emotional lives of our children.

References

California State Department of Education. (2007). *Reading/language arts framework for California public schools*. Sacramento: California Department of Education Press.

Calkins, L. M., et al. (2003). *Units of study for primary writing: A yearlong curriculum (Grades K-2)*. Portsmouth: Heinemann.

Dyson, A. Haas. (1990). Symbol makers, symbol weavers: How children link play, pictures, and print. *Young Children, 45*(2), 50–57.

Dyson, A. Haas, & Smitherman, G. (2009). The right (write) start: African American Language and the discourse of sounding right. *Teachers College Record, 111*, 973–998.

Engelmann, S., Haddox, P., & Bruner, E. (1983). *Teach your child to read in 100 easy lessons*. New York: Simon & Schuster.

Genishi, C., & Dyson, A. Haas. (2009). *Children, language, and literacy: Diverse learners in diverse times*. New York: Teachers College Press & Washington: National Association for the Education of Young Children.

Goetzman, G., & Kurfirst, G. (Producers), & Demme, J. (Director). (1984). *Stop making sense*. United States: Palm Pictures.

Hohmann, M., Banet, B., & Weikart, D. (1979). *Young children in action*. Ypsilanti: High/Scope Press.

Kenneally, C. (2007). *The first word: The search for the origin of language*. New York: Viking.

Miller, E., & Almon, J. (2009). *Crisis in the kindergarten: Why children need to play in school*. College Park: Alliance for Childhood.

Momaday, N. S. (1999). *In the bear's house*. New York: Harper Perennial.

Nelson, K. (2007). *Young minds in social worlds: Experience, meaning, and memory*. Cambridge: Harvard University Press.

Russo, H. L. (2009). *Play, peer relationships, and academic learning: Exploring the views of teachers and children.* (Unpublished doctoral dissertation). Teachers College, Columbia University, New York.

US Census Bureau. (2009). *Characteristics of the U.S. foreign-born population.* Press release. Retrieved from http://www.census.gov

Vygotsky, L. S. (1978). *Mind in society: The development of higher psychological processes.* Cambridge: Harvard University Press.

Chapter 7
Education That Is Multicultural and Promotes Social Justice: The Need

Yvonne De Gaetano

We are living in fascinating and exciting, as well as conflicted and complicated times. Because of accessible travel, instant media coverage, and advanced technology, we are more in contact with those who are different from ourselves in ethnicity, religion, race, social class, political thought, and so many other ways. While these differences make life more interesting, they can also cause discomfort and fear. This becomes clear when one opens up a newspaper and reads about the terrible conflicts that are happening all over our world—Iraq, Afghanistan, Israel, and Darfur. Global conflicts over ethnic, religious, economic, and political differences affect everyone, young and old alike.

On a local level we also experience conflicts due to differences, despite the fact that some of them may not be as dramatic as the ones cited above. Think about the overt racism that emerged during the recent presidential elections in our country, and the subsequent shocking racist depictions of the president that continue to crop up. Think about the teens who desecrate religious cemetery sites, or youngsters who scrawl hateful things about groups of a different race, religion, or sexual orientation on city walls. What happens when someone very different from the neighbors to whom one is accustomed moves into the house next door? What comments are made? These negative reactions are evidence of discomfort, uneasiness, and ignorance about differences.

In this new and "smaller" world, how can we begin being more open to human differences of all kinds? How do we get more fairness in our lives and in the lives of others? How can we learn to live peacefully and productively, embracing rather than rejecting all of our differences? When and how do we begin?

I think that we need to begin when children are very young—in the home, schools, childcare centers, parks, playgrounds, camps, museums—in sum, in the institutions that educate the youth in our society. As a teacher educator, I believe that focusing on multicultural and social justice education early in the lives of children and throughout their schooling provides a strong foundation for the development of behaviors and attitudes that lead to a more just, peaceable, and equitable environ-

Y. De Gaetano (✉)
School of Education, Hunter College, New York, NY, USA
e-mail: ydegaeta@hunter.cuny.edu

B. S. Fennimore, A. L. Goodwin (eds.), *Promoting Social Justice for Young Children,* Educating the Young Child 3, DOI 10.1007/978-94-007-0570-8_7,

ment. Early on, young children need to be exposed to positive ways of responding to differences and to an antiracist stance in their lives before racism takes hold in their thinking and before they have to "unlearn racism and other problematic stances" (Cochran-Smith 2004, p. 13). Comer (1989) also stresses that it is difficult to change racist attitudes and values and that an antiracist focus should begin in the early childhood years.

In this chapter I give a brief outline of the growth of multicultural education in early childhood programs and in the broader educational arena. I define education that is multicultural and promotes social justice within the context of early childhood education. I go on to argue that today, though greatly needed, a focus on multiculturalism and social justice in early childhood settings is almost nonexistent. I believe this has happened because of a series of events such as the large influx of new immigrants which has resulted in antiimmigrant attitudes, government policies such as *No Child Left Behind* (NCLB) which focuses disproportionately on standardized tests as the measure of student learning, and lack of consensus on ways to implement multicultural education. As I see it, these problems have unfortunately shifted attention away from a focus on persistent educational initiatives to help young children to develop positive attitudes toward diversity in the early years. I conclude the chapter with examples of how some teachers, despite the odds, are focusing on education that is multicultural and promotes social justice.

History and Context

It is impossible to separate the schooling of children from the political context of the society in which that schooling is taking place. For example, the initial call for multicultural education began after the Civil Rights Movement in the 1960s when determined minorities began to counteract inequities and omission of opportunity in schools for children who were racially and culturally diverse or living in poverty (Banks 1993; Nieto 1995; Sleeter and McLaren 2000). At that time, even as efforts were being made to create programs and services for children who were in need, children of diversity were defined by negative labels and terminology. The common view among some social scientists was that poverty created major deficits in language and experience that caused an inevitable gap in their abilities when compared to children of the middle class (Jensen 1972; Bereiter and Engelman 1966).

With the belief that preschools could remedy these, "deficits," programs such as Head Start and other subsequent preschool programs were developed to provide children living in poverty with the experiences and skills needed for school success. Although these programs were initially focused on a "cultural deficit approach" to the children, the voices of leaders in multicultural education began to question and challenge that viewpoint (Ramsey et al. 1989). As a result, there was a move by the federal government in the 1970s to fund the development of curricula that would be culturally responsive as well as developmentally appropriate for young children's cognitive and social emotional growth (Ramsey et al. 1989).

Early Multicultural Models for Young Children

Four early childhood preschool curriculum models that addressed multicultural, bilingual education for the young child were developed in the late 1970s. Although the authors of the curriculum models differed in their views on culture, as well as on their educational approaches and goals, each of the four curriculum models (*ALERTA, Amanecer, High Scope*, and *Nuevas Fronteras*) were multicultural and bilingual models for early learning (Ramsey et al. 1989). The curriculum developers challenged the deficit stance and deliberately focused on cultural and developmentally appropriate approaches, strategies, and materials for young children's learning. The language, skills, and experience that culturally diverse children brought to schools were viewed as strengths to be acknowledged and built upon for learning. For several years as the coauthor of one of these models (*ALERTA*), I conducted training primarily for Head Start centers across the country, as did the developers of the other models. Other approaches and ways of addressing multicultural education were also being developed (Banks 1993; Kendall 1996; Ramsey 2004) and implemented in the United States and in England. Among the most noteworthy additional perspectives were Derman-Sparks' *Anti Bias Curriculum Task Force* (1989), Ramsey's *Teaching and Learning in a Diverse World* (1987), and Kendall's *Diversity in the Classroom: New Approaches to the Education of Young Children* (1983).

Multicultural Education: New Approaches

From the early 1960s to the late 1990s, multicultural education went through a variety of changes in its goals and content including movement from an initial focus on human relations, to ethnic group studies with its inclusion of the contributions and heroes of different groups, and finally, to increasingly politicized concepts of multicultural education. These politicized forms of multicultural education (sometimes referred to Multicultural Education, or Education that is Multicultural and Social Reconstructivism) (Sleeter and Grant 1987) focus on change and challenge to the status quo. In particular, the concept of social reconstructivism has a focus on the analysis of race, class, power, privilege, and justice—content that most teachers find difficult to address (Grant and Tate 1995).

By the 1980s and 1990s, the concept of multiculturalism began to be attacked as divisive (Schlesinger 1991; Nieto 1995; Sleeter and Mclaren 2000). Despite the attacks, the concept of multicultural education continued to survive and for the next 20 years many scholars wrote excellent articles and books about cultural diversity, multicultural education, and social justice in early childhood education. Unfortunately, however, there was a dissonance between what researchers and academics were writing about and what was happening or not happening in early educational settings. In my experience and that of others, multicultural education in real classrooms often emerged as a superficial focus in different foods, cultural festivals, and ethnic holiday celebrations. Sadly, by the end of the 1990s, I believe that less-than-fully developed forms of multicultural education had largely limped their way out of early childhood classrooms. Paradoxically, the numbers of culturally and linguistically diverse immigrant children and those living in poverty are increasing (Lim 2010) as the focus on diversity and social justice is decreasing.

In the many classrooms that I have visited over the last 25 years, I have heard children say things that tell me that they have learned the ugly messages of racism, sexism, and other "isms" that can harm their emotional and cognitive growth. For example, recently I heard a child say loudly and clearly that she didn't want to hold Sharon's hand because, "Sharon is black." Another child, Brianna, said that the boys could not play within a specific area in the classroom, because "no boys allowed." In class Billy announced that, "The Arabs are terrorists."

I have found that many parents, teachers, and administrators either reprimand children because, *it's not nice to say those things*, or they choose to ignore these statements and change the topic. Some of the teachers in my classes tell me that they know that these are "teachable moments," but they are unsure about how to tackle these statements in ways that "will not take time from the curriculum." More often than not, they are left not knowing what to say or do.

In classrooms that are multicultural and promote social justice these situations are not viewed as "taking time away from the real learning" nor deviating from the "normal curriculum" because the issues raised by the comments are integral to what children must learn to become members of fair and equitable communities. They are not "add ons" to the curriculum. Teachers who endorse and implement education that is multicultural and promotes social justice in their classrooms enhance, enrich, and broaden children's learning by putting emphasis on antibias learning (avoiding prejudice and addressing unfairness) in early childhood classrooms. In fact, among the components most vital to teaching in early childhood are the issues and topics addressed in classrooms that are multicultural and promote social justice.

Multicultural and Social Justice Education in the Early Childhood Classroom: Definitions

Kendall (1996) outlines the primary goals of multicultural education for early childhood classrooms as follows: to teach children to function positively in a multicultural and multiracial world; to help children experience differences and similarities in people in a positive way, and to value and respect them; and to enable children of color, who are "most affected by racism," (p. 10) to develop positive self concepts.

According to Ramsey (2004), multicultural education in early childhood means helping children to "learn how to navigate contradictions and ambiguities and to challenge the injustices that divide and diminish their world" (p. 6) in developmentally appropriate ways. De Gaetano et al. (1998) write that multicultural education in classrooms is a process that enables teachers to connect children's cultures to their learning "in ways that address issues of equity and commitment to social action" (p. 5). Ultimately, these, and other early childhood teacher educators and scholars who are committed to multicultural and social justice education emphasize that such education is about promoting academic excellence for *all* children, children who are from the majority as well as those who are from minority groups. This happens because in classrooms that promote education that is multicultural, children's experiences, skills, and understandings are acknowledged and used to teach new knowledge, resulting in interested and motivated learners. In addition, education that is multicultural promotes equity in the quality of teaching for children, and provides adequate resources and multiple opportunities to learn. Practitioners who understand how schools function and how they can be changed to value diverse human experiences enable equitable learning for all. With such practices children can attain academic excellence.

Education that is multicultural and promotes social justice is essential to our society and, consequently, to schooling where children not only acquire formal knowledge and new skills, but also learn the fundamentals of living in a democracy. In addition, through education that is multicultural, children's families, cultures, language(s), and differences are validated (Kendall 1996; Lee 1998; Ramsey 2004).

The complexity of multicultural education is not always understood. This was brought home to me recently when one of my early childhood education students commented that she didn't really need to take multicultural education courses as part of her course work because she knew that good early childhood education naturally situates the child and family at the center of the early childhood curriculum, and "that is multicultural education." Although placing the child at the heart of the curriculum is critical, the more difficult issues of racism, sexism, classism, and other "isms" that need to be addressed as integral components of multiculturalism and social justice should never be omitted.

Social Justice

According to Nieto (2004), social justice is an integral part of education that is multicultural and it enables children to recognize and challenge injustices toward themselves and others. Social justice has been defined as beliefs that focus on care, justice, respect, and equity issues (Marshall and Oliva 2006). Darling-Hammond (2002) defines social justice as knowing oneself and understanding others' viewpoints, perspectives, and opportunities. Teaching for social justice is "teaching what we believe ought to be" (Greene 1998, xxix). Rawls (1971) posited that social justice is essentially about fairness. Fairness is a concept that young children can understand and relate to and, therefore, it fits neatly into early childhood classrooms.

Multiculturalism and Social Justice Education: The Focus Today

Goffin and Washington (2007) posit that in the field of early childhood education, many "resist(s) doing what our knowledge base says is necessary for achieving good results for children" (p. 5). There is a mismatch between what the principles of good early childhood education are and how they are implemented. The authors go on to say that many early childhood practitioners submissively follow the "federal, states, and local policy decisions" without adhering to what is known to be vital in early childhood education.

My experience as an early childhood teacher and teacher educator has taught me that many early childhood teachers are patient, caring, and creative. Good early childhood teachers honor children's experiences, languages, and cultures. Recently, however, too many early childhood teachers function differently. Largely because of NCLB, teachers are urged to prepare children in academics earlier and earlier and they are hard pressed to meet the demands made on them. As a result, currently in early childhood classrooms there seems to be less conversation, less play, less exploration, and more paper and pencil tasks. Meiers (2009) states that: "The latest research indicates that, on a typical day, children in all-day kindergartens spend 4–6 times as much in literacy and math 'instruction' and taking or preparing for tests (about 2–3 hours per day) as they do in free play or 'choice time' (30 minutes or less)" (p. xx). This is distressing information; yet, too many teachers are worried that their children will not be ready for the next level of schooling, so they act in ways that are antithetical to how they have been taught to teach and how they know is best to teach.

Reasons for the Decline of Multicultural and Social Justice Classrooms

As mentioned earlier, I believe that the quiet erosion of multicultural education in early childhood classrooms today has been caused by three main phenomena. First of all, there appears to be a strong negative reaction towards the large numbers of non-European immigrants entering the nation, particularly those who are undocumented. Next, there seems to be a general lack of knowledge and consensus about what multicultural education is (Villegas and Lucas 2001) or how it should be implemented in classrooms (Grant and Tate 1995). Finally, NCLB has created a strong focus on early academic achievement as measured by standardized tests. Many teachers feel daily pressure to prepare children for those tests and lack the time to focus on a more inclusive curriculum. It appears to be most important in many schools and programs to accelerate early development of literacy and numeracy in preschool so children can begin to read and do formal mathematics in kindergarten.

It is important to recognize that formal knowledge and academic skills are critical components of education that is multicultural and promotes social justice. In no way do I want to give the impression that early learning and the development of skills are in opposition to an education that focuses on fairness and justice. A dynamic focus of multicultural and social justice education is that of equity in the learning process for all children. Consequently, children's individual and age readiness for certain skills and learning, as well as their cultural and linguistic differences, have to be taken into consideration for learning to occur. This is essentially what is meant by developmentally appropriate practice (Bredekamp and Copple 1997).

The gains made in the 1970s and early 1980s in multicultural education have been replaced by a developmentally *in*appropriate emphasis of forcing all children into the same mold. Sadly, what I have observed and experienced has been that whatever focus on multicultural education existed in early childhood education has become, at best, superficial and, at worst, almost nonexistent.

How Adults Engage Children in Multicultural and Social Justice Education

How can we respond to the negative comments made by the young children I quoted in this paper? How can teachers respond in ways that teach antiracism and critical thinking? The first thing I tell teacher candidates or other adults who work with children is that these comments cannot be ignored nor should they be forbidden. The moment one says, "You are not allowed to say that," the possibility for learning is stifled. Derman-Sparks (1989) recommends that teachers "engage children in 'critical thinking' discussion about the problem" (p. 191). By asking open-ended questions, children can be guided toward new ideas. The focus in classrooms and at home must be on fairness. Teachers and other adults can address these comments in developmentally appropriate ways through literature, discussions, and through contact with people from the community who can counteract stereotypes children may have about certain groups. Children quickly learn to recognize bias and injustice if adults emphasize and personalize these concepts.

Teachers Who Give Us Hope

Although I have lamented the lack of multicultural and social justice education in early childhood classrooms today, the reality is that there are still some brave and talented teachers who, despite the focus on testing in schools, are teaching through multicultural perspectives and with a social justice stance.

> A teacher asked about fairness and unfairness in her students' own lives, after she had read a story that had these elements in her third grade classroom. The students immediately began

> complaining about the unfairness of not being able to talk at all during lunch time in the cafeteria. The teacher guided the students through a conversation about why they thought that the principal had made that rule and what they could do about it. After much discussion and learning how to write a letter, the students wrote a class letter to the principal requesting that the lunch time silence rule be changed to quiet talking. They sent the letter to the principal who came to talk with the class after she received it. As a result of the children taking action and having discussions with the principal, the principal changed the rule on a trial basis. The children were able to learn and experience that group action can make a difference. In addition, the teacher was able to teach the skills of letter writing and negotiation.

> When a teacher noticed that most of his kindergarten children divided themselves along racial lines as they played, he searched out books and read stories that focused on color and race. He led discussions on what he had read, and asked the children questions regarding what they thought about what he had read. At first the children didn't make connections between what was read to them and their own behaviors. Then the teacher began to pair some of the white children with some of the black children for special classroom activities such as painting, planting, or the observation of caterpillars for science. Soon after the children began to make connections between what the teacher was reading and how they were responding to one another in the classroom. With time, and the teacher's persistence, the children engaged in rich and powerful discussions of color/race and behaviors that were discriminatory or unjust.

The teachers in these scenarios and others are committed not only to high academic standards, but also to fairness and justice in the lives of all children. Such teachers are the ones who observe carefully and pay attention to children's backgrounds and to their capabilities, so that they can teach using the children's strengths and experiences. These teachers are attentive to what children say and do, and they respond actively and plan appropriately so that children can become antiracist and action-oriented individuals. They make sure that families and communities in which the children live are acknowledged, honored, and included in the teaching process. Attention is paid to the relationships established between children, and between adults and children, in a multicultural setting or classroom. Differences are acknowledged, named, and discussed (Fennimore 2000), and biases and stereotypes are examined and addressed.

Recommendations

Education that is multicultural and promotes social justice is not a simple concept for adults to understand and address, and in educational settings there is not only one way to implement this type of education. Parents, administrators, and teachers who care about these issues, however, must focus on equity and fairness in the lives of young children. Teachers in such classrooms hold all children to high standards and give them every opportunity to learn. Respect, caring, and community building are the cornerstones of multicultural and social justice classrooms (Pang 2005; Cummins 1989). They are places where children feel safe, supported, and connected with one another (Sapon-Shevin 1999).

Teachers and administrators of multicultural and social justice education also need to be advocates for their students, in their own classrooms, in the school, and in the community. They need to investigate current information related to their advocacy interests, and to evaluate different perspectives on the issues. Most importantly, they need to help children learn to make informed decisions on how to take social action (De Gaetano et al. 1998; Fennimore 1989). Education that is multicultural and that promotes social justice is transformative, focuses on academic excellence, and guides children to become champions of justice.

References

Banks, J. (1993). Approaches to multicultural curriculum reform. In J. A. Banks and C. A. M. Banks (Eds.), *Multicultural education: Issues and perspectives* (2nd ed.) (pp. 195–214). Boston: Allyn & Bacon.

Bereiter, G., & Engelmann, S. (1966). *Teaching disadvantaged children in the preschool.* Englewood Cliffs: Prentice Hall.

Bredekamp, S., & Copple, C. (1997). *Developmentally appropriate practice in early childhood programs serving children from birth through age 8.* Washington: National Association for the Education of Young Children.

Cochran-Smith, M. (2004). *Walking the road: Race, diversity, and social justice in teacher education.* New York: Teachers College Press.

Comer, J. P. (1989). Racism and the education of young children. *Teachers College Record, 90*(3), 352–361.

Cummins, J. (1989). *Empowering minority students.* Sacramento: California Association for Bilingual Education.

Darling-Hammond, L., French, J., & Garcia-Lopez, S. (2002). *Learning to teach for social justice.* New York: Teachers College Press.

De Gaetano, Y., Williams, L. R., & Volk, D. (1998). *Kaleidoscope: A multicultural approach for the primary school classroom.* Upper Saddle River: Merrill Prentice Hall.

Derman-Sparks, L. (1989). *Anti-bias curriculum: Tools for empowering young children.* Washington: National Association for the Education of Young Children.

Derman-Sparks, L. (1998). Activism and preschool children. In E. Lee, D. Menkart, & M. Okazawa-Rey (Eds.), *Beyond heroes and holidays: A practical guide to K-12 anti-racist, multicultural education and staff development* (pp. 188–192). Washington: Network of Educators on the Americas.

Fennimore, B. S. (1989). *Child advocacy for early childhood educators.* New York: Teachers College Press.

Fennimore, B. S. (2000). *Talk matters: Refocusing the language of public schooling.* New York: Teachers College Press.

Goffin, S. G., & Washington, V. (2007). *Ready or not: Leadership choices in early care and education.* New York: Teachers College Press.

Greene, M. (1998). Introduction. In W. Ayers, J. Hunt, & T. Quinn (Eds.), *Teaching for social justice* (pp. xxvii–xlvi). New York: Teachers College Press.

Grant, C. A., & Tate, W. F. (1995). Multicultural education through the lens of the multicultural research literature. In J. A. Banks & C. A. M. Banks (Eds.), *Handbook on multicultural education* (pp. 145–166). New York: MacMillan.

Jensen, A. R. (1972). *Genetics and education.* New York: Harper and Row.

Kendall, F. (1983/1996). *Diversity in the classroom: New approaches to the education of young children* (2nd ed.). New York: Teachers College Press.

Lee, E. (1998). Anti-racist education: Pulling together to close the gaps. In E. Lee, D. Menkart, & M. Okazawa-Rey (Eds.), *Beyond heroes and holidays: A practical guide to K-12 anti-racist, multicultural education and staff development* (pp. 402–406). Washington: Network of Educators on the Americas.

Lim, T. (2010). *Early childhood education update-Dec. 2009.* Washington: Center for Law and Social Policy.

Marshall, C., & Oliva, M. (2006). *Leadership for social justice: Making revolutions in education.* Boston: Allyn & Bacon.

Meiers, D. (2009). *Early childhood. The Forum for Education.* http://www.forumforeducation.org/blog. Retrieved March 10, 2009, from

Nieto, S. (1995). From brown heroes and holidays to assimilationist agendas: Reconsidering the critiques of multicultural education. In C. E. Sleeter & P. L. McLaren (Eds.), *Multicultural education, critical pedagogy and the politics of difference* (pp. 191–220). New Paltz: State University of New York Press.

Nieto, S. (2004). *Affirming diversity: The sociopolitical context of multicultural education* (4th ed.). Boston: Pearson Education.

Pang, V. O. (2005). *Multicultural education: A caring-centered, reflective approach.* Boston: McGraw Hill.

Ramsey, P. G. (1987/2004). *Teaching and learning in a diverse world* (3rd ed.). New York: Teachers College Press.

Ramsey, P. G., Vold, E. B., & Williams, L. R. (1989). *Multicultural education: A sourcebook.* New York: Garland Publishing.

Rawls, J. (1971). *A theory of justice.* Boston: Harvard University Press.

Sapon-Shevin, M. (1999). *Because we can change the world.* Needham Heights: Allyn & Bacon.

Schlesinger, A. M. (1991). *The disuniting of America: Reflections on a multicultural society.* New York: Norton & Company.

Sleeter, C., & Grant, C. (1987). *An analysis of multicultural education in the United States. Harvard Educational Review, 57,* 421–444.

Sleeter, C., & Mclaren, P. (2000). Origins of multiculturalism. *Rethinking Schools Online, 15*(1), 1–2.

Villegas, A., & Lucas, T. (2001). Preparing culturally responsive teachers: Rethinking the curriculum. *Journal of Teacher Education, 53*(1), 20–32.

Chapter 8
Revolutionary Pedagogy: Art, Culture, and Place-Based Education in an Era of Standardization

Paula G. Purnell

Social Justice for Children Through the Lens of the Arts

BZ: Dear Paula, I have tremendous regard for you as a creative artist and educator on many levels of aesthetic experience. We have talked over the years about the relationship of the arts to social justice and children, so I hope you will accept our invitation to write a chapter for our upcoming book on children and social justice. I am not sure that many people realize the historic discrepancy between arts exposure in public and independent schools, and this gap is currently widening due to economic and federal education policies. There seems to be a lot of evidence that the *No Child Left Behind* (NCLB) legislation has created pressure for school districts to eliminate art and music classes so more time can be spent on subjects that are tested. This pressure may be greatest in the districts serving our poorest children who are already most often shortchanged by a lack of equitable district resources. What impacts will the increased disappearance of aesthetic experience in school have on the development of children and the future of society? Please let us know if you are willing to take on this important subject in a chapter for our book!

Paula: Yes, I accept your invitation! As an educator and artist-in residence I have seen the power of art, music, dance, and theater in the classroom. There is abundant, current research supporting my observations, indicating that learning and important social skills are enhanced through participation in the arts. Currently, however, there is no national mandate for arts education. As a result, the implementation of arts programming is left solely to the discretion of local superintendents, principals, and school boards. In the current test-driven school environment, funds earmarked for the arts are often redistributed to pay for supplemental test-preparation classes and materials. This is especially true in struggling urban and rural school districts where, the arts have been shown to have the most positive social and academic im-

P. G. Purnell (✉)
Indiana University of Pennsylvania, 424 Davis Hall, 507 South 11th Street,
Indiana, PA 15705, USA
e-mail: p.g.purnell@iup.edu

B. S. Fennimore, A. L. Goodwin (eds.), *Promoting Social Justice for Young Children*,
Educating the Young Child 3, DOI 10.1007/978-94-007-0570-8_8,

pact. The inequitable distribution of resources denies children in struggling school districts opportunities to develop their aesthetic interests and abilities in school. This trend has consequences that reach far beyond the classroom. Innovation, imagination, and creativity have been identified as essential tools for success in the new global economy. By denying some children access to learning in and through the arts, current policies reinforce the long-standing achievement gap that, ironically, they were designed to eliminate.

In addition to losing our arts programming, I am also very concerned that public education's overdependence on standardized tests and textbook-driven curriculum is marginalizing the role of local history, heritage, and culture in the classroom. The elimination of arts programs combined with the devaluing of the humanities and local culture send a clear message to children that our system of education does not value their cultural heritage or creative expressions of self. I believe that this depersonalizing of education breeds apathy and indifference, a consequence with dangerous social implications, particularly in communities with little political or economic power.

In this chapter, I will explore the role of art and culture in the classroom, and examine the impact of textbook-driven curricula and high-stakes testing on each. Finally, I will describe an alternative educational approach, place-based education, which has the potential to ameliorate the negative effects of mass-produced texts and tests by providing arts-rich, interdisciplinary instruction based on meaningful encounters with students' immediate physical and cultural surroundings.

The Arts in Public Education

The arts have never enjoyed a central place in America's school system. We know intuitively that the arts are integral to a quality life, but despite decades of research on arts education, shifts and changes in policies and administrations, and millions of private and public dollars invested, we still cannot decide where the arts belong in the public school curriculum. On the one hand, we want our children to be educated with an aesthetic appreciation for the world around them, in an educational system that fosters creativity, imagination, and critical thinking. On the other hand, we demand quantifiable evidence that all children have mastered basic language and math skills. These two goals, however, are rarely accomplished through similar pedagogies and assessments. Currently, our test-driven system is skewed toward producing quantifiable measures of mastery in a very narrow set of specific, academic skills.

Schools' singular focus on raising standardized test scores has resulted in decreased time for the arts, more reliance on mass-produced curriculum materials, fewer creative projects and activities in the general classroom, fewer field trips and community visitors, and less time for the study of the humanities. Dr. Susan Fuhrman, the President of Teachers College, Columbia University, states, "all children—but especially those in impoverished neighborhoods where basic skills dominate classroom time—need rich curriculum that includes challenging content, the arts, physical education, exposure to cultural institutions and more" (2008, p. 24). In reality, however, current policies have narrowed the curriculum and diminished instructional time in the arts and humanities, especially for children living in poverty (Chapman 2007; Klein 2007).

The *NCLB* Act of 2001 reauthorized the Elementary and Secondary Education Act (ESEA), passed in 1965 and is the main federal law guiding public education from kindergarten through high school in America. Proposed by President Bush shortly after his inauguration, NCLB was signed into law on January 8, 2002. NCLB implemented new academic accountability measures to be evidenced through standardized test scores in English, math, and science. NCLB had immediate impacts, both positive and negative, on arts education policies. For the first time ever, the arts were included in the legal definition of "core academic subjects," making federal funds available to research-based arts education programs (Chapman 2004). NCLB also, however, required schools to test students in grades three through eight each year in math and reading. Arts advocates worried that the high-stakes emphasis on reading and math might threaten existing arts education programs, as policy makers and administrators redesigned their budgets to meet the demands of NCLB. Indeed, by 2003, federal funding originally earmarked for arts programs had been cut in favor of "higher priorities" (United States Department of Education 2003). High-stakes testing helped portend a drastic reduction in the amount of time and funding devoted nationally to arts instruction (National Art Education Association 2008).

The standardized tests imposed by NCLB are considered "high-stakes" because schools must meet the government's specified benchmarks for Adequate Yearly Progress (AYP) in order to be eligible for federal funding. An overarching goal of NCLB has been the elimination of the achievement gap between children attending school in poor and affluent school districts. One unintended consequence of NCLB's mandates, however, is that schools with fewer resources are now under greater pressure to raise test scores. As a result, underfunded school districts are more likely to reduce or eliminate their arts programs in favor of additional test preparation. Test preparation materials are expensive and generally designed to achieve quick results through direct instruction, repetition, and rote memorization of facts. By contrast, the benefits of arts education accumulate slowly and may take years to be evidenced in a quantifiable way. In 1749, statesman Benjamin Franklin wrote, "As to their studies, it would be well if they could be taught everything that is useful, and everything that is ornamental. But art is long, and their time is short" (Beck Green 1948, pp. 25–26). In today's high-stress, high-stakes classrooms, Benjamin Franklin's words ring especially true—art is long and time is short. Research shows, however, that arts participation develops important skills that are not currently being addressed elsewhere in the public school curriculum, including persistence, innovation, creative problem solving, observation, self-evaluation, and reflection (Winner and Hetland 2008). These skills and habits of mind are not easily quantified, but they are essential to developing higher-order thinking skills. And evidence shows that these are exactly the skills that will be most in demand as we move away from an economy based on the production of goods toward an economy based on ideas (Florida 2002; Freedman 2006).

NCLB's system of assessment was designed to assure that all students would have the basic academic skills by the time they graduated from high school. In our rush to standardize and quantify education, however, we are denying some of our youngest citizens access to the creative and aesthetic experiences that—so much more than the mere accumulation of facts—will help them to develop the skills and knowledge needed to participate fully in a democracy, and to engage effectively in a new era of innovation.

Culture in the Classroom

Sir E. B. Taylor (1871) defined culture as "the complex whole which includes the knowledge, belief, arts, morals, law, custom, and any other capabilities and habits acquired by man as a member of society" (p. 1). Contemporary American culture is often described as a culture of mass production and consumerism. Pull off any major highway in the country, for example, and you are bound to find the same super-stores and fast food chains, whether you are in Ohio, Florida, or California. Walk into any classroom in the country and you will see students and teachers using the same textbooks, worksheets, and standardized tests.

Textbooks and fast food have a lot in common—both serve a purpose, but you wouldn't want to live on a steady diet of either. Both offer convenience, uniformity of content, and predictability. But these are often gained at the expense of individuality, uniqueness, character, and regional flavor. In schools across the county, dependence on standardized tests and mass produced curriculum materials is supplanting other valuable resources, including teacher-created activities and projects, arts and music classes, field trips and community visitors, and student-directed, inquiry-based projects. I suggest that our growing reliance on mass-produced curriculum materials and assessments threatens to depersonalize education, and to devalue the role of local culture and community in the lives of young children.

Multicultural theorist James Banks' definition of culture distinguishes between the culture of nation-state, or *macroculture*, and smaller cultural communities, or *microcultures.* Microcultures include religious affiliations, socioeconomic status, gender, ethnic heritage, and a wide array of variations. It is through our associations with microcultures, Banks posits, that we "mediate, interpret, reinterpret, perceive, and experience these overarching national values and ideals differently" (2006, p. 72). Cognitive psychologist, Bruner (2004), writes that personal interactions with one's family and community culture, including histories and narrative stories, greatly influence children's construction of reality and are essential in developing positive self-identity. In an ideal learning environment, skilled teachers carefully navigate the intersections of cultures within their classroom—creating bridges between home and school cultures, and inviting children to learn about, appreciate, and participate in their home communities. Currently, however, the standardized curriculum is so narrow, and the school day so jam-packed with content, that this kind of individual attention to the cultural makeup of a class or school is virtually impossible.

In 1987, author and environmental activist Wendell Berry warned that when educators relinquish their teaching responsibilities to policymakers and big business they "are easily replaced by bureaucratic and methodological procedures, 'job market' specifications, and tests graded by machines" (Berry 1987 p. 86). Our ambivalence towards the arts and the role of culture in the classroom, combined with our current dependence on high-stakes, high-stress testing, portends a very banal educational landscape, one in which students' and teachers' unique cultures and creative self-expression are considered extraneous and are easily usurped by the avarice of a profit-driven industry.

America's Testing Machine

Currently, a handful of publishing companies including Harcourt-Brace, Pearson, and McGraw Hill, constitute a more than US $40 billion industry, and are responsible for creating the texts and tests that dominate American classrooms. School districts across the country select and purchase their published curriculum materials through a complicated and highly competitive textbook adoption system. Textbook publishers target just three states for sales: Texas, California, and Florida. Since adoption in these states is imperative for the companies' financial success, representatives from those states receive special preference in deciding what information should, and should not, be included in the scope and sequence of each subject area. Unfortunately, this means that publishers first create products specifically designed for adoption in those three states, and then sell the very same products to everyone else (Ansary 2004).

In this tail-wagging-the-dog system, the same mega-publishers also create, disseminate, collect, and score the standardized tests that are currently used as the sole measurement of public schools' success. To ensure that individual students pass the test and that schools meet the government-set benchmark of AYP, teachers are strongly encouraged to teach from the text. As a result, instead of tests being created to assess achievement in knowledge identified as important by educators, the tests themselves have established and standardized what is considered to be knowledge. "Standardized tests create uniformity in the knowledge taught in public schools. In other words, these tests standardize knowledge" (Spring 2007, p. 135). In 2007, students in 92,000 American schools took over 50 million standardized tests (Glovin and Evans 2007). The Bush Administration's US Deputy Secretary of Education, Raymond Simon, stated, "The whole teaching system is based on the results of those tests" (Gloven and Evans 2007, p. 21).

The educational resources that dominate America's classrooms are created by an industry that is neither motivated nor equipped to address the unique characteristics of each state, let alone the history, ecology, and arts of specific communities, or the creative self-expressions of individuals. Like fast food chains, the textbook industry provides uniformity, consistency, and convenience. But text-driven curricula and scripted lessons can't replace the role of a teacher, skillfully guiding a child's curiosity-driven discovery of their immediate cultural and physical surroundings.

Place-Based Education

Since the 1990s, advocates of Place-based Education (PBE) have been "striving to make the boundaries between schools and their environs more permeable by directing at least part of the students' school experiences to local phenomena, ranging from culture and politics to environmental concerns and the economy" (Smith 2007, p. 190). The term PBE was popularized in the 1960s and 1970s when environmental educators recognized that students could not comprehend the global impacts of pollution, over-population, and misuse of natural resources until they became aware of, and engaged in, understanding and addressing these concepts at a local level. Environmental educators created outdoor classrooms and invited students to investigate locally significant issues, such as the consequences of industrialization on local water and air quality. These real-life PBE, experiences enhanced students' comprehension of complex issues, and engaged students in community service and civic action. Through place-based environmental education students learned the true meaning of the bumper-sticker slogan, "Think Globally: Act Locally."

The environmental application of place-based learning may have been a new idea in the 1960s, but the concept has been a mainstay of progressive education for quite some time. Dewey (1915) stated, "experience has its geographical aspects, its artistic and its literary sides, its scientific and its historical sides. All studies arise from aspects of the one earth and the one life lived upon it" (p. 91). Mitchell (1934) recognized the educational importance of connecting young children to their immediate social environments before introducing them to more broad concepts such as governance and law; "the school's job," she stated, "is to begin with children's own environment whatever or wherever it may be" (p. 16). The well-known early childhood educational philosophy developed in the Reggio Emilia region in Italy in the 1940s is based on a deep knowledge of community-constructed values. The school, in fact, is considered to be a natural extension of the community, not separate from it.

As with the arts and culture, however, the recognition in theory of the importance of establishing a sense of place in education has not translated into viable policy or practice in America's schools. In *The Culture of Education* (1996), Jerome Bruner urged educators to reevaluate the direction of public education and "consider education and school learning in their situated, cultural context" (p. ix). Over the ensuing years, a growing number of educators have responded by developing a range of educational programs designed to immerse students in local culture, ecology, history, government, and arts.

Interdisciplinary place-based activities explore the interconnections in subject areas across the curriculum, including mathematics, social studies, science, literacy, and the arts. Teachers, often working collaboratively with local experts and artists, create lessons and hands-on activities that align with state and national academic standards while fostering meaningful connections and affiliations with the places where students live. By addressing subject content in a situated context, PBE engenders civic pride, social consciousness, and cultural and environmental stewardship.

PBE has significant implications for arts education as well. Place-based arts programs spotlight locally produced works of art and encourage students to actively participate in the arts within their immediate cultural environment. Bringing colloquial art, traditions, celebrations, and narrative histories into the classroom helps to dispel the consumer-culture perception that "real" art is created in far-off places for national or international audiences. Ball and Lai (2006) suggest that place-based arts programs "contribute to the well-being of local communities by highlighting and encouraging expressive cultural practice through which residents can participate in local life" (p. 279).

Revolutionary Pedagogy

Brazilian activist and author of *Pedagogy of the Oppressed*, Freire (1995), recognized that those holding political and economic power create systems of education within a given society. To counteract the social injustice inherent in such systems, Freire proposed something revolutionary—pedagogies based on students' own cultural experiences and daily lives, designed to raise social consciousness, and ultimately, incite civic action. In a review of current educational trends, Smith (2007) concludes, "Not much revolutionary pedagogy is happening anywhere in the United States or elsewhere. But that doesn't mean that such a pedagogy can't happen at all" (p. 205). Like Smith, I see little to suggest that institutionalized education will be renouncing standardization and embracing art, culture, and revolutionary pedagogies any time soon. I also agree with Smith, however, that revolutionary pedagogy—the critical examination of curriculum within the students' immediate physical and cultural environment—is not beyond the scope of current classroom practice. In fact, such instruction is imperative for sustaining a vibrant educational system that is responsive to the needs of the population it serves. Critical pedagogy requires students and teachers to vigilantly examine, question, and transform the generalizations and assumptions that are present in any system of institutionalized education. In an article titled "The Best of Both Worlds: A Critical Pedagogy of Place," Gruenwald (2003) states, "articulating a critical pedagogy of place is a response against educational reform policies and practices that disregard places and that leave assumptions about the relationship between education and the politics of economic development unexamined" (p. 3).

The arts and culture are integral to developing children's sense of place in the world. Locally produced works of art, songs, poetry, and drama are primary documents that tell the dynamic, human stories intrinsic to specific locales. Consider, for example, the powerful cultural and social messages embedded in the murals of

Diego Rivera, the plays of August Wilson, and the songs from the bituminous coal fields of West Virginia. Far from being ancillary to "real" academics, the arts can inform, educate, motivate, and inspire. Validating self-produced and locally produced artworks is empowering for all children, but particularly for children living in poor rural and urban communities where local culture and art may be undervalued or stigmatized by the mainstream. Place-based arts education endows children with the skills, knowledge, and self-awareness they will need to confidently add their own stories to the global conversation.

Conclusion

For decades, educators striving to meet the needs of students in an ever-changing society have fluctuated between a philosophy of progressive, child-centered education, and a demand for pragmatic, "back to basics" tactics in the classroom. Contrary to many Americans' perceptions, research strongly indicates that the arts are not merely "fluff" or pleasant distractions from "real" academic work. In fact, participation in the arts enhances vital social and cognitive skills, many of which will be integral to individuals' success in the burgeoning global economy of invention and innovation. Currently, inequitable school funding, text-driven curriculum, and narrow, standardized assessments are denying many children, particularly those living in struggling school districts, access to these essential tools for future success. Rigorous academics, arts-rich learning, and strong connections to home and community are not mutually exclusive. In fact, each is imperative in providing the high quality of education that Americans must demand for all children.

References

Ansary, T. (2004). *A textbook example of what's wrong with education.* www.edutopia.org. Accessed 11 May 2009.

Ball, E., & Lai, A. (2006). Place-based pedagogy for the arts and humanities. Pedagogy: Critical Approaches to Teaching Literature, Language, Composition, and Culture, 6(2), 261–287.

Banks, J. (2006). Cultural diversity and education: Foundations, curriculum and teaching. Boston: Allyn & Bacon.

Beck Green, H. (1948). Proposals related to the education of youth: The introduction of art as a general education subject in American schools. Unpublished Doctoral Dissertation, Stamford University.

Berry, W. (1987). *Home economics*. New York: North Point Press.

Bruner, J. (1996). *The culture of education*. Cambridge: Harvard University Press.

Bruner, J. (2004). Life as narrative. *Social Research, 71*(3), 691–710.

Chapman, L. (2004). No child left behind in art?. *Art Education Policy Review, 106*(2), 3–17.

Chapman, L. (2007). An update on No Child Left Behind and national trends in education. *Arts Education Policy Review, 109*(1), 25–36.

Dewey, J. (1915). *The school and society*. New York: McMillan.

Florida, R. (2002). The rise of the creative class: And how it's transforming work, leisure, community, and everyday life. New York: Basic Books.
Freedman, K. (2006). *Leading creativity: Responding to policy in art education.* http://portal.unesco.org/culture/en/files/30187/11415088311winfried_kneip.pdf/winfried%2Bkneip.pdf. Accessed 27 December 2009.
Freire, P. (1995). *Pedagogy of the oppressed.* New York: Continuum.
Fuhrman, S. (2008). If we're talking about race, let's talk about education. *Education Week, 27*(36), 24.
Glovin, D., & Evans, D. (2007). Standard error: Testing industry undercuts quality control for profit margin. *The IRE Journal, 30*(5), 21–22.
Gruenwald, D. (2003). The best of both worlds: A critical pedagogy of place. *Educational Researcher, 32*(4), 3–12.
Klein, A. (2007). Survey: Subjects trimmed to boost math and reading. *Education Week, 26*(44), 7.
Mitchell, L. S. (1934). *Young geographers.* New York: Bank Street College.
National Art Education Association (2008). New study reports on revitalizing arts education in six urban areas. *NAEA News, 50*(4), 1.
Smith, G. (2007). Place-based education: Breaking through the constraining regularities of public school. *Environmental Education Research, 13*(2), 189–207.
Spring, J. (2007). *Deculturalization and the struggle for equality* (5th ed.). New York: McGraw-Hill.
Taylor, E. B. (1871). *Primitive culture* (Vol. 1). London: John Murray.
US Department of Education (2003). Fiscal year 2004 education budget summary and background information, Section III: Programs proposed for elimination. http://www.ed.gov/about/overview/budget/budget04/summary/edlite-section3.html. Accessed 8 Feb 2007.
Winner, E., & Hetland, L. (2008). Art for our sake: School arts classes matter more than ever—but not for the reasons you think. *Arts Education Policy Review, 109*(5), 29–32.

Part III
Children of the World in Our Classrooms—Honoring Multiple Identities, Languages, and Knowledges

Chapter 9
Working with Immigrant Children of "Undocumented" and "Mixed" Families

Xue Lan Rong, Liv Thorstensson Dávila and Jeremy Hilburn

Major demographic shifts that have taken place over the past 40 years in the United States have resulted in a variety of significant transformations in US schools. Most striking is the increased language and cultural diversity of students in elementary, middle, and secondary classrooms. Since the passing of the 1965 Immigration Act, which eliminated country-by-country quotas, more and more Americans are racial minorities, foreign-born, and multilingual. Today, approximately 42% of students in public elementary and secondary schools in the United States are members of a racial or ethnic minority, up from 28% in 1981. Sixteen percent of all students are Black, 20% are Latino, 4% are Asian, and 2% are classified as minority students of other races. Almost half of all American children under the age of five are Latino, Black, Asian, or other minorities. Moreover, minority groups account for more than one-half of children under the age of 18 in six states: Arizona, California, Hawaii, Florida, New Mexico, and Texas (NCES 2006; US Bureau of the Census 2003, 2007).

Just as minority populations constitute a rising share of the total US population, the children of immigrants—both foreign and US-born—also comprise a growing proportion of the nation's K-12 student population. The number of children whose parents are immigrants tripled from 6 to 20% between 1970 and 2000. Between 1979 and 2005, the number of school-aged children who spoke a language other than English at home increased from 3.8 to 10.6 million, or from 9 to 20% of the population in this age range (NCES 2006). In addition, the estimated population of undocumented immigrants has nearly tripled over the past three decades (see Fig. 9.1) (Passel 2005). In 2004, approximately 1.7 million school-aged children were undocumented, and 3 million US-born children were living in mixed families, i.e., households headed by one or two undocumented immigrant parents. Consequently, US schools are facing enormous challenges posed by this demographic transition, and one of the greatest challenges is smoothly navigating the necessary reforms to accommodate the tremendous needs of the children of this immigration movement.

X. L. Rong (✉)
School of Education, University of North Carolina, Chapel Hill, NC, USA
e-mail: xrong@email.unc.edu

B. S. Fennimore, A. L. Goodwin (eds.), *Promoting Social Justice for Young Children*, Educating the Young Child 3, DOI 10.1007/978-94-007-0570-8_9,

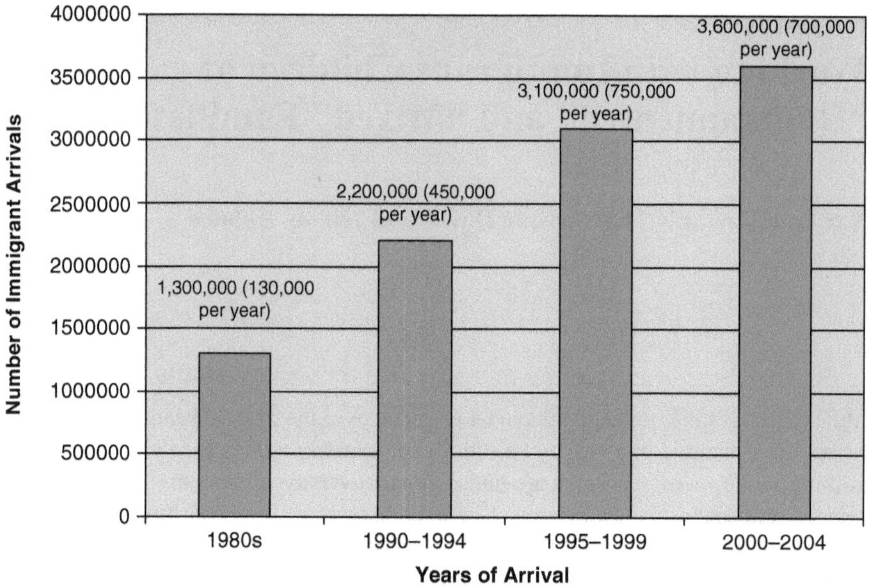

Fig. 9.1 Number of undocumented immigrants arrived by years. (Data from Passel 2005)

The Study

This chapter focuses on the particular conditions and needs of undocumented PreK and elementary students. It is a conceptual paper. We first established a quantitative context for this paper based on an examination of current population studies. We then drew on the existing literature and other documents across the fields of education, anthropology, sociology, population studies, and psychology, narrowing our scope to children of undocumented or mixed families in the United States only, to answer the following questions:

1. Who are the children of undocumented and mixed immigrant families?
2. What are their special needs?
3. What can and should schools and educators do to help these children adjust?

We classify undocumented immigrants as those who entered the United States without valid documents (passports or visas) or who have overstayed their student, work, or other visas without permission from the BCIS (Bureau of Citizenship and Immigration Services). About half of the growing undocumented immigrant population is comprised of those who arrived without legal documentation, having crossed the border without being apprehended, and the rest are those who have overstayed their visas without authorization (Martin and Midgley 2006). We use the term "undocumented immigrant" throughout this paper, but this group is also referred to as illegal immigrants, unauthorized immigrants, or illegal aliens in much governmental, media, and scholarly discourse. A child may exist in one of several undocumented family situations. For example, they may be a foreign-born child with undocumented parents, or a US-born child with one or both parents being foreign-born and undocumented. In the former case, the child may also be an undocumented immigrant; in the latter case, the child is an American citizen in a "mixed" family with parents and siblings who may be undocumented.

Theoretical Framework

The framework for this paper follows the theory of segmented assimilation (Portes and Zhou 1993). This theory posits that immigrant children's acculturation is based on their immigration experiences, including the extent to which they are received by and incorporated into the host society (Rong and Preissle 2009). The theory of segmented assimilation allows us to account for situational or environmental factors that bear on the particular needs and obstacles of undocumented immigrant youth. Previous research based on this theory, for example, uncovered differing outcomes of legal and undocumented Central American immigrants, and underscored the significance of state policy as either facilitator or deterrent of children's and adults' assimilation (Portes and Rumbaut 1996). Several studies (e.g., Portes and Zhou 1993) have concluded that the context of reception largely determines the kinds of adjustments newcomers must make. An additive model in practitioners' scholarship has also been advocated (e.g., Valenzuela 1999) as the more effective approach to take when working with children of undocumented or mixed immigrant families on their initial and continued adjustment in the United States.

Undocumented Immigrants and Their Children in the United States

Data on the precise number of undocumented immigrants living in the United States is unavailable due to obvious technical and legal reasons. However, several population studies have shed light on the estimated size of the undocumented population in the United States through examinations of the basic demographic characteristics of this group by region of origin, geographical concentration, and gender, family, and legal status (Camarota 2005; Mather et al. 2006; Passel 2005).

In 2004, it was estimated that 10.3 million undocumented immigrants were living in the United States, with numbers increasing annually. Of these undocumented immigrants, 57% emigrated from Mexico while 24% came from other Latin American countries, 9% from Asia, 6% from Europe and Canada, and 4% were from the rest of the world (Passel 2005). One out of every six undocumented immigrants in the United States is a school-aged child.

Children of immigrants are the fastest growing segment of the overall child population in the United States, including the steadily increasing proportion of immigrant children who are undocumented or from mixed families. In 2000, an estimated 1.5% of all elementary school children were undocumented immigrants, and 5% were children of undocumented immigrants (Capps and Fix 2005). However, the majority of children with an undocumented immigrant parent live in families with mixed legal status. This means that of all children with undocumented immigrant parents, two of every three are US citizens and, therefore, accorded rights guaranteed by the US Constitution.

Zhou (2003) noted that, since 1981, 40 to 45% of undocumented immigrants have been female. This figure suggests that immigration to the United States often involves the resettlement and establishment of families, a notion that defies earlier arguments that male undocumented workers merely wanted to remit their income to their country of origin and return after a few years of work in the United States. The exigency of this issue is particularly relevant in eight states (California, Texas, Florida, New York, Arizona, Illinois, New Jersey, and North Carolina) where two-thirds of undocumented immigrants currently reside (Passel 2005). With Zhou's and other studies in mind, schools can no longer assume that undocumented children are but temporary residents of their communities. Instead, educators must consider the unique needs of undocumented immigrant children and initiate long-range planning in terms of developing educational policies and pedagogical practices to work effectively with this population.

The following sections will address the special needs of preK and K-5 children from undocumented and mixed families based on their particular vulnerabilities, and provide recommendations for educators.

Special Needs of Children from Undocumented and Mixed Families

Approximately five million children (two-thirds of them being US citizens) live in either mixed or non-mixed undocumented families. These are the children of America's most invisible and lowest paid workers. The majority of these workers experience labor exploitation and are unprotected by US laws governing workplace safety, and employee benefits. These workers are also subject to arrest, retention, deportation, and jail time. Children who live in households affected by these conditions are likely to suffer from severe hardship. These children also face multiple individual vulnerabilities produced by language barriers, dislocation, cultural differences, and familial separation. Studies (e.g., Gaytan et al. 2007; Rong and Preissle 2009) indicate that these vulnerabilities could have a substantial counterproductive impact on the school performance and academic achievement of these children. Though all immigrant groups experience difficulties associated with relocating to a new country, this paper will focus on challenges particular to undocumented immigrants, such as structural deficiencies, psychological stresses, language barriers, as well as conditions that affect this population in what we call New Gateway States, i.e., states whose immigrant populations have tripled in the last decade.

Structural Vulnerabilities

Children from families with questionable legal status are structurally vulnerable in several unique ways due to the current anti-immigrant political climate and inconsistent government immigration policies across states. Researchers (e.g., Edelman and Jones 2004) have cautioned us that, in the past, the issues of social class and poverty have not received enough attention from researchers and practitioners studying the education of immigrants. Poverty rates increased between 2001 and 2005 with two of the poorest segments being children 0 to 5 year old, and the other poorest segment being recent immigrants. Findings reported by Rong and Preissle (2009) with 2000 Census data show that the poverty rate for all US families in 2000 was about 11%, about 15% for children aged 5 to 18, and more than 27% for immigrant children aged 5 to 18 (33% for Hispanic children). The highest poverty rate was found among second-generation Hmong children (44%) and among Hmong immigrant children (59%). Child poverty poses a significant social problem because it is linked to a number of long-lasting health, developmental, and education-related issues that often translate into poor socioeconomic outcomes in adulthood (Edelman and Jones 2004). For example, because undocumented immigrants are not eligible for welfare, food stamps, Medicaid, or other public benefits, children from undocumented immigrant families are substantially more likely than other immigrant children to be poor and to experience food and housing-related hardships (Capps and Fix 2005). Additionally, children in undocumented immigrant households are more likely to be in fair or poor health and to lack health insurance.

One of the major barriers to fighting poverty for this group of children is the lack of governmental support and public services available to them. US-born children living in mixed families receive welfare and public services at a substantially lower rate than other US children, despite being equally qualified to receive benefits such as food stamps and health insurance. Some factors that may prevent parents from applying for benefits for themselves or their children include confusion or lack of knowledge about eligibility, limited English proficiency, and parental noncitizen status. Anxiety over possible deportation among families with mixed citizenship status also inhibits their use of benefits for their children (Shields and Behrman 2004).

Furthermore, preK children of immigrants are less likely to be in center-based child care or participate in federal or state programs offering early education such as Head Start, Even Start, Smart Start, or other similar programs for children from low-income families. They are also excluded from some special programs designed for English language learning, as well as some general special education programs for learning-disabled children, all of which potentially limits their preparation for schooling (InFocus 2005).

Psychological Stress

According to a study by Greenberg and Rahmanou (2004), in 2002, nearly three-quarters of all children with immigrant parents were themselves US citizens living with one or more noncitizen parents in families of mixed legal status. Living in undocumented or mixed families under harsh social conditions can be very stressful for both children and parents. Children not only face uncertainties about their parents' employment, they also tend to live in crime-ridden neighborhoods, and in multi-family living arrangements, and are often responsible for caring for younger siblings. Moreover, they must also move frequently from place to place, either between their country of origin and the United States or within the United States itself (Hamann 2001).

In addition, 49% of children in these populations are separated from at least one parent for extended periods of time while 36% are separated from both parents. Prolonged separation can be emotionally taxing and often results in complicated periods of adjustment for all family members. Recent studies have revealed that children in separated undocumented or mixed families develop "significantly more depressive symptoms" than immigrant children whose families stay together (Gaytan et al. 2007, p. 11).

Many undocumented children are traumatized by well-publicized immigration raids in restaurants and factories, and the subsequent deportation of illegal immigrants across the United States. Even worse, some of the children's parents, their friends' parents, and fellow countrymen have been arrested, jailed, and deported. Furthermore, these children are likely to experience unfriendly treatment and hostility from schools, fellow students and their parents, and society in general. Unfortunately, stigma and exclusion from school and society pose challenges to these children's psychological adjustment.

Young children are particularly likely to be confused regarding their ethnic identity due to their uncertain legal status. They may not be certain if they "belong" to the Unted States or to their parents' country of origin. Researchers (e.g., Suarez-Orozco et al. 2008) have reported that these emotional stresses might be carried over into K-5 students' school experiences. Unstable family arrangement often undermines the capacity of parents to retain authority to educate their children (Fernandez-Kelly and Curran 2001). The fact that undocumented children often grow up in unstable environments and are unable to participate in federal and state early childhood education programs or K-5 after school programs available to many legal citizens, may add to their sense of alienation, or lack of motivation in school. In addition, children of undocumented and mixed families often experience shame associated with poor academic performance linked to high-stakes achievement tests. "[Standardized tests] that do not acknowledge a student's cultural background and related knowledge … will mislabel a student's skills and capabilities, and will construct a student's school struggles as an individual problem…rather than a multilateral failure" (Hamann 2001, p. 51).

Language Transition

In many ways related to psychosocial well-being, barriers encountered in language transition are another vulnerability associated with children in undocumented or mixed families. For this paper, language transition refers to the lifelong process involving the interplay between learning English, and the retention and attrition of the native or heritage language (Rong and Preissle 2009).

"Learning English" was cited by 56% of undocumented students as the greatest barrier to their education, ranked ahead of lack of resources, being undocumented, or discrimination (Gatyan et al. 2007). Traumatic experiences and lack of familial and social support can hinder language acquisition (Suarez-Orozco and Suarez-Orozco 2001); language acquisition in turn also affects the school experiences and the psychosocial wellbeing of undocumented students. Young children are particularly apt at learning languages. However, language minority students must be immersed in environments that support bilingualism and biculturalism at home, in school, and in their communities. Lack of social and academic proficiency in both English and the heritage language, can result in underachievement in school as well as fractured family and peer relationships.

Due to their uncertain immigration legal status and frequent moving experiences, children from undocumented immigrant families may be shuttled back and forth between two kinds of language stages: pseudo-bilingualism with a preference for English, and pseudo-bilingualism with a preference for their native language. These linguistic shifts may be particularly confusing to young children and may eventually delay their learning of English. Moreover, because children are often the only English-speaking member of the family, they must take on extra familial responsibilities, such as serving as translators in stores, hospitals, and at parent–teacher meetings in school. While increased responsibility often has such positive benefits as improving communication and leadership skills, excessive responsibility can cause intergenerational conflicts (e.g., parent–children role reversal), as well as other psychological burdens in young children. It also takes away time better spent on academic pursuits. Schools must be fully aware of these issues and work to cross language barriers to reach children of undocumented or mixed families.

New Gateway State[1] *Factor*

The foreign-born population in many new gateway states has tripled or quadrupled since the 1980s. Atlanta, for example, as a new immigrant destination, re-

[1] The "traditional" gateway states (California, New York, Texas, Florida, Illinois, and New Jersey) have historically hosted large foreign-born populations; "new gateway" states (also labeled "new growth" states by demographers) are states such as North Carolina, Georgia, Iowa, and Utah which have tripled or quadrupled their immigrant populations in the last 15 years (see Passel and Suro 2005).

ceived four times as many newcomers in the 1990s as it did in the 1980s. In areas with an increasing population, particularly the new gateway states, with large numbers of international as well as internal migrants, schools should expect a continued overflow of immigrant children, many of whom are undocumented. This challenge is compounded by the fact that these states' service organizations and personnel have historically had very little preparation for working with immigrants.

In contrast to the populations of traditional gateway states, the immigrant population in new gateway states such as Georgia, North Carolina, and Nevada is disproportionately made up of recent arrivals. More than 50% of all immigrants living in these states arrived during the 1990s, compared with 40% in traditional gateway states (Fix and Passel 2003). On the one hand, this increase means that demands for various types of social services are on the rise. The influx of domestic migrants in these states has boosted the demand for construction, service, and retail jobs. These have been increasingly filled by recent immigrants who are more likely to have moderate incomes, fewer marketable skills, and a weaker command of English than their counterparts in traditional gateway states and the United States as a whole, as well as either domestic migrants or long-term residents (Passel and Suro 2005). For this reason, recent immigrants in new gateway states are more likely to need benefits and services such as health insurance, bilingual translators, and English language education. Unfortunately, new gateway states have "limited experience and infrastructure for settling newcomer families" (Fix and Passal 2003, p. 8) as they have historically received few immigrants in the centuries following colonial conquest and expansion. All of these factors may create challenges for schools and other social institutions in terms of designing educational programs that sufficiently meet the needs of these children while also involving their parents.

Many schools, particularly elementary schools, in these areas are struggling to accommodate growing student enrollments, including domestic migrant students and immigrant students, into already-oversized schools and overcrowded classrooms (Hernandez 2004). Meanwhile, these schools are being challenged to focus their attention and resources on meeting testing requirements mandated by the NCLB federal laws, while simultaneously accommodating the cultural and linguistic needs of the newcomers. To address these demographic changes, traditional gateway states may need to reevaluate their laws and policies while new gateway states need to author new legislation to, for example, build new schools, recruit and train more teachers, and so on.

The government agencies should understand that restricting public benefits does the most harm to school-aged children. In spite of the fact that undocumented families are avoiding contact with government, and thus, not receiving public services, many states restrict services to undocumented immigrants with the hope that restricted social services will "drive out" undocumented immigrants (e.g., Propositions 187 and 227 in California). A survey in 2000, however, revealed the folly of this logic, as only 1% of undocumented immigrants moved to a new state for social services (Berk et al. 2000).

Recommendations

We have addressed the special needs of children in undocumented or mixed immigrant families based on the four main vulnerabilities synthesized from existing literature. In this section, we make recommendations to schools and educators for how to work effectively with undocumented preK and elementary school students. Our five recommendations are based on an additive model (Valenzuela 1999), which recognizes the structural barriers that certain immigrant groups face, and places value on the primary languages and cultures of all students. Valenzuela (1999) has argued that additive schooling advocates providing equal opportunities to immigrants and assimilating them into society through a bicultural process. This process recognizes heritage languages and cultures as assets to a positive acculturative process and involves teaching in ways meaningful to students' bicultural experiences. Additive schooling within this framework also emphasizes maintenance of community and formation of home–school relations. Additive schooling has posited that promoting mutual respect and cooperation between schools and immigrant communities and including immigrant families in school decision-making helps children maintain a healthy identity as well as social and psychological well-being (Valenzuela 1999). We also argue that health, social and legal services, as well as community outreach and advocacy should embody this additive model.

Provide In-Service Training for School Personnel

Morse and Ludovina (1999) offer several suggestions for in-service training of school personnel regarding serving undocumented students. School personnel must realize that economic and other structural issues might limit students' school attendance and participation. School personnel must hold high expectations for all students and keep in mind that undocumented immigrants are often motivated to come to the US to provide a better education for their children. Staff must receive training in the cultural backgrounds of undocumented students and their families and their experiences and expectations with regard to education. Staff must also receive ongoing training in procedures that affect undocumented students, such as language proficiency and placement tests and how to modify lesson plans to accommodate the language and social needs of this population. These staff development workshops must also address issues that include educators' beliefs, attitudes, and awareness regarding the students from undocumented or mixed immigrant families.

In working with children from mixed or non-mixed undocumented immigrant families, educators need to hold beliefs compatible with democratic values and ethics as professional educators. First of all, they should be aware that all children residing in the United States have a legal right to a free public K-12 education regardless of their immigration status owing to the outcome of a 1982 landmark Supreme Court case, *Plyer v. Doe*. According to *Plyler v. Doe*, schools (a) must provide educational services to all students regardless of immigration status, (b) may not legally inquire into a student's legal status, and (c) may not engage in practices that make students feel unsafe and thereby compromise their attendance in school. *Plyler v. Doe* also ruled that schools are not allowed to require students to present their Social Security numbers (Morse and Ludovina 1999).

In spite of the protections granted to undocumented students under *Plyler v. Doe*, debates on if and how to educate this population in US schools persist among the educators and general publics. We believe that US educators' beliefs and attitudes towards these debates can influence the quality of the teaching and other services children of this population may receive. School personnel should recognize that persistent and widespread anti-undocumented immigrant sentiments in the US toward Latino immigrants, especially Mexican and Central American immigrants, are often based on a combination of misinformation and political rhetoric. Policymakers and educators should also realize that, regardless how one might feel about US immigration policies, there is no turning back the clock on the children of immigrants already living here, and that these children's well-being affects all aspects of our lives at the present time and for years to come. Furthermore, US educators not only need to sort out these issues for themselves in unbiased ways, they should also use the classroom as a vehicle to communicate this information to students and the community. For example, Bryant (2004) believes that Social Studies classes can play an important role in easing community tensions of Hispanic and non-Hispanic citizens by opening discussions on contentious issues that have been driven for decades by anti-immigration forces against the low wage-earning and poor Latino immigrants.

Maintaining awareness of the complex situations of undocumented families is also essential when working with Latino immigrant students. Educators need to be aware of the particular arrangements of some families. For example, many children have split from their families and live in the United Sates with relatives or family friends as they were sent from Central and South America without their parents to escape military conflicts. On the other hand, some immigrants cross the border while leaving their children with family members and are unable to reunite with their children for extended periods because they cannot afford the risks or costs of returning home to retrieve them. These parents face the difficult choice of allowing others to raise their children or hiring smugglers to bring their children into the United States (Romo 2007). When children finally reunite with their parents in the United States, their families often need to work through numerous family issues that arise during long periods of separation. For instance, conflict can arise in reunited families when a parent perceives that their child has become over-Americanized (absorbing values and behaviors that conflict with those of the heritage culture) during the period of separation.

Educators must also be aware that students with undocumented or mixed immigrant families often suffer greater stress and anxiety than other immigrant children. People who work with children of undocumented parent(s) or siblings should recognize the stresses (including fear of losing parents, uncertainty in their future, etc.) these children have experienced. They also must understand the complicated child care arrangements that need to be made before, during, and after the deportation of the parents (World Daily 2007).

Create and Maintain a Welcoming and Friendly Human Environment in School

Schools must make efforts to welcome students from undocumented or mixed immigrant families who may feel particularly vulnerable due to their illegal status. Bilingual signs, maps of the school, color coding, and the assignment of "buddies" to new students can make them feel more welcome (Morse and Ludovina 1999). Students' perceptions of school climates (including suspicion and discrimination) are strongly and consistently related to their behaviors in school and their academic performance. Studies looking at factors that impact students' schooling behaviors and achievement highlight the benefits of a friendly and supportive learning climate (Stone and Han 2005).

School personnel should be particularly sensitive to these children's fears and insecurities and to the issues surrounding their right to a free education in the United States. For example, in compliance with *Plyer v. Doe*, schools should avoid actions that might imply to undocumented families that their right to access to education is in jeopardy. Actions that should be avoided include asking about a student's immigration status and requesting immigration-related documentation. Schools should provide services to all migrant students that are comparable to services offered to other students in the school district and ensure that migrant students are involved in the regular school programs offered to other students. Schools should provide counseling services to children who show signs of immigration-related stresses and ensure children feel safe and secure. Counseling of this kind can also provide alternatives and options for families and children regarding their difficulties without having to ask about immigration status.

Overcome Language Barriers

Educators must recognize that English language acquisition and heritage language retention are vital components of language minorities' psychosocial and educational adjustment. First, we address several practices serving linguistic minority immigrant children that we believe may also work for children of undocumented and mixed immigrant families. The National Association for the Education of Young Children (NAEYC 1996), in their position statement regarding linguistic and cultural diversity, states that educators must accept the legitimacy of the children's home language in order to promote the optimal development and learning of all children. The NAEYC's position requires schools to provide support in the heritage languages for students whose first language is not English until those students are proficient in English. Programs that switch to English-only for political reasons, as highlighted in the Baquedano-Lopez case study, do not best serve students. Educators should recognize the connection between national attitudes toward immigrants in the US and language education, and must resist political pressure to use English-only instruction with English language learners (Baquedano-Lopez 2004). In addition, standardized achievement tests that do not account for language barriers also harm students' sense of self-worth (Hamann 2001). Schools should serve as a linguistic bridge between the language of the country of origin and the language of the settlement country. For example, schools could post school rules in English around the school building, but the published school rules and procedures sent home to the families could be printed in English and the home languages in order to prevent misunderstanding and to create a sense of belonging (Green 2003).

In terms of assisting children of undocumented and mixed families to overcome language barriers, educators need to understand two interrelated processes: English acquisition and heritage language retention. According to Flores et al. (2005), children of undocumented or mixed immigrant families are most likely to live in a household where no adult speaks fluent English, and parents of these children are likely to speak no English at all. These children may lack any motivation to learn English due to their uncertain future. Therefore, schools need to work effectively with these children to help them learn English. At the same time schools must encourage or assist with heritage language maintenance considering families' sojourner experiences and also the possibility that families will return to their native country. These are unlikely to be easy tasks since elementary school is a key time for immigrant children to learn English effectively as well as a time when children rapidly lose their heritage language abilities.

Work with Families and Community

Suarez-Orozco et al. (2008) emphasize that schools must explore ways to welcome undocumented parents, and teachers must form caring relationships with parents. For instance, Bernhard et al. (1998) illustrate how a group of Latino parents of elementary school children in Canada met monthly to discuss issues regarding their children's schooling. The group learned to assert their interests and concerns and collaborate with teachers and administrators. Additionally, the parents gained insight into how to best support their children with school while valuing and promoting their native language and culture.

Community outreach is critically important to children of undocumented or mixed families. For 5 or 6 year old children, school recruitment is the first step to being integrated into a US educational institution. Green (2003) believes that unless children are identified and enrolled in school, educational opportunities are nonexistent. In terms of schools serving as the link between available social services and the children of undocumented or mixed families, Schoorman (2001) studied the effectiveness of a project undertaken by Florida's Palm Beach County school system to provide community-based support services and to facilitate a community–school partnership in order to enhance the educational achievement of immigrant students, specifically those with limited English proficiency. The project relies on school and community resources, including guidance counselors, teachers of English as a second language (ESL), health and mental health professionals, churches, and migrant services personnel. It engages in a variety of multilingual activities, including school visits, tutoring, mentoring, home visits, parent workshops, counseling, guidance to community services, and college/career awareness.

Research also reports on other school-community activities (e.g., Huerta-Macios et al. 2000). The community can systematically link children of undocumented or mixed families with a mentor, preferably a successful member of the community (Gaytan et al. 2007). Finally, community members, especially educators, must exhibit understanding and empathy about the vulnerabilities specific to children of undocumented or mixed families. For example, Green (2003) has stated that educators must be aware that economic survival is a high family priority which might limit school attendance and participation. Crosnoe has argued further that undocumented youth typically endure more "problematic [educational] contexts, such as resource deprivation, impersonal structure, and low academic focus" (Crosnoe 2005, p. 272).

Schools can also help families to gain access to governmental support and public services. Because many undocumented parents are afraid of being "exposed," they will often refrain from seeking public benefits. In extreme cases, undocumented parents who did not seek public services for fear of deportation might be at an even greater risk of homelessness (Huerta-Macios et al. 2000). While most children in this population do not end up homeless, it is the responsibility of the school to help undocumented families identify outlets to provide basic services, such as food and shelter, in order to prevent homelessness (Huerta-Macios et al. 2000).

Advocate for Social Policies for Children of Undocumented Immigrant Families

The current economic downturn will likely result in more difficult times ahead for undocumented or mixed immigrant families. In addition to having to live through continued economic hardship, these families must also endure the public's hostilities. Public opinion polls have shown that a majority of Americans do not favor large-scale long-term immigration (Meissner 2001). Public attitudes toward immigrants may become increasingly hostile if the economic conditions in the United States worsen. As the Latino population in the US continues to grow rapidly and the nation is substantially transformed in terms of race and ethnicity, the issues of immigration continue to polarize our nation. Hispanic immigrants, especially Mexican–Americans, are likely to be targeted by hate groups. In fact, there have been reports on the increasing number of organized anti-Hispanic activities in the Southern states (Associated Press 2005) and also a greater number of recorded hostile attitudes and beliefs about Mexican immigrants in American schools (e.g., Shannon and Escamilla 1999). Schools must take actions to resist the public's attempts to fuel anti-immigrant sentiment among teachers and other school staff members. Instead, educators, regardless of their personal beliefs toward American immigration policies, should advocate for equal educational opportunity for all children (Midobuche 2001). Schools should serve as resource centers and encourage social-service agencies and other institutions to strengthen their bilingual staff and to work with community-based organizations. The joint efforts from different agencies can enhance schools' outreach efforts and facilitate greater access to benefits for eligible children in immigrant families, including those in undocumented or mixed immigrant families (Shields and Behrman 2004).

Moreover, the decline in resources to facilitate efforts to work with immigrant students presents an additional barrier to be overcome. For example, although more immigrants are arriving, the federal government has reduced or restricted the few programs that assist new immigrants in integrating into the economic, social, and civic life of the US Federal funding for refugees, legalized aliens, and immigrant education programs has been delayed or cut substantially. For the most part, the responsibility for integrating immigrants into society has been left to state and local governments, educational and other social institutions, private organizations, and immigrants themselves (Morse 1994).

Policy scholars believe that any national strategy for reducing child poverty, promoting children's well-being, and helping low wage-earning workers must address the needs and circumstances of immigrants and their children. Federal policy must take a new course—one that moves away from the goal of restricting assistance to immigrant families but instead acknowledges the need to provide family support and employment services to help ensure that the children of immigrants thrive and that their parents can progress in the labor force (Greenberg and Rahmanou 2004).

Future Research on Children of Undocumented and Mixed Families

More rigorous studies are needed that focus specifically on P-12 children from undocumented or mixed families. Specifically, research is needed to provide more accurate demographic data on this population, as well as information regarding the social and economic characteristics of these children, their academic achievement, language learning, special needs, and so on. Furthermore, there is a need for more research to help identify how programs can best serve newcomers and/or ELL students. These programs should be evaluated qualitatively and quantitatively for their effectiveness with children of undocumented or mixed families, either within a specific school setting or evaluated comparatively across school districts in different social and economic contexts. However, if schools and policy makers want to have accurate information about this school population and develop insights in terms of how to best work with this population, there should be some explicit policies to protect the identity of the informants, as well as granting immunity for researchers who will keep the confidentiality of the informants even under the pressure of revealing the identities of the informants from the court.

The ongoing large-scale immigration to the United States will affect all aspects of life in America over the next 50 years, and US schools will continue to be an initial point of contact between immigrant newcomers and the surrounding community. How schools cope with the declining federal and local support while still effectively integrating immigrant children into US society will greatly affect the future of our nation. The literature reviewed for this paper suggests there is a need for additive approaches to working with undocumented immigrants as well as further research into the particular needs of preK and elementary school-aged children of undocumented or mixed families.

References

Associated Press (2005). *Hate groups turn focus on Hispanic immigrants*. http://azbilingualed.org/News%202005/hate_groups_turn_focus_on_hi. Accessed 7 Jan 2008.

Baquedano-Lopez, P. (2004). Traversing the Center: The politics of language use in a Catholic religious education program for immigrant Mexican children. *Anthropology and Education Quartery, 35*(2), 212–232.

Berk, M., Schur, C., Chavez, L., & Frankel, M. (2000). Health care use among undocumented Latino immigrants. *Health Affairs, 19*(4), 51–64.

Bernhard, J. K., Freire, M., & Pacini-Ketchabaw, V. (1998). A Latin-American parents' group participates in their children's schooling: Parent involvement reconsidered. *Canadian Ethnic Studies, 30*(3), 77–99.

Bryant, J. J. A. (2004). Tinderbox economics, immigration, and education in a North Carolina town. *Social Education, 68*(6), 414–417.

Camarota, S. A. (2005). Immigrants at mid-decade: A snapshot of America's foreign-born population. http://www.cis.org/articles/2005/back1405.pdf. Accessed 1 June 2007.

Capps, R., & Fix, M. E. (2005). *Undocumented immigrants: Myths and facts. The Urban Institute.* http://www.urban.org/publications/900898.html. Accessed 19 Nov 2008.

Crosnoe, R. (2005). Double disadvantage or signs of resilience? The elementary school contexts of children from Mexican immigrant families. *American Educational Research Journal, 42*(2), 269–303.

Edelman, M. W., & Jones, J. M. (2004). Separate and unequal: America's children, race, and poverty. *The Future of Children, 14*(2), 134–137.

Fernandez-Kelly, P., & Curran, S. (2001). Nicaraguans: Voices lost, voices found. In R. G. Rumbaut & A. Portes (Eds.), *Ethnicities: Children of immigrants in America* (pp. 127–156). Berkeley: University of California Press.

Fix, M., & Passal, J. (2003). *Proceedings from US Immigration: Trends and implications for schools.* New Orleans: National Association of Bilingual Education.

Flores, G., Abreu, M., & Tomany-Korman, S. C. (2005). Limited English proficiency, primary language at home, and disparities in children's health care: How language barriers are measured matters. *Public Health Reports, 120,* 418–430.

Gaytan, F., Carhill, A., & Suarez-Orozco, S. (2007). Understanding and responding to the needs of newcomer immigrant youth and families. *Prevention Researcher, 14*(4), 11–13.

Green, P. (2003). Educating the children of migrant workers. *Bilingual Research, 27*(1), 57–71.

Greenberg, M., & Rahmanou, H. (2004). Commentary 1. *The Future of Children, 14*(2), 139–145.

Hamann, E. T. (2001). *Theorizing the sojourner student. Digital Commons at the University of Nebraska-Lincoln.* http://digitalcommons.unl.edu/teachlearnfacpub/73. Accessed 5 Nov 2008.

Hernandez, D. J. (2004). Demographic change and the life circumstances of immigrant families. *The Future of Children, 14*(2), 17–48.

Huerta-Macios, A., Gonzales, M. L., & Holman, L. (2000). Children of undocumented immigrants: An invisible minority among homeless students. In R. Mickelson (Ed.), *Children of the streets of the Americas* (pp. 238–248). New York: Routledge.

InFocus (2005). *Children in immigrant families. The Center for Health and Health Care in School.* http://www.healthinschools.org/News-Room/InFocus/2005/Issue-1.aspx. Accessed 22 July 2006.

Martin, P., & Midgley, E. (2006). Immigration: Shaping and reshaping America. *Population Bulletin, 61*(4), 3–28.

Mather, M., Rivers, K. L., & Jacobsen, L. A. (2006). The American Community Survey (2005). *PRB Population bulletin, 60*(3), 3–28.

Meissner, D. (2001). *After the attacks: Protecting borders and liberties (Policy Brief No. 8).* Washington: Carnegie Endowment for International Peace.

Midobuche, E. (2001). More than empty footprints in the sand: Educating immigrant children. *Harvard Educational Review, 71*(3), 529–535.

Morse, A. (1994). *America's newcomers.* Washington: National Conference of State Legislatures.

Morse, S. C., & Ludovina, F. S. (1999). *Responding to undocumented children in the schools (Information Analyses).* Charleston: Rural Education and Small Schools.

NAEYC (National Association for the Education of Young Children) (1996). Position statement: Responding to linguistic and cultural diversity. *Young Children, 51*(1), 4–12.

NCES (National Center for Educational Statistics) (2006). *Concentration of enrollment by race/ethnicity and poverty.* http://nces.ed.gov/programs/coe/2006/section1/table.asp?tableID=440. Accessed 5 July 2007.

Passel, J. S. (2005). The size and characteristics of the unauthorized migrant population in the US. http://www.Pewhispanic.org. Accessed 16 May 2006.

Passel, J. S., & Suro, R. (2005). *Rise, peak, and decline: Trends in US immigration 1992–2004.* Washington: Pew Hispanic Center.

Portes, A., & Rumbaut, R. G. (1996). *Immigrant America: A portrait* (2nd ed.). Berkeley: University of California Press.

Portes, A., & Zhou, M. (1993). The new second generation: Segmented assimilation and its variants. *Annals of the American Academy of Political and Social Science, 530,* 74–96.

Romo, H. (2007). Immigrant children. In S. Oboler & D. J. Gonzalez (Eds.), *The oxford encyclopedia of Latinos and Latinas in the United States.* http://www.oxford-latinos.com/entry?entry=t199.e411. Accessed 1 Feb 2008.

Rong, X. L., & Preissle, J. (2009). *Educating immigrant students in the 21st century.* Thousand Oaks: Corwin Press.

Schoorman, D. (2001). *What difference do we make? The challenges of evaluating community-based efforts in immigrant education.* Paper presented at the Annual Meeting of the American Educational Research Association, Seattle.

Shannon, S. M., & Escamilla, K. (1999). Mexican immigrants in US schools: Targets of symbolic violence. *Educational Policy, 13*(3), 347.

Shields, M., & Behrman, R. (2004). Children of immigrant families: Analysis and recommendations. *The Future of Children, 14*(2), 4–16.

Stone, S., & Han, M. (2005). Perceived school environments, perceived discrimination, and school performance among children of Mexican immigrants. *Children & Youth Services Review, 27*(1), 51–66.

Suarez-Orozco, C., & Suarez-Orozco, M. M. (2001). *Children of immigration.* Cambridge: Harvard University Press.

Suarez-Orozco, C., Suarez-Orozco, M. M., & Todorova, I. (2008). *Learning a new land–Immigrant students in American society.* Cambridge: Belknap Press.

US Bureau of the Census (2003). *2000 Census of population and housing-public use microdata samples 5%.* Washington: US Bureau of the Census.

US Bureau of the Census (2007). *The American community Survey 2005*. Washington: US Bureau of the Census.

Valenzuela, A. (1999). Subtractive schooling: US–Mexican youth and the politics of caring. Albany: SUNY Press.

World Daily (August 15, 2007). Where can the children look for help if parents are deported? C3.

Zhou, M. (2003). Contemporary trends in immigration to the US: Gender, labor market incorporation, and implications for family formation. *Migraciones Internacionales, 2*(2), 77–95.

Chapter 10
Challenging the Text and Context of (Re)Naming Immigrant Children: Children's Literature as Tools for Change

Mariana Souto-Manning

> *I think my greatest wish is to be called María Isabel Salazar López. When that was my name, I felt proud of being named María like my papá's mother, and Isabel, like my grandmother Chabela.... If I was called María Isabel Salazar López, I could listen better in class because it's easier to hear than Mary Lopez.*
>
> (Ada 1995, pp. 49–51)

This essay entitled *My Greatest Wish*, from the children's book *My Name is María Isabel* (Ada 1995), was written by a young girl named María Isabel Salazar López. On the first day at her new school, María Isabel Salazar López was (re)named "Mary Lopez" by her teacher simply because there were already too many "Marías" in the classroom. Through such a seemingly innocent act (and perhaps even unintentional), the teacher communicated a powerful message: that she disregarded the personal history behind the name María Isabel, a name that honored and represented both of her grandmothers, her grandfather, and her father. Additionally, by omitting Salazar, the teacher attempted to use American conventions for normalizing *nombres Latinos*. Assuming that first and last names comprise the shortened version of one's full name in every culture and ignoring a student's given name, the teacher employed assimilation tools that discounted María Isabel's Puerto Rican heritage. In this book authored by Ada (1995), the teacher failed to comprehend how language shapes identities and did not fully consider the implications of (re)naming an immigrant child.

As a former early childhood teacher and now a teacher educator, I have seen incidents such as this story featured by Ada (1995) in many early childhood classrooms. This "(re)naming" phenomenon (Souto-Manning 2007) has become a common practice enacted by both teachers and parents. Teachers might decide to (re)name a child because they cannot pronounce a name, or because, like María's teacher, there

M. Souto-Manning (✉)
Teachers College, Columbia University, New York, NY, USA
e-mail: ms3983@columbia.edu

B. S. Fennimore, A. L. Goodwin (eds.), *Promoting Social Justice for Young Children*, Educating the Young Child 3, DOI 10.1007/978-94-007-0570-8_10,

are already too many of the same name in the classroom, or because they think that giving the child an "American name" will be advantageous in some way. Parents might choose to (re)name their children in hopes that their child will fit in (Souto-Manning 2007), or so that other people will be able to pronounce their child's new name properly. Such practices are motivated by dominant discourses which frame immigrants and differences in terms of deficits. By (re)naming a child, a teacher and/or parent engages in an attempt to reposition that child in a more "acceptable" way. Ultimately, (re)naming encompasses both rejecting a name and conferring a new one which is positioned more favorably within specific contexts—e.g., the privileging of Anglicized names in US schooling contexts.

Certainly, there are many positively motivated or perceived reasons for (re)naming, but it is necessary to fully consider the complexities pertaining to the ways in which (re)naming can affect children's learning and cultural repertoires. By embracing the institutional discourses (Chouliaraki and Fairclough 1999) that frame immigrants as needing to be Americanized in order to succeed, parents and teachers are being colonized. By using the term *colonized*, I recognize and highlight the alignment of this situation with the historical way in which colonizers "imposed their language onto the peoples they colonized, forbidding natives to speak their mother tongues…systematically prohibit[ing] native languages. Many…students were demoted, humiliated, or even beaten for speaking their native language in colonial schools" (Margulis and Nowakoski 1996, para 1). This process is akin to what is happening to immigrant children who are given English/American names and are often encouraged to learn English as a replacement for their native languages. In addition to linguistic choice, language colonization also means that the ideas of the more powerful are being imposed onto minoritized, immigrant populations.

Those who work with children must challenge the resulting stances which position immigrant children and families in certain negative ways. Rather, it is important to engage in appropriating these institutional discourses, problematizing and deconstructing traditional definitions of success in school, normalcy, and naming. Within this context, this chapter extends from the practices and realities of teachers to other contexts, being of value to those who are interested in better understanding immigrant children or who work with immigrant children in a variety of professional capacities.

The Problem of (Re)Naming Young Children

A name underscores an individual's identity. The process of giving a name to a child is heavily laden with cultural ideals and norms. When a child is named, that name often carries deeper social and cultural meaning. (Re)naming a child, then, can be read as an act of assimilation, where those who are deemed to be culturally different, through a simple act of "(re)naming," become as close to the norm as possible (Parmentier 1994).

By the time a child enters school, she is already accustomed to her name. In Ada's book, each time someone called "María Isabel," María Isabel responded.

Although a child in elementary school, María Isabel knew that María Isabel indexed and signified her person. Over time, the name came to signify her very identity. That is, until she was assigned a new name. (Re)named and relabeled as "Mary Lopez" María Isabel reacted with resistance, not responding when anyone called Mary Lopez. As illustrated by Ada's (1995) *María Isabel,*, in many classrooms students feel so disoriented by their (re)naming that they lose motivation, failing to respond to their new nomenclature and ultimately shutting down. (Re)naming can deeply affect students' learning in the classroom. María Isabel spent much of her time daydreaming in the classroom, did not realize the teacher was calling her when she heard Mary, and was frustrated by her (re)naming. All of these feelings started to affect her self-perception as a learner.

Often early childhood teachers ask me why it is so difficult for "(re)named children" to answer to a newly assigned name. In my experience, even in cases where there is no overt resistance, children typically yearn for their original, given name. A name might be one of the few constants as children immigrate and cross linguistic, cultural, and geographic borders.

If this is the case, why do well meaning teachers and families (re)name immigrant children? To help them fit in? In reality, these well meaning intentions often have further and deeper implications—that the child's name, language, and culture are not valued and need to be replaced. This is definitely not the message immigrant children need; they require support and encouragement to develop bilingually and biculturally (Souto-Manning 2006, 2007). By recognizing the importance of children's names and honoring them in schools and classrooms, teachers are not denying the child access to the dominant American culture (Delpit 1995). Instead, they are recognizing the multiplicity of cultures and identities immigrant children embody, and valuing cultural and linguistic diversity as capital (Gutiérrez 2006) in classrooms.

While we might initially conceptualize stories such as the one described above within the realm of fiction, similar cases come to life every day in US schools. Here, I briefly describe selected instances of (re)naming in an urban setting in the Southeast. I identify them as learning cases because they are situated representations of prevalent trends and issues, yet these instances do not possess the level of detail and contextualization present in a case study (Dyson and Genishi 2005). While both cases briefly described in this chapter portray instances in which parents (re)named their own children, it is important to look into the reasons why immigrant parents "choose" to (re)name their children as they enter US schools. Additionally, the story portrayed above (the one told by Ada) illustrates another prevalent trend—(re)naming by teachers. Thus, the issue of (re)naming is an important one as it is being embraced by both teachers and families.

The first case is that of Idelbrando (Souto-Manning 2007). When Idelbrando entered my first grade classroom, he did not know that his mother had decided to (re)name him Tommy. I immediately noticed that Tommy was not on the class roll and thought that he might have entered the wrong classroom. After much back and forth, I learned from one of his older brothers in the same school that his mother had decided to (re)name him. Upon talking to his mother, I learned that she was so frustrated by how her two older sons had been stereotyped and had not received an appropriate education due to their identities as Mexican immigrants that she decided to (re)name her youngest son so he would not be treated as a *Mexicano*. She said that she gave him an American name so that teachers would not know of his Mexican immigrant heritage. In the midst of a busy daily life, she forgot to inform her young son of his name change prior to his first day at school, thereby causing Idelbrando great distress. Even though I assured her I would provide him equal learning opportunities in my classroom and my opinion was that he should keep the name Idelbrando, she decided in favor of the name change because he would not always have *una maestra hispana*. She believed that maintaining the name Idelbrando could hinder her son's opportunities for schooling success in future years.

A similar case is that of Min-su, a Korean boy who entered my classroom with the new name of Michael. He knew Michael was his new name but could only rarely respond when other children called him Michael. Upon talking to Min-su's father and trying to understand the reason why he had (re)named his son, I learned that he did not want his child to be viewed as Korean, as so different that special classes were required. He wanted his child to have equal opportunities at school and firmly believed that (re)naming him was a way to secure such opportunities.

Both Idelbrando's mother and Min-su's father innocently thought that their child's chances in school would improve with name changes (practices reflecting colonization by way of institutional discourses which position immigrant children with "broken English" as needing to be fixed). They also recognized the disadvantages of being cast as immigrants in US schools, contexts that largely frame bilingualism and cultural diversity in terms of deficits (Volk and Long 2005; Souto-Manning 2006). Nevertheless, in trying to protect their children, they were uncritically embracing an institutional discourse that correlated success with "American" and schooling with speaking English.

While these families wanted to counter the cultural deprivation paradigm (Carter and Goodwin 1994; Goodwin et al. 2007), they were embracing simplistic solutions that had been offered to them via institutional discourses. Thus, they too were being colonized by the discourses of Americanization (Chouliaraki and Fairclough 1999). When such a discourse is adopted by schools and educators, it frames children who are not English speakers as needing fixing and their homes/communities as somehow deprived. Thus, the action of these families was a reaction to schools conceptualizing difference as undesirable and unfitting.

The families' attempts to ensure their children succeed in schools by simply (re) naming them points toward the need to reconceptualize differences from a diversities paradigm. A diversities paradigm conceptualizes multiple cultural practices and legacies as equally worthy and valid. From such a perspective, teachers recognize children's unique gifts and strengths and build upon them. As educators and child advocates, we need to challenge the issue of (re)naming as well as the very reasons which encourage families to engage in such practices—difference defined as deficits in so many educational settings (Souto-Manning 2006). We need to question and deconstruct larger institutional discourses which frame immigrant children and families as necessitating educational interventions so that we can engage in changing assimilationist practices which frame the (re)naming of immigrant children day in and day out.

Discourse in/of (Re)Naming

Fennimore (2000) wrote that "Educators never 'just talk.' The language environment of any school or other educational institution serves as a dynamic platform for powerful attitudes and behaviors" (p. 4). Thus, it is very important to pay close attention to language, as language can be conceived as action, as behavior that makes things happen (Fennimore 2007). To promote change, we need to first recognize a particular situation or event, to identify (or read, if you will) institutional discourses (language in use) by engaging in the problematization of injustices and inequalities, and contesting unfair realities.

Taking a critical approach to analyzing language in use, Chouliaraki and Fairclough (1999) explained the process of colonization and appropriation through language. They posited that if language is accepted and not contested, it becomes part of an individual's repertoire and has the potential to colonize that person. For example, if individual people accept unequal and unfair access in educational settings, they are then colonized by such unfair realities. This colonization is what was happening when children were being (re)named in my classroom. On the other hand, by contesting language and concepts within specific contexts and taking socio-historical and cultural issues into account, one gains the power to appropriate language, and utilize it to promote change. Challenging the status quo (or what *is* as defined by the dominant culture) becomes very important as one seeks to uncover the historicity of certain issues. Through language appropriation, individuals can acquire the necessary tools for transformation.

But, how do we critically pose problems, seeking to deconstruct the sociocultural and historical influences shaping the phenomenon of (re)naming without singling out those who were (re)named and making them feel even more like misfits? Here, I propose that children's literature can serve as a way to represent the phenomenon while moving the focus away from specific children. Children's books can provide entryways into critical and transformative practices which challenge such colonizing discourses. In the following section, I explore a way to name such a practice in order to start changing, transforming it.

Reading and Representing Institutional Discourses: Children's Books as Tools for Change

While it is important to name unjust issues in order to promote change, it can be challenging to bring a personal issue to discussion in the classroom without placing any specific young child in a vulnerable position. I suggest that a way to critically deconstruct (re)naming practices is by using children's books—such as the ones described below—as codifications of generative themes.

Generative themes portray social and cultural issues relevant to individuals and communities. They are generated from students' lives and experiences via a thematic investigation (Souto-Manning 2010). These themes come directly from the learners who are participants in their own learning (Freire 2000) and are "literally hand-made from the social fabrics of the students' lives" (Salvio 1998, p. 69). Such a process recognizes that actions cannot be separated from the context in which they take place (Wertsch 1991). The process starts with thematic investigations, which involve the exploration and documentation of the social, cultural, and linguistic contexts of the learners. A thematic investigation is initially done by the teacher, who takes on the role of an ethnographer, learning about the culture of the learners' communities. As the teacher learns about relevant themes in the lives of students, she/he seeks to identify common experiences (across time and space). Such experiences are generative themes. As the name implies, they are themes generated from the individuals' lives.

Prior to planning engagements and teaching, educators learn from the communities and cultural practices which participants navigate. According to Freire (2000):

> The concept of a generative theme is neither an arbitrary invention nor a working hypothesis to be proved. If it were a hypothesis to be proved, the initial investigation would seek not to ascertain the nature of the theme, but rather the very existence or non-existence of themes themselves. In that event, before attempting to understand the theme in its richness, its significance, its plurality, its transformations, and its historical composition, we would first have to verify whether or not it is an objective fact; only then could we proceed to apprehend it. Although an attitude of critical doubt is legitimate, it does appear possible to verify the reality of the generative theme—not only through one's own existential experience, but also through critical reflection on the human-world relationship and on the relationships between people implicit in the former. (p. 97)

Generative themes represent complex experiences in the lives of the participants. They have political significance and are likely to generate dialogue geared toward action.

To be able to access these generative themes, teachers must embrace fluidity in the roles of teacher and learner (Freire 2000). Only by blurring these roles can teachers truly engage in surfacing these generative themes. Such a stance "allows us to transform whatever sense of certainty and cultural superiority we might bring to school into a genuine search for the history and meaning behind specific practices" (Ayers 2001, p. 77).

Following identification, generative themes are codified into words, drawings, vignettes, or other representational formats. Here, I suggest that children's books, such as those identified below, can serve as a codification of generative themes emanating from students' lives. They are especially appropriate for the early childhood classroom because of their acceptance in the classroom and because of the richness of detail provided by a realistic fiction picture book (as opposed to a word or picture as Freire had used in adult education). For instance, one of the children's books mentioned here could be used as codification, a representation of the (re)naming phenomenon. Because it is often a representation of a phenomenon commonly experienced by several participants, a generative theme may represent a collective experience which includes details of many situated representations as opposed to details of one single case.

(Re)Naming in Children's Literature

Due to its prominence, the "(re)naming" phenomenon has become a frequent topic within children's literature. Consider, for instance, the children's books about (re)naming that have been published recently—e.g., *My Name is Yoon* (Recorvits 2003), *The Name Jar* (Choi 2003), *Hannah is My Name* (Yang 2004), *My Name Is Jorge: On Both Sides of the River* (Medina 2004). Such books can be placed at the center of the critical cycle (Souto-Manning 2007). They can act as representations of situations lived by children in the classroom (i.e., generative themes) and serve as catapults for authentic dialogue and action. They also provide situated perspectives as they tell the stories of children who experienced or considered being (re) named (by choice or not) and expose the reader to some possible solutions and feelings associated with this common phenomenon. While children's books may help get the critical conversation started, they do not promote change themselves but can serve as tools for change, as codified generative themes to be discursively deconstructed. As you read these books with children and adults, I invite you to pose problems, and consider multiple perspectives to move toward problem solving and transformative action. Some questions are listed below as the critical cycle is explained.

Children's literature can depict common immigration and (re)naming scenarios and point toward the need to affirm and study multiple cultures and heritages and may serve as learning cases for early childhood teachers and students as well as any professional working with immigrant children and families. Books can portray, in accessible ways, solutions negotiated by immigrant children who were (re)named. After reading the books, we can problematize such situations, such stories, and seek to uncover larger institutional discourses which are powerfully (yet silently) shaping the (re)naming of immigrant children, together engaging in dialogue and seeking to collectively problem solve and negotiate a plan for action.

Applying the Critical Cycle to Collectively Negotiate a Possible Solution

While it is important to identify themes relevant to the lives of children and select picture books which illustrate specific phenomena, in order to get past naming the issue and move toward transforming or changing the situation, it is important to engage in the critical cycle. Thus, it is important to read these books aloud to the children. As specific books are read, the role of the teacher becomes that of facilitating a problem posing process—encouraging children to ask questions, to challenge injustices, etc. This allows children to engage in critical dialogue, seeking to overcome innocent and simplistic views of the world or any specific situation, critically disagreeing, engaging in conflict, and transforming the situation in place.

Problem solving and action are mediated dialogically; transformation happens through dialogue and problem solving in a cyclical and recursive process which leads to transformative action. These common aspects are illustrated as the critical cycle (p. 119). The critical cycle is representative of what happens in Freirean culture circles (Souto-Manning 2010). Even though Freirean culture circles were initially employed in adult education, their inherent critical cycle approach provides fertile grounds for disrupting the status quo and promoting change in early educational settings with both children and adults (see for example, how culture circles were employed to challenge and change segregationist pull-out programs in a primary classroom—Souto-Manning 2009).

The critical cycle has five dynamic phases:

1. *Generative themes* (including thematic investigation and codification): During this phase, the situated representations of a phenomenon (such as (re)naming immigrant children) are identified via thematic investigations of the individual's lives and practices. A prominent and recurring phenomenon is then represented by a chosen or created artifact (such as a book, picture, or vignette). In early childhood settings, I suggest using children's books. Some of the books presented in this chapter are realistic fiction stories representing the (re)naming phenomenon across settings. Other artifacts, photographs, and cases may also work here depending on the children participating.
2. *Problem posing:* During this phase, the representational artifact is decoded (or decodified) through questions which seek to uncover the reasons shaping such situations. The focus is on sociocultural and historical forces shaping the specific issue. For example, why are immigrant children being (re)named? What are some of the causes and consequences of the phenomenon? How do children feel when they are given other names upon entering a new school/classroom/country? Why do people give them other names? Please bear in mind that these are merely suggested questions and that questions should be relevant to each group while seeking to uncover institutional discourses shaping the specific phenomenon being problematized.
3. *Dialogue:* This happens throughout the critical cycle, as participants consider multiple perspectives and move from posing problems to collectively negotiating solutions recursively and cyclically. This is not a completely distinct phase as it starts with the problems and questions being posed and moves toward problem solving. During dialogue participants can offer their own perspectives and engage in considering multiple beliefs shaping an event. The idea in this situated representation is to try to understand not only why families and teachers are

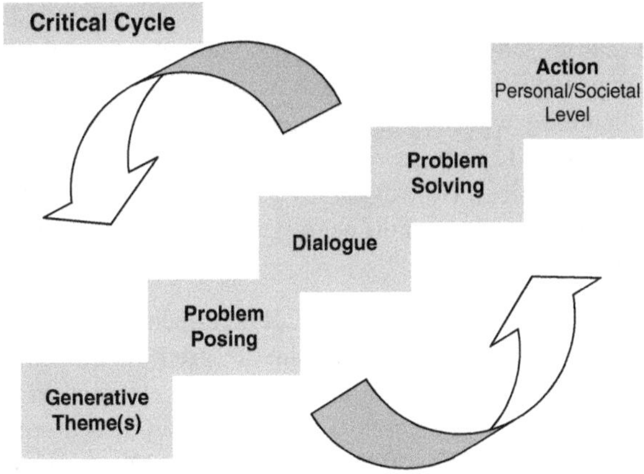

(Souto-Manning, 2007, 2010)

engaging in (re)naming, but in what ways (re)naming may be affecting immigrant children, and what forces lead parents and educators to (re)name. How would you feel? How did María Isabel/Yoon/Jorge (or another character of a story read aloud) feel? Why? What are some of the ways that children may feel? These are questions that may help mediate the dialogue. Here, listening and considering a multitude of perspectives is essential so that children and/or adults can uncover and recognize how varying points of view impact positionalities (how children are positioned).

4. *Problem solving:* This is the phase in which participants consider ways to change the issue being problematized. Contextual specifics are considered as well as personal preferences. The idea is not to arrive at one solution cathartically, but to consider a variety of possibilities that are real and may be applied—e.g., raising awareness of how children feel in terms of motivation when they are (re)named as well as shedding light onto the reasons why families are (re)naming their children—for example, English being considered a more desired language and more closely associated to success, even in terms of names. Problem solving might happen through study groups and/or forums that consider an issue directly. Children may engage in making sure that everyone's name is pronounced properly, for example. Here it is important to note that the solutions will be as unique as the members of the group who are part of this critical cycle. There are no canned solutions for issues in a critical cycle. The key is to make visible the institutional discourse colonizing a person/a group of people and examine it, question it, collectively moving toward co-constructing possible solutions and envisioning possible futures.
5. *Action* (at the personal and/or societal level/s): Solutions negotiated through dialogue are implemented at the personal and/or societal level/s. Sometimes this phase leads to change and transformation. Other times it generates more themes to be collectively problematized. This action step can mean that a teacher strives

> not to (re)name a child on the personal level or that a teacher/advocate seeks to raise awareness of the reasons why immigrant families are (re)naming their children. Beyond that, it may lead to raising awareness of the importance of not (re)naming children, but honoring who they are—which starts with honoring a child's name. Children may decide to learn about and educate their families regarding a variety of naming practices. Here again my examples serve as mere illustrations and not as prescriptions. Any actions negotiated and carried out will be unique and context-specific.

As illustrated above, this approach is a recursive process. It is reflective in nature because it starts with data from participants' lives and aims to promote transformative action. Additionally, the critical cycle takes individual characteristics and interests under consideration as it is an applied approach to education. It is a process which refutes panoptical definitions of time (Genishi and Dyson 2009), and is therefore not hurried. The process is as important as the topic being approached.

The critical cycle does not focus on the transmission or mastery of some specific body of knowledge, but on how people can make sense of their own worlds—i.e. reading institutional discourses which are colonizing, challenging and changing them, instead of living in a world that someone else is making sense of on their behalf. As evident in other studies (Souto-Manning 2007, 2009, 2010), participation in the critical cycle exemplified by Freirean culture circles is also internalized, and allows participants to engage in and develop personal, critical meta-awareness—not only recognizing the issue per se, such as (re)naming, but identifying and challenging colonizing discursive practices. As participants approach a situation, they consider multiple perspectives and trouble the issues in a critically conscious manner.

Critical Dialogue Toward Action

Freire proposed that through dialogue, individuals could reframe education as a problem posing process, problematizing issues as opposed to seeking clear-cut solutions. In the case of the (re)naming phenomenon, it was important to come to see (re)naming as a culturally-loaded practice as it disregards the histories behind individual names. Asking why and questioning the practice as opposed to accepting it due to unintentionality is important. Appropriating language rather than being colonized by it is paramount (Chouliaraki and Fairclough 1999).

Such language appropriation happens via the critical cycle which takes place in Freirean culture circles. Culture circles start from the very issues which affect participants' everyday lives. Generative themes which are common experiences across participants' lives or relevant to participants' realities serve as starting points to problem posing. As problems are posed, participants engage in dialogue, considering a multitude of perspectives, and seek to move toward problem solving. As a group engages in collective problem solving, it charts a course for action at the personal and/or societal levels.

Toward Social Justice: Fostering a Broader View of Diversity and Naming

As I consider the phenomenon of (re)naming immigrant children, I am reminded how important it is that we early childhood professionals foster the broadest view of diversity and naming by learning with and from our students and their families. A broad view of diversity "asks us to reject any action that treats other people like objects, anything that *thingifies* human beings. It demands that we embrace the humanity of every student" (Ayers 2004, p. 35). By embracing the humanity of each student and valuing their cultural, social, and linguistic backgrounds and practices, we can broaden our view of diversity and shy away from stereotyping or attempting to assimilate our students. A broad view of diversity includes problematizing issues with children and their families, issues from their own lives such as (re)naming. One way of doing so is by bringing books to early childhood classrooms, as conversation starters aimed at promoting a critical reading of the world (Freire 2000).

Through engagement in the critical cycle, early childhood teachers and advocates can disrupt the common practice of (re)naming immigrant children by understanding such a practice as socioculturally- and historically-shaped (Shor 1987) and by problematizing the privileging certain names over others. We can also strive to change the discourse surrounding immigrant children in schools (Souto-Manning 2006), who are so often framed as culturally-deprived and need to be seen for all the strengths they have (Goodwin et al. 2007).

The stories portrayed by these children's books and the learning cases from my own classroom point toward the need for a classroom (and school) culture which values diversities. Such an environment appreciates the beautiful patchwork quilt represented by children's names, languages, and cultural experiences, rather than forcing immigrant children to fit the teacher's cultural models (simplistic representations or descriptions of how prototypical events are to unfold) and linguistic experiences (e.g., all children must speak English in order to succeed in US schools) (Gee 1999). As an integral part of a child's heritage and identity, a name needs to be celebrated and not replaced in classrooms as it is integrally connected to an individual's sense of self, group membership, and cultural identities (Parmentier 1994).

A paradigmatic shift needs to happen so that schools can become inclusive and welcoming places for *all* children. I propose that the first step toward promoting change is to identify the issue—to become aware of the rampant (re)naming of immigrant children. After recognition of the issue, then it is important to try to uncover the complexities and forces shaping the specific phenomenon from cultural, social, and historical perspectives. With regard to (re)naming, what is prompting families and teachers to (re)name immigrant children? This process of identifying and questioning initiates an important critical cycle.

Implications

A beginning point in moving from a cultural deprivation paradigm toward a diversities paradigm is to continuously interrogate multiple viewpoints (Lewison et al. 2002) and make differences visible (Harste et al. 2000) rather than trying to invisibilize differences present in our classrooms, schools, and society. Thus, implications point toward a need to re-envision policy, honoring first hand and culturally-specific knowledges (Grant and Sleeter 1996) in order to take immediate transformative action. Obviously, more research needs to be done in this area as we move from seeking to find solutions to the problems of immigrant populations to rethinking education so as to embrace multiple bodies of knowledge and expertise. As Banks (2004) pointed out, the field of multicultural education (which builds on the work of ethnic scholars) is relatively new. Research on truly multicultural schools needs to take place, from a critical and inclusive stance. Pouring immigrants into US schools, asking them to adapt, and then placing the blame for academic difficulties on individual children and families is at best unfair. Research needs to document what schools promote as desirable (in terms of linguistic and cultural preferences), scrutinize and deconstruct the institutional discourses of schools regarding immigrants, and point toward promising practices and schooling situations.

The consideration of multiple perspectives points toward the need to move away from the concept of policy as a separate field. To honor diverse perspectives, policy must emanate from practices. When it stands separate from critical practice, policy mirrors the cultural experiences of policy makers (who in the US are mostly white males), further reinforcing the (mono)cultural nature of so many of the developmentally appropriate or evidence-based bodies of knowledge. Thus, policy should take into account first-hand knowledge of immigrant populations and of populations which are underrepresented among policy makers. Listening to the stories immigrant families and children tell and addressing the issues which continue to colonize them must become a priority. Policy then should develop in tandem with practice, and with research which emanates from practice. Immigrant families need to be invited and involved.

In terms of action, I propose that the critical cycle (Souto-Manning 2010) can provide a framework for transformative change, for collectively appropriating institutional discourses which have shaped and continue to shape immigrant children's and families' experiences in schools and society. We who work with immigrant children and families must listen to the stories they tell and try at all costs to challenge and push back those colonizing discourses which attempt to thingify (Ayers 2004) human beings, to (mono)culturally position curriculum (Goodwin et al. 2007), and to see knowledge as culture-free (Grant and Sleeter 1996). After all, moving toward social justice involves examining competing stories dialogically and collectively writing counter-narratives to dominant (re)naming practices.

References

Ada, A. F. (1995). *My name is María Isabel.* New York: Alladin Paperbacks.

Ayers, W. (2001). *To teach: The journey of a teacher* (2nd ed.). New York: Teachers College Press.

Ayers, W. (2004). *Teaching toward freedom: Moral communication and ethical action in the classroom*. Boston: Beacon Press.

Banks, J. A. (2004). Multicultural education: Historical development, dimensions, and practice. In J. A. Banks & C. A. Banks (Eds.), *Handbook of research on multicultural education* (2nd ed., pp. 3–29). San Francisco: Jossey Bass.

Carter, R., & Goodwin, A. L. (1994). Racial identity and education. In L. Darling-Hammond (Ed.), *Review of Research in Education* (Vol. 20, pp. 291–336). Washington: American Educational Research Association.

Choi, Y. (2003). *The name jar*. New York: Knopf Books.

Chouliaraki, L., & Fairclough, N. (1999). *Discourse in late modernity*. Edinburgh: Edinburgh University Press.

Delpit, L. (1995). *Other people's children: Cultural conflict in the classroom*. New York: The New Press.

Dyson, A. H., & Genishi, C. (2005). *On the case: Approaches to language and literacy research.* New York: Teachers College Press.

Fennimore, B. S. (2000). *Talk matters: Refocusing the language of public schooling*. New York: Teachers College Press.

Fennimore, B. S. (2007). Talk about children: Developing a living curriculum of advocacy and social justice. In C. Genishi & A. L. Goodwin (Eds.), *Diversities in early childhood education: Rethinking and doing* (pp. 185–199). New York: Routledge Falmer.

Freire, P. (2000). *Pedagogy of the oppressed* (30th ed.). New York: Continuum.

Gee, J. (1999). *An introduction to discourse analysis: Theory and method.* London: Routledge.

Genishi, C., & Dyson, A. H. (2009). *Children, language, and literacy: Diverse learners in diverse times*. New York: Teachers College Press.

Goodwin, A. L., Cheruvu, R., & Genishi, C. (2007). Responding to multiple diversities in early childhood education: How far have we come? In C. Genishi & A. L. Goodwin (Eds.), *Diversities in early childhood: Rethinking and doing* (pp. 3–10). New York: Routledge.

Grant, C., & Sleeter, C. (1996). *After the school bell rings*. Bristol: Falmer Press.

Gutiérrez, K. (2006, February). *Wrap-up*. 2006 NCTE Assembly for Research Mid-winter Conference. Chicago.

Harste, J., Breau, A., Leland, C., Lewison, M., Ociepka, A., & Vasquez, V. (2000). Supporting critical conversations. In M. Pierce (Ed.), *Adventuring with books*. Urbana: National Council of Teachers of English.

Lewison, M., Flint, A., & Van Sluys, K. (2002). Taking on critical literacy: The journey of newcomers and novices. *Language Arts, 79*(5), 382–392.

Medina, J. (2004). *My name is Jorge: On both sides of the river.* Honesdale: Boyds Mill.

Margulis, J., & Nowakoski, P. (1996). *Language*. http://www.english.emory.edu/Bahri/Language.html. Accessed 9 July 2009.

Parmentier, R. (1994). *Signs in society: Studies in semiotic anthropology*. Bloomington: Indiana University Press.

Recorvits, H. (2003). *My name is Yoon.* New York: Frances Foster Books.

Salvio, P. (1998). On using the literacy portfolio to prepare teachers for "willful world traveling." In W. F. Pinar (Ed.), *Curriculum: Toward new identities* (pp. 41–74). New York: Garland.

Shor, I. (1987). *Freire for the classroom: A sourcebook for liberatory teaching*. Portsmouth: Boynton/Cook.

Souto-Manning, M. (2006). A critical look at bilingualism discourse in public schools: Auto/ethnographic reflections of a vulnerable observer. *Bilingual Research Journal, 29*(2), 439–458.

Souto-Manning, M. (2007). Immigrant families and children (re)develop identities in a new context. *Early Childhood Education Journal*, *34*(6), 399–405.

Souto-Manning, M. (2009). Negotiating culturally responsive pedagogy through multicultural children's literature: Towards critical democratic literacy practices in a first grade classroom. *Journal of Early Childhood Literacy*, *9*(1), 53–77.

Souto-Manning, M. (2010). *Freire, teaching, and learning: Culture circles across contexts*. New York: Peter Lang.

Volk, D., & Long, S. (2005). Challenging myths of the deficit perspective: Honoring children's literacy resources. *Young Children*, *60*(6), 12–19.

Wertsch, J. V. (1991). *Voices of the mind: A sociocultural approach to mediated action*. Cambridge: Harvard University Press.

Yang, B. (2004). *Hannah is my name*. Cambridge: Candlewick.

Chapter 11
Creating Meaningful Contexts in Schools for English Language Learners

Min Hong

I learned how to speak English when I was seven years old, three months after my family and I immigrated to the United States from Korea. Although people are amazed at the speed with which I learned to speak a new language, at the time it seemed more like a necessity than a gift or talent. School was an extremely lonely place—there was not one person I could identify with culturally and linguistically. While I was not shy about initiating conversations or playing with my peers, it seemed that when I approached them, they often frowned, shouted, and walked away from me.

Both of my parents worked two jobs (each working about 14–16 hours a day) and I hardly saw them throughout my childhood. For me, learning how to speak English became a mission, a way to communicate and make friends, but more importantly, a way to survive. After school, I would go to a nearby playground and watch how children would talk to their peers and parents. I watched their hand gestures, body language, and facial expressions with certain words. Then I would rush home to watch television. As I watched different television shows, I would phonetically write down in Korean all the words, phrases, and conversations that I heard at the park and that I would hear again on these shows. Before going to bed, I would practice saying the words and phrases that I jotted in my notebook. Three months of this ritual led me to finally have full conversations at school and in the playground.

My determination to survive among my peers led me to strategize and implement a system to learn a new language. I do acknowledge, however, that this is a sophisticated "system" and one that may not be shared among other young English Language Learners. Because of my own challenges and struggles to "fit in" and survive within a new culture and language, I have become an advocate to preserve the right of English Language Learners and their families to be fairly educated in school.

Although my list of worries about the future education of young children is longer than my son's Christmas list to Santa Claus, my pivotal concern is the overall lack of urgency to equitably educate our young children who are English Language Learners. I have been an urban educator in New York City for almost two decades

M. Hong (✉)
Department of Education, New York, NY, USA
e-mail: minsang91@verizon.net

B. S. Fennimore, A. L. Goodwin (eds.), *Promoting Social Justice for Young Children*, Educating the Young Child 3, DOI 10.1007/978-94-007-0570-8_11,

and the most difficult times I have faced were ironically not the years at the beginning of my new career. Rather, I face the toughest struggle now in my journey as a veteran educator. I have never felt as unsure or anxiety-filled as when I consider how to better prepare our young children to become adults.

Ten years ago, in order to make my voice and my fight for equity more public, I began to work on my doctorate, published my research in the form of books and articles, and became nationally board certified (NBPTS). I ultimately received my doctorate and moved on to teach higher education, but then chose to return to public education in order to work closely with young children on a daily basis. Today, all of these credentials, rich resources, and background knowledge have actually placed me at a disadvantage in my career. It appears that my continuous advocacy for children's rights to learn "naturally" and my fundamental belief that learning is a process and a journey conflict with current systemic changes in education. Luckily, my saving grace is that I am now part of a school community of leaders, educators, and families who strongly believe that without putting children's needs first, we are merely running a factory, not a school.

How can it be that federal legislation designed to promote equity and accountability poses so many serious concerns for educators? "The main problem with NCLB lies not with its core commitments to equity and accountability for results, rather in its failure to establish a realistic theory of action and mechanism for actually achieving these important ends" (Rebell and Wolff 2009 p. 263). I worry that the "failure to establish a realistic theory of action" related to the *No Child Left Behind* Act (NCLB)—will severely "leave" young children behind. Therefore, I wonder what will become of our next generation of citizens, especially our English Language Learners.

I write this chapter not so much as an "expert" in the field, but as a veteran educator of young children and as a mother of a young child. As both, I am extremely concerned about the future of English Language Learners as they invest their lives in a school system that disappoints them more than prepares them to succeed and become productive future citizens. In this chapter, I will discuss the problems that English Language Learners encounter in schools and share strategies and solutions to make learning more purposeful for them. Our challenge is also the ultimate goal: How do we create meaningful contexts in schools for young English Language Learners?

The Problems of English Language Learners

> Since the historic 1954 ruling in *Brown v. Board of Education*, our national goal has been to provide equal educational opportunity to disadvantaged students. Today, under NCLB, we have the additional challenge for producing excellence in academic outcomes for *all* children. For students from non-English-speaking families, however, educational "reform" as we have practiced it, particularly since the NCLB legislation, has had almost no impact; six years into the NCLB reforms, wide achievement gaps persist between these students and their English-only peers. (Garcia 2009, pp. 83–84)

Due to NCLB and the rigidity and implementation of standardized testing, the climate of schools and the ways in which young children have been taught have not been changed dramatically in the past several years. In particular, schooling for *young* children has changed drastically in this time for various reasons. Cuts in funding have eliminated numerous centers and preschools as a way of downsizing programs, and public kindergarten classes have moved from half days to full days and follow more of a first-grade curriculum. In New York City, parents who once opted to keep their young children at home until kindergarten no longer have that choice for fear that once their children enter formal schooling, they may be labeled "at risk" in meeting grade-level standards.

Currently, young children entering schools are inundated with assessments and scripted curricula (Gelberg 2008). In New York City, these assessments are administered in September each year to evaluate the level of each child's reading and writing development (Calkins and Colleagues 2003; NYCDOE 2009a). A child may be labeled as an English Language Learner (ELL) at the start of registration. For instance, for the New York City Department of Education, families who register their children for pre-kindergarten or kindergarten are required to fill out a family/language survey which asks for the dominant language spoken by the child. If a parent indicates that the home language is other than English, the child is automatically labeled an "ESL" student (even if the child can speak the English language). If a parent indicates that the child speaks English at home even though English is not the dominant language, the child is not labeled an English as a Second Language (ESL) student (NYCDOE 2009b). If a child is labeled in the system an "ESL," the school is required to provide ESL services until the child reaches mastery on a statewide exam and thus is no longer considered an English Language Learner (NYSESLAT 2009).

As a result of the passage of NCLB, the United States has become more focused on test scores and many early childhood programs are more concerned with providing an academic program. While schools should incorporate rigorous standards for academic excellence, such a narrow focus on academics can become a restriction that sacrifices what is critical for our young children—access to a social curriculum. Therefore, as a consequence of overemphasizing test scores, schools are no longer emphasizing and, in some cases, eliminating—subjects such as the arts, social studies, science, and play (Nichols et al. 2006). A natural question that must be asked in the face of such changes is: What does this mean for our English Language Learners?

When all involved parties (i.e., families, teachers, school administrators, legislators, higher educators, etc.) neglect the important aspect of meeting the child's social, cultural, and language needs, the achievement gaps widen among English Language Learners (Rebell and Wolff 2009). Schools now focus on whether children are able to identify alphabet letters (lower and upper), letter sounds, concepts about print (CAP), and basic sight words (NYCDOE 2009a). These initial assessments have certainly helped me as an early childhood teacher to get to know the child as a literacy learner and assisted me in determining what he or she has not yet learned or mastered. The unfortunate aspect of administering these assessments so early on to English Language Learners or children who speak two or more languages, however, is that they do not account for: (1) what the child may *already* know about language and literacy (i.e., simple words in English; traditional melodies like the Alphabet song; the letters that make up his or her name; words used to communicate with others; pictures that match the text on the page; etc.), and (2) the fact that most children entering kindergarten are only four and a half or five. Therefore, if a child does not meet grade-level standards or move at a level comparable to a child who is making progress, the English Language Learner is labeled "at risk."

As described earlier in my own personal childhood scenario, I believe that it is critical for all children to learn the English language when living and attending school in the United States. However, it is vital that we do not "push" and impose the learning of a new language and its skills or else it will result in superficial, rather than purposeful, learning. Rather, if schools utilize and incorporate the primary/home language and its resources (i.e., family, cultural activities and experiences, etc.) to immerse and teach into the new language, young children will be able to make meaningful connections as they acquire and learn the new language (Cazden 1988; Rogoff 1990).

If we are to preserve the social life, culture, and language of our English Language Learning students, schools must embrace all English Language Learners' backgrounds and diverse languages and "examine" how the school's "approach to students' linguistic diversity either includes or pushes out our most vulnerable learners" (Christensen 2008, p. 60).

Learning from My Professional Experience

I taught for 15 years in a New York City urban public school that served a high population of Latino children who spoke fluent Spanish. Some of these children were classified as "ESL." Through all those years, I did not know how to speak Spanish, yet I taught hundreds of students who were often looked upon as "deficient" in learning how to read and write in English. Not only did these groups of children learn a new language, but they also excelled, often meeting and exceeding New York State and City standards.

I often reflect back on what made learning a new language so successful for the English Language Learners in my classroom. It was not a particular handbook or curriculum on how to teach English Language Learners. Rather, it was my core belief that every child came to school owning a language he or she can *share* with others. When it comes to acquiring a new language, we often look at how "different" it is from our home language instead of looking at how similar our home language is to other languages (Chomsky 2000). For instance, when I taught my kindergarten children 15 different ways to say "hello" and "thank you" in other languages, they noticed more similarities across languages than differences. As long as a child believes that he or she is able to create and participate in shared experiences with peers, then the work of acquiring a new language is a tangible possibility. Below I share two intimate examples of how English Language Learners are often "misdiagnosed" by the school system in its effort to educate young children who are labeled ESL.

Three years ago, a child with great energy and enthusiasm entered my kindergarten class. Her home language survey indicated that she only spoke Spanish. After meeting Jenny and her mom, it was evident that Spanish was their only language. While she acclimated into my kindergarten room as a typically developing kindergartner, she could not identify the letters and sounds of the alphabet nor read and "respond" to stories in English in any of the assessments that were administered. Although the school labeled Jenny an ESL child, she presented herself as a typical kindergarten student. For instance, she was interested in playing with her peers, and loved the color pink and princesses. Jenny had a crush on our gym teacher, as did all of the girls in class, and wrote letters to me (scribbles and pictures constituted her words) about how she loved her mom.

Although she did not "pass" the ongoing assessments (meet grade-level expectations/benchmarks), it was not because she could not understand the content of the assessment. Rather, she did not fully speak and use the English language at the time of the assessment. Therefore, she was labeled "at risk" by the administration and was added to the "list" for possible holdover.

Another child who comes to mind is a seven-year-old boy named Isaac. He had been attending this particular school for the last three years. Isaac is what I call an English Language Learner who has been severely "misdiagnosed" from the start and labeled "at risk" of meeting grade-level standards for the wrong reasons. Far below grade level, he is receiving special educational services (as noted on his Individualized Education Plan (IEP)—Classification for his disability: Speech and Language Delay). I watched him at work earlier this year and wondered whether he would still be mislabeled or misdiagnosed if he had been given a real opportunity to show what he can do as an English Language Learner. Action plans determined for Isaac when he started kindergarten did not include: respecting his "silent period" (Hong Kingston 1976); watching how he uses his home language with his peers and adults; and connecting with his home language as part of a strategy to immerse him in learning a new language (Rogoff 1990).

After my initial assessment of his reading, I worried about the following aspects of Isaac's literacy development: (1) the lack of vocabulary in his repertoire; (2) his struggle to sound out or recognize basic sight words; (3) the challenges of fluently reading his "independent leveled" books (level D/E—beginning of first grade); and (4) his disconnect from any of the units of study being taught. The possibility of delay could hardly be determined with accuracy at this point when Isaac did not have the opportunity to show what he knew and could do at his pace and within meaningful contexts. While some educators may argue that it is not too late for Isaac, playing "catch-up" is clearly not an option for him. Because he did not properly work through a "series of revelations," it is too late to determine if Isaac is an English Language Learner with typical academic development or an English Language Learner with a delay or disabilities. Tabors (1997) writes:

> Young children must work through a series of revelations: 1) not everyone understands or speaks their language; 2) the people who do not understand and speak their language understand and speak a *different* language; and 3) if they want to communicate with these people, they will need to learn this new and different language. (p. 59)

Young children do not know how to discriminate among those who cannot speak or do not share similar cultural backgrounds. Only by naturally engaging in active experience do they come to realize the kind of learner they are within the context of others. For English Language Learners, acquiring a language different from their home language is a process that they need to sort out for themselves. Learning the English Language is a vital component of every child's repertoire of socialization, schooling, and learning. It is only a concern when English Language Learners are quickly misdiagnosed and inaccurate assumptions are made that interfere with and delay the child's educational experience. If English Language Learners are given ample time to sort out what makes sense in their world of learning a new language, each child will be more likely to encounter successful learning outcomes that beneficially impact on his or her long-term knowledge and social experiences.

Perspectives and Possible Solutions

> There is hardly an oral culture or a predominantly oral culture left in the world today that is not somehow aware of the vast complex of powers forever inaccessible without literacy. This awareness is agony for persons rooted in primary orality, who want literacy passionately but who also know very well that moving into the exciting world of literacy means leaving behind much that is exciting and deeply loved in the earlier oral world. (Ong 1982, pp. 14–15)

Echoing Ong's statement, young English Language Learners and their families are certainly aware that being a part of the school community and its culture requires them to somewhat "leave behind" what is culturally connected to their identity. But why must we accept this as a norm? Young English Language Learners and their families should feel privileged to make decisions that are purposeful and meaningful for their children. If English Language Learners need a "lengthy non-verbal" period (Tabors 1997) to create a system to learn a new language, schools should accept that reality and work within the confines surrounding each English Language Learner.

In summary, we have not made much progress in the history of equitably educating English Language Learners in schools. Society views not speaking the English Language as a deficit, and thus gives up too quickly on the idea that English Language Learners can eventually learn to speak the language. With this stigma comes the idea that learning the English language should be *pushed* on them, rather than focusing on what English Language Learners already can do and know within a new language. With this reluctance or inability to look at what English Language Learners can utilize culturally and linguistically, schools are quick to misdiagnose and label children as deficient and at risk. I cannot say enough that it is incredibly important for English Language Learners to learn English while maintaining their cultural and linguistic identity. Although I believe that everyone has an opportunity and a responsibility to make a difference, I focus in this chapter specifically on what teachers and schools can do via school policy and curriculum to preserve the rights of children who are learning English. Thus, the following are possible approaches and solutions that will support fair and equitable treatment of English Language Learners in schools. The list does not contain any new ideas or unattainable solutions. Rather, these recommendations are premised on the ideology that common sense is often the best solution to a problem.

Schools must stop pressuring English Language Learners and their families to "give up" their home language in order to learn English (Hong 2003). Schools must be prepared to teach English Language Learners by rethinking and reexamining the existing pedagogy (e.g, assessments, curriculum, scripted curriculum, etc.). In teaching English Language Learners, we must look for explicit statements that recognize the diverse nature and range of learners. For instance, how do the curriculum, lesson plans, and assessments explicitly highlight differentiation of all learners? If scripted curricula do not highlight differentiation for English Language Learners, teachers must ask: How do we provide differentiation in our planning for and teaching of English Language Learners? Schools must urge early childhood teachers to think long-term when planning for the school year. While planning social and academic curricula, early childhood teachers must become cognizant of what our young English Language Learners are to face when they reach middle school, high school, and beyond (Levine 2007).

Teachers must look beyond traditional competencies to prepare English Language Learners for academic success (e.g., rote learning, teaching of vocabulary words disconnected from child's experience and relevance, etc.). Rather, early childhood teachers should plan curricula that will give English Language Learners opportunities to use socialization as a tool for learning (Hong and Genishi 2005; Lindfors 1986). Schools and teachers should treat English Language Learners in the same way as they would treat children who are considered to be successful learners. Teachers must relinquish control and "encourage students to construct their own understandings, their own theories about the world…about the language and social relationships" (Genishi 1988, p. 16).

We must develop a sociocultural approach to teaching children. Teachers must adopt a routine of presenting new possibilities and must extend their instruction to tap into other available resources. English Language Learners must be able to understand that they do not have to rely only on schools to learn a new language, but that valuable learning and resources can also include their own familiar cultural and social networks. Thus, they can more easily connect with less familiar learning experiences in school (Moll 1992; Volk 1999).

Recommendations for Research and Implications for Practice

Last year, I enrolled my two-year-old son in a child care program near where we live. My son has predominantly been in the care of his maternal grandparents and learned how to speak Korean when he was one year old. My husband and I decided that we wanted our son to be fluent in both Korean and English. Therefore, while my parents interact and communicate with him in Korean, my husband and I interact with him in English. By 18 months, our son spoke both languages fluently and never struggled with nor became confused by learning the two languages. He is now a confident language user, knowing when to code-switch easily (when he is talking to his grandparents vs. to my husband and me). When he entered school, his teacher told me that my son was learning new English words and was learning to speak more English everyday. I was frankly shocked by this information and investigated this further with my son. When I asked him how he spoke to his teacher in school, he looked at me and simply said, "I talk to her like I talk to Hami [grandma] and Habi [grandpa]." When I asked him why he did not speak to her the way he speaks to me (in English), he again simply replied, "Because I don't want to."

We should all feel empowered to make choices that make sense to us, that will help us reach learning and mastery in ways that are purposeful and connected to who we are. My son has reminded me that language defines who we are and is a part of our identity. Young English Language Learners are far more confident and competent in English than they might appear. For most English Language Learners who enter school and see that others do not share their culture and language, they may in fact feel more comfortable using the language they speak with caregivers and that connects them with their everyday experience. Although my son's teachers did not teach and promote language learning as organically as I would have liked, over time, like my son, other children will also feel comfortable with code-switching from the home language to English and/or transitioning to English. My son, who now exclusively speaks English to his teachers and the school community, made that choice on his own terms and within his own meaningful context.

For future research and classroom practice set in a context of social justice and fair treatment for English Language Learners, we must look at teaching through the lens of equity for *all* children, not only with one child or one group of children in mind. Our goals should include creating a classroom that recognizes the core beliefs of social justice teaching and becoming "miracle workers" who believe and acknowledge that all children have the same rights to be educated. For English Language Learners, learning to speak, listen, read, and write English is not an option; it is a "must." As a nation, we are obligated to ensure that they learn to do this with excellence. If I do not expect a mediocre and inequitable education for my own son, my expectations and vision are the same for my students. Equity is accomplished when English Language Learners are given multiple opportunities to learn English in meaningful contexts.

In reality, our work as teachers in urban schools is incredibly challenging and will likely remain so. I honestly feel that on some days, I too have more excuses than solutions for the problems that persist in our educational system. However, I have stopped feeling sorry for having to face all these challenges and difficulties. Instead, I repeatedly ask myself what will happen to our young English Language Learners who look to us to navigate their learning. How will they know what they are capable of becoming if we do not believe in their potential? Our passivity as teachers will negatively impact how our next generation of citizens thinks and makes decisions.

Despite the inherent challenges in today's education, the fundamental essence of what is important for all of our children is simple. "Teachers should not be held accountable for the outcome of high-stakes test scores, but for *documented progress* of growth over time. It is only through the collaborative process of all those vested in this journey, that successful school experiences for all can be created" (Hong 2003, p. 136).

To create schools and classrooms where English Language Learners feel empowered to see themselves as learners is to create environments where *all* children can have equal access points to lessons, projects, tests, and assessments. This must be the driving goal that inspires us as we teach and learn alongside our children. We must put an end to imposing on our students our preconceived notions that non-English speakers are deficient and at risk. These assumptions are beyond biased—they are harmful in predetermining a child's destiny and what kind of citizen a child will become.

References

Calkins, L. M., & Colleagues. (2003). Units of study for primary writing: A yearlong curriculum (Grades K-2). Portsmouth: Heinemann.

Cazden, C. (1988). *Classroom discourse: The language of teaching and learning.* Portsmouth: Heinemann.

Chomsky, N. (2000). *New horizons in the study of language and mind.* New York: Cambridge University Press.

Christensen, L. (2008). Welcoming all languages. *Educational Leadership, 66*(1), 59–62.

Garcia, E. E. (2009). Educational policy for linguistically and culturally diverse students: Foundation or barrier? In M. A. Rebell & J. R. Wolff (Eds.), *NCLB at the crossroads: Reexamining the federal effort to close the achievement gap* (pp. 83–105). New York: Teachers College Press.

Gelberg, D. (2008). Scripted curriculum: Scourge or salvation? *Educational Leadership, 65*(6), 80–82.

Genishi, C. (1988). Children's language: Learning words from experience. *Young Children, 44*(1), 16–23.

Hong, M. (2003). *Kindergartners' literacy-related talk: Case studies of three English language learners.* Unpublished doctoral dissertation, UMI® Dissertation Services, Ann Arbor, MI.

Hong, M., & Genishi, C. (2005). Voices of English language learners. In L. Diaz-Soto & E. Swadener (Eds.), *Power and voice in research with children* (pp. 165–175). New York: Peter Lang.

Hong Kingston, M. (1976). *The woman warrior.* New York: Vintage Books.

Levine, M. (2007). The essential cognitive backpack. *Educational Leadership, 64*(7), 16–22.

Lindfors, J. (1986). Research currents: English for everyone. *Language Arts, 63*(1), 76–84.

Moll, L. C. (1992). Bilingual classroom studies and community analysis: Some recent trends. *Educational Researcher, 21*(2), 20–24.

New York City Department of Education (NYCDOE). (2009a). Early childhood language assessment system 2. http://Schools.NYC.gov;Accountability/ResourcesforEducators/PeriodicAssessments/ECLAS2andEPAL/default.htm. Accessed 18 Jan 2010.

New York City Department of Education (NYCDOE). (2009b). Home language survey. http://schools.nyc.gov.NR/rdonlyres/3A4AEC4C-14BD-49C4-B2E6-8EDF5D873BE4/74496/NEWDRAFT_12_09_FINAL.PDF. Accessed 18 Jan 2010.

New York State English as a Second Language Achievement Test (NYSESLAT). (2009). Albany: University of the State of New York: State Education Department.

Nichols, S. L., Glass, G. V., & Berliner, D. C. (2006) High-stakes testing and student achievement: Does accountability pressure increase student learning? *Education Policy Analysis Archives, 14*(1), 1–175.

Ong, W. J. (1982). *Orality and literacy: The technologizing of the word.* London: Methuen.

Rebell, M. A., & Wolff, J. R. (2009). *NCLB at the crossroads: Reexamining the federal effort to close the achievement gap*. New York: Teachers College Press.

Rogoff, B. (1990). *Apprenticeship in thinking.* New York: Oxford University Press.

Tabors, P. O. (1997). *One child, two languages.* Baltimore: Paul H. Brookes.

Volk, D. (1999). The teaching and the enjoyment and being together: Sibling teaching in the family of a Puerto Rican kindergartner. *Early Childhood Research Quarterly, 14*(1), 5–34.

Part IV
Educating Professionals for Social Justice Commitments

Chapter 12
Beyond Inclusion: Disability Studies in Early Childhood Teacher Education

Beth A. Ferri and Jessica Bacon

> *The principal distortion, of course, is the institutional practice of special education, which reaffirms the paradigm by removing students for whom it does not work. In effect, this prevents teachers from recognizing anomalies in their paradigms, and thus, ultimately, removes a valuable source of innovation from the system.*
>
> (Skrtic 1991, p. 169)

> *In this sense, disability is a teacher. It disrupts our conventional views of the "normal body," of what it means to educate and be educated, and of what it means to be human. Thus, the trouble of disability, when reconceived as the "disruption of teaching," can become the rich and fertile ground from which we can cultivate the desire to understand ... difference.*
>
> (Michalko 2008, p. 414)

Since its inception, the field of early childhood special education has been steeped in deficit model understandings of disability. From this vantage point, disability has been reduced to a set of problems or deficiencies inherent in individuals' bodies. Entangled with problematic ideologies of racism and classism, disability labels soon became a tool for othering "other people's children" (Delpit 1996), resulting in the over representation of students of color in special education. Recently, however, scholars in Disability Studies in Education have begun the task of troubling these shared histories of exclusion (Ferri and Connor 2006) and rewriting the very text of dis/ability (Kliewer 2006). Central to this work involves questioning taken-for-granted ideas about diversity and difference, as well as our responses to difference in the classroom. As Michalko (2008) explains, "Disability is not merely something to be educated about, thereby contributing to the solution to the trouble of disability" (p. 414). Nor, he argues, should we as educators seek to ignore or homogenize difference. Instead, he argues that disability, like other aspects of diversity, must be embraced as

B. A. Ferri (✉)
Syracuse University, Syracuse, NY, USA
e-mail: baferri@syr.edu

B. S. Fennimore, A. L. Goodwin (eds.), *Promoting Social Justice for Young Children*, Educating the Young Child 3, DOI 10.1007/978-94-007-0570-8_12,

an essential aspect of what it means to be human and what it means to live in a community. As Skrtic (1991) contends, disability should be valued in education because it invites complexity and serves as a "valuable source of innovation" (p. 169).

In this chapter, we will explore what it might mean to embrace a disability studies perspective in early childhood special education. Specifically, we show how this shift would entail: (1) confronting ableism in theory and practice; (2) adopting an ethic of belonging and becoming; and (3) moving beyond inclusion toward honoring disability identity, culture, and politics.

Confronting Ableism in Theory and Practice

From its infancy, the science of child development sought to establish universal stages of normal maturation. Cognitive as well as other aspects of development were thought to develop in a linear and predictable progression. In the various classification systems and developmental models that followed, the unstated normative reference point reflected dominant codes of power (Baker 2002; Harry et al. 1999). In other words, so-called universal parameters of normal development reflected the experiences of the privileged classes and pathologized people who were poor or from non-majority racial and ethnic backgrounds.

Children who did not conform to these norms, according to conventional wisdom, came to be defined as having special needs (Kliewer and Raschke 2002) or as being "at risk" (Mutua 2001). Thus, when children were seen as not keeping up with normative conceptualizations of development or standardized curriculum, they themselves became constituted as abnormal or "at risk." With this new designation, when schools failed to teach all students, these failures were not seen as failures of curriculum, pedagogy, or of the underlying normative assumptions of child development, but of deficits inherent in the bodies and minds of individual learners. Of course, this left schools off the hook for accounting for their own failures to teach an increasingly diverse student population. The designation of "at risk" was also disproportionately applied to children who were poor or from racial minorities. Over time, and drawing legitimacy from the science of psychometric testing, a great deal of power was concentrated in those invested with the ability to define the boundaries between normalcy and abnormalcy (Skrtic 1991).

Drawing from pathology or deficit models of medicine and statistical models of norms borrowed from psychology (Kalyanpur and Harry 1999), a new field of early childhood special education soon emerged to serve these "special" populations (Kliewer and Raschke 2002). This new branch of early childhood education drew on a completely different set of intellectual traditions and discourses from its predecessor. Focusing on a "functional" curriculum, behavior modification, and clinically-focused remedial instruction and therapies, early childhood special education (ECSE) modeled itself after a laboratory or clinic rather than the constructivist, student-centered, and holistic early childhood classrooms, where young children were encouraged to develop through language experience, social interaction, and symbolic play.

Paralleling this same trajectory, segregated classes in public schools arose in the United States during the Progressive Era[1] as a way to deal with social changes brought about by increased urbanization, immigration, and industrialization (Danforth, et al. 2006). Ideas about mental "fitness" were grounded in eugenic ideologies of the time—such that the cognitive abilities of children from racial/ethnic minorities, immigrant backgrounds, and working class families were assumed to be delayed or deficient compared to children from more privileged backgrounds (Baker 2002). Along with the proliferation of special classes, a whole set of professions gained legitimacy during this time, including special education, school psychology, and social work. As Skrtic (1991) argues, however, special education emerges historically to contain general education's failure to teach all students. The host of professions that emerged as a result of the creation of the category of disability share one thing in common—they are all in *need* of "special" needs students to justify their existence. Thus, in this symbiotic relationship, the field must continue to produce the problem it was created to serve.

Unfortunately, many of the ideas that first informed ECSE continue to hold sway. Recently, however, scholars in disability studies have begun to critique traditional developmental models and disability classification systems for creating disability and reinforcing difference in negative ways. By adhering to deficit models of disability, schools function as gatekeepers—sorting out students who are deemed unfit or defective from those who are seen as normal. As stated, such widespread dividing, sorting, and classification practices were informed by eugenic ideologies. Although these practices permeate all aspects of schooling, they are perhaps most pronounced in the early grades, where there is a heightened "production of and hunt for different forms of disability, unreadiness, and at-risk-icity" (Baker 2002, p. 673).

Rather than address hegemonic notions of normalcy or the adverse social, economic, and political factors that give rise to the category of "at risk," when a child's development strays from rigidly defined frameworks, these differences are cast as "deficits" within the child. In what Baker refers to as a "hunt for disability," discourses of risk are codified in social policy, early intervention programs, and educational discourse, working together to pathologize children who are poor or who are from non-dominant backgrounds. Moreover, as Mutua (2001) suggests, the designation of "at risk" is increasingly applied to poor children long before the child even enters school or experiences academic difficulties. The Individuals with Disabilities Education Act (IDEA), further reifies this "hunt for disability" (Baker 2002) under the child find mandate (IDEA 1997). According to this federal mandate, states are required to have in place a system that will "identify, locate, and evaluate" all children with disabilities who reside in the state, (34 C.F.R. §§ 30.125(a)(2)(i)). For very young children, early intervention regulations (34 C.F.R. §§ 303.321) mandate that states must locate and identify children who are simply suspected of having the potential to be diagnosed as disabled. These mandates place all children, but

[1] For a more detailed discussion of the history of special education and ECSE see Danforth et al. (2006); Franklin (1989); Kliewer and Raschke (2002).

particularly those from non-dominant backgrounds, who are subject to what Collins (2003) has called "ability profiling," at risk of being hunted out as disabled.

Once labeled "at risk" the child is then funneled into a host of ever more restrictive programs, such as early intervention services and ECSE (Mutua 2001). As Michalko (2008) explains, early childhood practitioners conceive students with disabilities as having "special" needs—"not the 'ordinary troubles' that all children bring with them into the classroom. They are seen as extraordinary troubles and these troubles require extraordinary solutions such as a degree in special education" (p. 413). Thus, through the use of labels and categories of disability, schools function as a "social sieve," identifying, sorting, and separating children in the guise of better meeting their needs (Mutua 2001, p. 291). Early intervention programs position children as objects to be treated or fixed. Students who are deemed abnormal during early years become the target of individualized interventions, which attempt to "fix" the problem of disability and make such "deviant" children more normal.

Yet, rather than uncritically assuming that it is the child who has "special needs," we might do well to consider whose needs are really served by early childhood special education programs? We would argue, in fact, that it is often the school's (or the general education teacher's) need for "order, calm, routine, and predictability" that is transmogrified as the child's need for special services (Thomas and Glenny 2000, p. 286).

Moreover, although its focus on individual instruction and planning is often believed to be the most *special* aspect of early childhood special education, this focus on individual deficits and individualization can have problematic consequences (Harry et al. 1999; Kliewer and Landis 1999). What is typically meant by the focus on the individual child is that early childhood special education either aims to alter the child or remove them from his/her typically developing peers (Kliewer and Landis 1999). In other words, because the child is seen as so different from his or her typically developing peers, he/she is believed to require any number of specialized instructional programs, thought to require a completely different classroom setting and led by a specially trained professional. Referring to the way that individuals who are seen to *have* problems come to be seen *as* problems, Michalko (2008) calls for us to question the conventional "problem/solution dichotomy" upon which much of early childhood special education has been based.

Underlying this rush to label is a fundamental belief system, grounded in ableist thinking. According to Hehir (2005), ableism involves the uncritical assumption that it is "better for a child to walk than roll, speak than sign, read print than read Braille, spell independently than use a spell-check" (p. 15). When ableism grounds educational practice, teachers' hyperfocus on a child's weaknesses or individual characteristics, rather than changing educational structures and practices, creates unnecessary barriers for children who operate differently. Moreover, as we have seen, these individual characteristics often become the justification for the child's exclusion. When we forget that there is "more than one way to walk, talk, print, read, or write," we create barriers to active and full participation. Yet, settings that are responsive to difference allow a wide range of people to actively participate. As

Hehir states, "where people sign, deafness is not disabling, [likewise] buildings that are ramped allow people who use wheelchairs equal access" (Hehir 2005, p. 45). From a disability studies framework, the goal of education then is to honor different ways of learning and being in the world in ways that ensure equal access and active participation. In the remaining sections of this paper, we will discuss ways that a disability studies orientation would shift the ways we might think about early childhood teacher education.

Adopting an Ethic of Belonging and Becoming

In the title of this chapter we put forth the idea that we need to move beyond inclusion. Although this statement feels a bit premature when so many children with disabilities continue to be excluded in schools, as well as in community and neighborhood settings, we nonetheless want to shift the conversation from merely including students with disabilities to adopting an ethic of belonging and becoming in schools.

Danforth and Gabel (2006) provide several places where we might begin to reformulate early childhood teacher education from this ethic. First, they argue for the need to expand our notions of diversity to include disability. When thought of in this way, disability shifts from being a deficit within an individual to being recognized as an identity—an identity connected to a history of struggle for access. Like other marginalized identities, disability experience encompasses more than simply the experience of social inequality and has thus come to be thought of as a culture. This recognition of disability culture is important because it reminds us that "normalization" is not the goal, nor is erasure of difference (Michalko 2008). Rather, our classrooms must be places where differences are honored and respected—and where teachers and students come to understand that difference, diversity, and heterogeneity *is* normal. This infusion of disability as diversity should permeate all aspects of teacher education, beginning with early childhood.

When disability is seen as expected and inevitable, teachers can then focus on ways to accommodate the inevitable differences students will bring with them. The approach we are advocating is, at its core, a pragmatic stance—involving a shift in focus from individual student differences that we cannot (and perhaps even should not) change, to our own practices, which we most certainly can change. Rather than viewing disability as an individual tragedy or problem in need of a solution, disability becomes a respected way of being in the world (Hehir 2005) and a source of innovation and growth (Skrtic 1991). As Michalko (2008) argues, disability *is* a teacher—it can teach us quite a bit about how to improve our practice, not just for a particular student, but for all learners. The focus must shift from everyone being expected to operate in the same way, to learning from students how they learn best and adjusting our teaching to capitalize on those ways of learning. According to Ware (2006), a goal of such an approach would attempt to shift how teachers perceive, imagine, and think about disabilities—so they can then help their students shift their perceptions too.

Finally, to eliminate ableism in our practices, teachers must be willing to shed conventional meanings of disability as well as the special needs knowledge base of the field (Allan 2006; Kliewer et al. 2004). Teachers must be encouraged to question the very constructs of disability and normalcy, regardless of how natural or obvious these categories have come to seem. Placing less faith in knowing children from a medical or clinical lens means we regard children as always exceeding any of the categories that have been ascribed to them. Knowing children this way means that we put less stock in their labels and more of our focus on the whole child—the child who is always *becoming*, never as static or fixed as the labels used to describe them. A very simple, yet critical step is to first presume that each and every child is competent (Biklen 2005). We view this statement, elegant in its simplicity, as a kind of Hippocratic Oath of inclusive teaching. When you presume competence, you recognize every child as becoming, growing, and learning. You do not ask, "Is this child smart?" rather, "How is this child smart?" You do not question whether a particular child belongs, but rather ask yourself how can I ensure that this child can meaningfully participate?

Honoring Disability Identity, Culture, and Politics

When teachers begin to trouble their taken-for-granted assumptions about dis/ability[2], the next step is to shift from a medical model focus on "fixing" what is wrong with individuals to creating classrooms that are built upon values of "equality, solidarity, and respect" (Danforth and Gabel 2006, p. 1). In many ways, the values espoused by the disability community provide a model for what this kind of classroom community might look like. As we have already stated, a disability studies inspired classroom community would be skeptical of norms. Instead, teachers would encourage students to find creative ways around any obstacle. They would also work to ensure that their classroom structures do not create unnecessary barriers to learning or participation.

Such a classroom would place a high value on interdependence, rather than independence. Like other inclusive methods, interdependence pays dividends to more than the child with a disability. For instance, when students participate in cooperative learning, they are more likely to perceive others as friends and experience a sense of belonging (Johnson and Johnson 2001). Students and teachers alike would be seen as having strengths and weaknesses and the classroom would be a community where all students would feel supported and challenged. Rather than a competitive atmosphere, students would share in each other's successes. Thus, creative adaptation would be encouraged and celebrated.[3]

---

[2] We use a slash in the word dis/ability to signal that both ability and disability are socially constructed categories.

[3] An activity I (Beth) like to do with young children is something I call "40 ways to get there." In this activity I have a class line up on one side of the classroom. One at a time students think of a new way to get across the room. Some walk, some hop, some skip, some roll. All ways of moving are celebrated—so that the child that wheels simply offers one more, equally valid, way of getting from here to there. We finish the game by talking about, regardless of how we do things, the important thing is that we all get to the same place and we all have fun! I do this activity for several

All students and teachers would value diversity and difference as something that contributes to the life of the classroom. For instance, like the move toward multicultural education, teachers would infuse disability content into the curriculum. Curricular examples that include people with disabilities as integral members of the community can also have an important impact on how students perceive disability. It is an obvious fact that early childhood educators have an immense influence on children's perception of diversity and difference (Robinson and Jones-Diaz 1999). Through their daily practices, pedagogy, and curricula, early childhood educators can set the stage for all students to be valued. Students often take their cues from teachers in weighing the pedagogy and curricula, early childhood educators can set the stage for all students to be valued.

Students often take their cues from teachers in weighing the pedagogy and curricula, early childhood educators can set the stage for all students to be valued. Students often take their cues from teachers in weighing the relative status of individual peers. If the teacher welcomes and values a child's contribution to the class, students will often follow this lead. Unfortunately, the opposite can also hold true, where students come to take up negative perceptions held by teachers (Collins 2003).

Finally, as in the oft cited disability mantra, "Nothing about us without us" (Charlton 2000), inclusion must not be seen as a privilege or simply one among a menu of placement options, but as an issue of civil rights. When we teach students about the history of the civil rights movement, we should include the struggles of disabled people for access and accommodation. Disability experience should be incorporated seamlessly into our curricular repertoires, regardless of what we teach.[4] Moreover, just as students with and without disabilities should be taught to advocate for themselves and one another, teacher education candidates should see student advocacy as an integral part of their own professional ethic.

Conclusion

The emphasis of early childhood special education professional development and teacher education often focuses on intervention outcomes and efficient service delivery. Many current texts emphasize applied concerns and consist primarily of

---

reasons. Rather than thinking about disability as a deficit—this person can't move the way that I do—the game puts the focus on the ways that disability often involves creative adaptation. In other words, you and I may get there differently, but we both get there in our own ways. The game also puts no hierarchy on the normal way to get from here to there—all ways are valued equally. It also does not rely on simulation, a practice that although common, is seen as problematic and demeaning by many disabled people, who see them as provoking pity rather than mutual respect. Finally, the game focuses on the end goal of making sure we all get to the same place, regardless of the path we take.

[4] Simple examples might be to include a wheelchair wheel as an example of a circle. Students can learn about various assistive technologies used by students in the class or their families or ways that individuals with disabilities find creative solutions to everyday problems. Again, the focus would be on creative adaptation rather than on deficit or loss.

recommendations for "dealing with" the special needs child who does not follow linear trajectories of "normal" development (Mallory and New 1994). As Brantlinger (2006b) explains in her analysis of "big glossy" textbooks used in many university teacher education programs, rarely is the concept of normalcy or the "normal" child problematized. Children with disabilities are presented as "imperfect," "abnormal", and requiring specialized professional intervention. Although cultural-deficit perspectives are pervasive in these texts and in the field of special education more generally, questions about overrepresentation of racial and ethnic minorities and the structures of school practices are left largely unexamined and unquestioned.

Yet, these perceptions do not arise in a vacuum. Cultural perceptions of disability have accrued slowly over time, and have largely been informed by normalizing discourses from medicine and psychology and reinforced by institutions such as schools. Biological and cognitive sciences have also shaped educational practices. Due to such limited and deficit-based understandings, people with disabilities are often stereotyped as weak, pitiful, passive, dependent, and tragic (Ware 2001; Gilman 1985). As Brantlinger (2006a) argues, disability does not exist outside the social world that constructs it.

By understanding how concepts of normalcy are created and reified, we can see how the parameters of these concepts are socially constructed. The idea that disability is constructed relative to particular social, political, and cultural practices, independent of any individual corporeal or cognitive difference, has been taken up by many social theorists and disability studies scholars (Berube 1996, Bogdan and Knoll 1995; Kalyanpur and Harry 1999; Goode 1992). Instead, following a social model of disability, "obstacles to education, as well as to employment and personal relations [are seen to] exist, not due to inherent incapacities, but due to the physical and attitudinal barriers socially and politically constructed by the environment" (Peters 1991, p. 363).

According to Davis (2006), we must look further into the concept of the norm in order to fully understand the construct of disability. Davis tells us that there are seldom any places in contemporary life where the norm has not been calculated. We constantly compare our own activities against the "average" person. We "rank our intelligence, our cholesterol level, our weight, height, sex drive, bodily dimensions along some conceptual line from subnormal to above average.... Our children are ranked in school and tested to determine where they fit into a normal curve of learning, of intelligence" (p. 3). Of course, the "norm" has thus been constructed, and indeed relies on disability for its very existence. Therefore, it is only against this social idea of normalcy, founded later in human society, that disability categories become pathologized as negative and deviant.

There is much to gain by early childhood educators learning to critique and understand cultural and historical processes of disability. Using a disability studies perspective can help teachers problematize a range of unexamined beliefs, attitudes, and assumptions which work to hinder students with disabilities (Ware 2001; Davis 1995). It is critical that we encourage teachers to question taken-for-granted assumptions about ability and disability, normalcy and abnormalcy. Moreover, because early childhood teachers are often invested with the task of making life-changing decisions about disability referrals, it is thus vital for teachers to question the construction of these categories. Binaries which inform social categories such as race, class, gender, ethnicity, sexuality, and disability continue to powerfully operate in educational practices and policies. Thus, by challenging oppressive ideologies and practices that regardless of intension cause more harm than good (Brantlinger 2006a), more libratory practices informed by an ethic of belonging, can emerge.

References

Allan, J. (2006). Conversations across disability and difference: Teacher education seeking inclusion. In E. A. Brantlinger (Ed.), *Who benefits from special education? Remediating [fixing] other people's children* (pp. 347–362). Mahwah: Erlbaum.

Baker, B. (2002). The hunt for disabilities: The new eugenics and the normalization of school children. *Teachers College Record, 104*(4), 663–703.

Berube, M. (1996). *Life as we know it: A father, a family, and an exceptional child.* New York: Pantheon.

Biklen, D. (2005). *Autism and the myth of the person alone.* New York: New York University Press.

Bogdan, R., & Knoll, J. (1995). The sociology of disability. In E. L. Meyen & T. M. Skrtic (Eds.), *Special education and student disability: An introduction. Traditional, emerging, and alternative perspectives* (4th ed., pp. 609–674). Denver: Love.

Brantlinger, E. A. (2006a). Conclusion: Whose labels? Whose norms? Whose needs? Whose benefits? In E. A. Brantlinger (Ed.), *Who benefits from special education? Remediating [fixing] other people's children* (pp. 233–247). Mahwah: Erlbaum.

Brantlinger, E. A. (2006b). The big glossies: How textbooks structure (special) education. In E. A. Brantlinger (Ed.), *Who benefits from special education? Remediating [fixing] other people's children* (pp. 45–75). Mahwah: Erlbaum.

Charlton, J. (2000). *Nothing about us without us: Disability oppression and empowerment.* Berkeley: University of California Press.

Collins, K. (2003). *Ability profiling and school failure: One child's struggle to be seen as competent.* Mahwah: Erlbaum.

Danforth, S., & Gabel, S. (2006). *Vital questions facing disability studies in education.* New York: Lang.

Danforth, S., Taff, S., & Ferguson, P. M. (2006). Place, profession, and programs in the history of special education curriculum. In E. A. Brantlinger (Ed.), *Who benefits from special education? Remediating [fixing] other people's children* (pp. 1–26). Mahwah: Erlbaum.

Delpit, L. (1996). *Other people's children: Cultural conflict in the classroom.* New York: New.

Davis, L. (1995). *Enforcing normalcy, disability, deafness, and the body.* London: Verso.

Davis, L. (2006). Constructing normalcy: The bell curve, the novel, and the invention of the disabled body in the nineteenth century. In L. Davis (Ed.), *The disability studies reader* (2nd ed., pp. 3–16). New York: Routledge.

Ferri, B., & Conner, D. (2006). *Reading resistance: Discourses of exclusion in desegregation and inclusion debates.* New York: Lang.

Franklin, B. (1989). Progressivism and curriculum differentiation: Special classes in the Atlanta public schools, 1898–1923. *History of Education Quarterly, 29,* 571–593.

Gilman, S. L. (1985). *Difference and pathology: Stereotypes of sexuality, race, and madness.* Ithaca: Cornell University Press.

Goode, D. A. (1992). Who is Bobby? Ideology and method in the discovery of a Down's syndrome person's competence. In P. M. Ferguson, D. L. Ferguson, & S. J. Taylor (Eds.), *Interpreting disability: A qualitative reader* (pp. 197–212). New York: Teachers College Press.

Harry, B., Rueda, R., & Kalyanpur, M. (1999). Cultural reciprocity in sociocultural perspective: Adapting the normalization principle for family collaboration. *Exceptional Children, 66*, 123–136.

Hehir, T. (2005). *New directions in special education: Eliminating ableism in policy and practice.* Cambridge: Harvard Education Press.

Individuals with Disabilities Education Act (IDEA). (1997). 20 U.S.C. § 1400 et seq.

Johnson, D., & Johnson, T. (2001). Relationships between black and white students in intergroup cooperation and competition. *The Journal of Social Psychology, 125*(4), 421–428.

Kalyanpur, M., & Harry, B. (1999). *Culture in special education: Building reciprocal family-professional relationships.* Baltimore: Brookes.

Kliewer, C. (2006). Disability studies and young children: Finding relevance. In S. Danforth & S. L. Gabel (Eds.), *Vital questions facing disability studies in education.* New York: Lang.

Kliewer, C., & Landis, D. (1999). Individualizing literacy instruction for young children with moderate to severe disabilities. *Exceptional Children, 66*, 85–100.

Kliewer, C., & Raschke, D. (2002). Beyond the metaphor of merger: Confronting the moral quagmire of segregation in early childhood special education. *Disability, Culture, & Education, 1*, 41–62.

Kliewer, C., Fitzgerald, F., Meyer-Mork, J., Hartman, P., English-Sand, P., & Raschke, D. (2004). Citizenship for all in the literate community: An ethnography of young children with significant disabilities in inclusive early childhood settings. *Harvard Educational Review, 74*, 373–403.

Mallory, B., & New, R. (1994). *Diversity and developmentally appropriate practices: Challenges for early childhood education.* New York: Teachers College Press.

Michalko, R. (2008). Double trouble: Disability and disability studies in education. In S. L. Gabel & S. Danforth (Eds.), *Disability and the politics of education: An international reader* (pp. 401–415). New York: Lang.

Mutua, K. N. (2001). Policed identities: Children with disabilities. *Educational Studies, 32*(3), 289–300.

Peters, S. (1991). Book reviews [Review of the book *Women with disabilities: Essays in psychology, culture, and politics*]. *Harvard Educational Review, 61*(3), 357–368.

Robinson, K. H., & Jones-Diaz, C. (1999). Doing theory with early childhood educators: Understanding difference and diversity in personal and professional contexts. *Australian Journal of Early Childhood, 24*(4), 33–39.

Skrtic, T. (1991). The special education paradox: Equity as the way to excellence. *Harvard Educational Review, 61*(2), 148–206.

Thomas, G., & Glenny, G. (2000). Emotional and behavioral difficulties: Bogus needs in a false category. *Discourse, 21*(3), 283–298.

Ware, L. (2001). Writing, identity and the other, dare we do disability studies? *Journal of Teacher Education, 52*(2), 107–123.

Ware, L. (2006). Urban educators, disability studies and education: Excavations in schools and society. *International Journal of Inclusive Education, 10*(2–3), 149–168.

Chapter 13
Preparing Teachers of Young Children to be Social Justice-Oriented Educators

Celia Oyler

The elementary inclusive education program in which I teach receives hundreds of applications each year from prospective teachers. In their essays, more than a few applicants write about their love for children. However, when selecting students for our program we look for applicants who acknowledge the struggles teachers may face when working with young children and their families. Although we know that teaching must involve deep caring for children (and their families and communities), we also know that many prospective teachers' own life experiences have not adequately prepared them for the immense challenges inherent in a social justice-oriented approach to early childhood and childhood education. After all, in our public school classrooms are: Children whose basic needs for food, medicine and shelter have been ill-met; children raised within non-traditional family structures; children from families with unconventional religious beliefs or political ideologies; recent immigrants just starting to learn English who may or may not have literacy in their native language/s; children living in the midst of chronic illness (their own or their families'); children who punch and kick others, who cry all day, or who may be too anxious to talk; children who have learned not to trust adults; children who do not make eye contact or use other conventional social cues; and children who have documented disabilities that appear to interfere with their learning.[1] Yet teacher education from a social justice perspective involves much more than only meeting the enormous needs of all these learners; it is also involves planning both curriculum and instruction as well.

[1] Much of this list is from our collaboratively authored program position paper on inclusive education by the faculty of the Teachers College Elementary Inclusive Education Program.

C. Oyler (✉)
Teachers College, Columbia University, New York, NY, USA
e-mail: oyler@tc.edu

B. S. Fennimore, A. L. Goodwin (eds.), *Promoting Social Justice for Young Children,* Educating the Young Child 3, DOI 10.1007/978-94-007-0570-8_13,

What Is Social Justice-Oriented Teacher Education?

Teacher educators who work from a social justice perspective start with a few working assumptions. We understand that classrooms are sites of cultural and social reproduction and therefore cultural and social hierarchies must be carefully examined for the ways inequality and injustice are produced and perpetuated within the curriculum, the classroom, and the school. From this perspective, a "teaching tolerance" or "appreciating diversity," liberal-humanist perspective is insufficient; preservice teachers must graduate from their programs with knowledge about how racism, sexism, ableism, heterosexism, nationalism, linguistic privilege, religious intolerance and class bias operate in schools and society. Furthermore, teachers must have the skills to recognize how these forms of oppression are commonly expressed in the curriculum and in day-to-day school practices. Finally, awareness and critical analysis skills are not sufficient: Teachers must also have the tools to teach differently. This chapter begins with an overview and description of key attributes of social justice-oriented teacher education; continues by outlining some pedagogical approaches and practices; and concludes with some research findings and a theoretical framework for understanding social justice-oriented teacher education.

Definitions

The phrase "social justice" has proliferated in teacher education in recent years and is an umbrella term encompassing a large range of practices and perspectives (Adams et al. 2007), not limited to, but often including: building classroom communities of dialogue across and with difference (Sapon-Shevin 1999); critical multicultural and anti-bias education (Derman-Sparks and Ramsey 2006; Schniedewind and Davidson 2006; Sleeter 2005); culturally relevant pedagogy (Ladson-Billings 1994); culturally responsive and competent teachers (Irvine 2003; Irvine and Armento 2001); anti-racist teaching (Berlak and Moyenda 2001); equity pedagogy (Banks and Banks 1995); anti-oppressive teacher education (Kumashiro 2004); critical literacy practices (Comber 2001; Dozier et al. 2005; Vasquez 2004); disability rights (Charlton 1998; Linton 1998), ableism (Hehir 2002; Oliver 1996), and access to academics for students with disabilities (Kluth et al. 2003).

There are an increasing number of books designed specifically for social justice-oriented teacher education which build upon the missions of: teaching for social change (Darling-Hammond et al. 2002; Oakes and Lipton 2006; Sapon-Shevin 1999); teaching and learning in a diverse world (Nieto 2000; Ramsey 2004); and critical, social justice teacher education (Cochran-Smith 2004; Delpit 1995; Sleeter 2005; Soohoo 2006). In looking for the underlying commonalities across all the analyses and recommendations for social justice-oriented teacher education, two main themes emerge: (1) it is important for teachers to assume a capacity—rather than a deficit—orientation to young children, their families, and their communities; and (2) it is important for teachers to develop knowledge of oppression, a keen eye for inequity as it functions in schools, and a commitment to equity pedagogy.

Teaching a Capacity Approach to Young Children and Their Families

Social justice-oriented teacher educators challenge deficit constructions of young children, their families, and their communities. Instead, we advocate that teachers take up a capacity-oriented viewpoint. Such an orientation is often counter-hegemonic (Whitson 1991) and thus is often simultaneously attractive to some students, and destabilizing to others. Deficit constructions of public school children abound, both inside public schools and also in the popular press. Yet as Fennimore (2000) has noted,

> The language of educational deficiency is neither neutral nor benign…. Students invariably sense the attitudes and feelings of professionals who routinely describe them in terms of deficiency. They also experience serious repercussions from constant public dialogue about their presumed educational or familial inadequacies. (pp. 4–5)

A Capacity Approach to Children with Disabilities

In my program, we begin our challenge to taken-for-granted deficit constructions of children by examining the traditional notion of special education that is built upon a medical model of human difference. The dual system of special education and general education divides children into two categories: normal and abnormal. Thus, disability is viewed as pathology and after a full diagnostic process, a label is attached to the child. Special education professionals then relieve general educators of the responsibility for educating the child and design special, remedial educational services.

In contrast to this deficit-based special education orientation, a capacity-oriented teacher education program (with a critical special education perspective) prepares prospective teachers to carefully assess individual children's learning needs and work with special education partners to collaboratively plan multilevel and accessible curriculum (Oyler 2001). In this way, all children are provided with access to the general education curriculum, no one is banished (Kliewer 1998) from the regular education classroom based on a disability diagnosis, and children and teachers work to build classroom communities inclusive of the full range of human diversities (Sapon-Shevin 2007).

At Risk versus at Promise

The second main focus in helping prospective teachers develop a capacity rather than a deficit orientation to children, their families, and their communities, challenges mainstream notions encoded by the everyday term "underprivileged." When asked to imagine an "underprivileged" child, my preservice teacher education students most often describe a poor, child of color, or a rural white child living in devastating poverty. However, when children are framed in this way, educators are not able to explore the potentially rich "funds of knowledge" (Moll et al. 1992) that children from non-dominant groups bring with them from their homes and communities as they come to school.

As social justice-oriented teacher educators, we understand that school curricula and classroom discourse privilege certain forms of knowledge and certain forms of language. Thus, we aim for prospective teachers to carefully examine the discourses of middle class upbringing, ways of talking and acting that Annette Lareau (2003) has termed, "concerted cultivation." Through concerted cultivation, children learn how to negotiate with institutions and authority figures (such as teachers), and their parents have the confidence and knowledge (cultural capital) to negotiate with teachers on their behalf when necessary. Middle class cultural capital is further evidenced in norm- and criterion-referenced standardized achievement tests and thus reinforcing societal codes of power (Delpit 1995), privileging children who come to school immersed in the discourse and knowledge that has the greatest currency in schools. Therefore, central to any social justice-oriented teacher education program is an introduction for new teachers to the research that demonstrates the discourse and knowledge discontinuities for poor and working class children as they enter school (e.g., Delpit 1995; Heath 1983; Lareau 2003).

For teacher educators, some nuance is required here, as we assist our prospective teachers in developing lesson plans that start with careful assessment of young children's expertise and knowledge. Although by all standardized measures, the young child raised in poverty may score as delayed and deficient—particularly on tasks that tap academically-valued vocabulary—the very same child may be able to independently navigate the public bus system, protect a younger sibling, go to the corner store and bring home a gallon of milk, or get him or herself ready for school every morning. Teachers who develop an assets-based assessment strategy are then able to build upon the competencies of their young students, carefully scaffolding the building blocks to school-valued knowledge, and thus usher their students into the codes of power that circulate in mainstream society. Learning to see the unspoken assumption of white, middle class norms as the basis for many decisions in classroom pedagogy and curriculum, preservice teachers in social justice-oriented programs must be asked, "How can we create spaces where students not only attempt to merge their two worlds of home and school, but are rewarded and validated when they do so?" (Jones 2006, p. 40). We want our graduates to be able to critique deficit constructions of poor children that assert there is a "culture of poverty." Rather than viewing children as at risk, we challenge our students to see children as "at promise" (Swadener and Lubeck 1995). Rather than locating the problem in the individual families and within the individual children, social justice-oriented teacher education aims to develop socio-political understandings of culture, curriculum, and school change.

A Rich Curriculum for Poor Children

A third deficit-oriented perspective that social justice-oriented teacher educators challenge is that poor children require a pedagogy built on direct instruction and "basic skills," while middle class and wealthy children can be educated with a rich, integrated, experiential, inquiry-oriented, project method. Unfortunately, the current accountability movement has resulted in low-income children being subjected to endless rounds of test-prep curricula as desperate school leaders try to increase their achievement test scores. As Feinberg (1997) noted some time ago, "Minority children are more likely than their peers to spend time taking multiple choice standardized tests and to be taught a low-level curriculum designed around those tests—all in the name of 'raising standards,' of course" (p. 92).

As with the previous topic, this issue requires some nuanced instruction with prospective teachers; all too often, beginning teachers tend to conflate integrated, inquiry-oriented, project-based learning with a laissez-faire approach to instruction. Yet this should not be an either/or position. We have to assist our student teachers to learn to engage children in rich pedagogy that integrates strong and direct skills instruction. As Delpit (1995) points out, for poor students of color "to effect change which will allow them to truly progress we must insist on 'skills' *within the context of* critical and creative thinking" (p. 19). Furthermore, students "must be *taught* the codes needed to participate fully in the mainstream of American life, not by being forced to attend to hollow inane, decontextualized subskills, but rather within the context of meaningful endeavors" (Delpit 1995, p. 45).

Looking across these three capacity-oriented, assets-based orientations that problematize deficit constructions of children with disabilities, or poor children, or of families and communities of color, it is easy to notice a particular challenge those of us in teacher education face; that is, when so much of mainstream schooling positions children in deficit ways, we have to work diligently to find appropriate field placements for our students, particularly in urban centers. It is imperative to find individual cooperating teachers with capacity-orientations to children and to find building principals who create and sustain a learning environment that builds upon parents' skills and assets. Such schools certainly exist, and are usually grateful for the support of their local teacher education programs.

Oppression, Inequity, and Equity Pedagogy

The second main stance that unites social justice-oriented versions of teacher education relates to the importance of integrating issues of oppression and inequity into the university curriculum, along with their corollaries: equity pedagogy and multicultural curriculum design. Rather than have a stand-alone course on "diversity" or "teaching for social justice" or "integrating students with disabilities into the curriculum" or "school, society, and equity," it is important that matters of social justice, multicultural curriculum, and equity pedagogy are integrated into foundation courses, methods courses, and field-based courses. This is, of course, no simple task as such content evokes reactions from students. Two preservice teachers from another university provide some insight into this from the student perspective, writing:

> Why did it seem that so many people in our program had difficulty confronting issues of diversity and social change? We came into the program expecting solutions and practical results; we had overlooked some very real issues that arise when individuals raise questions about social justice. Issues of inequality, oppression, and racism often invoke feelings of fear, guilt, helplessness, and anger. These feelings are what make the discussions about social change so difficult; each of us came into the program with different kinds of understandings and experience. (French and Garcia-Lopez 2002, p. xv)

To prepare teachers from a social justice perspective requires sustained attention to racism and other forms of oppression at many levels: institutional, historical, professional, as well as interpersonal, and even intrapersonal. This sustained attention is not only for white students, but is essential for students of color as well (Knight 2002). The students of color in my program make up almost one-third of the student body, yet have major differences in their backgrounds: They come from a wide range of class positions; grew up in different parts of the world (including the suburbs and rural United States); and have different ethnic and cultural roots (including, of course, within similar racial groups). Noting the inherent dangers in assuming a prospective teacher's "minority" status will yield knowledge of culturally relevant teaching practices or even commitments toward social transformation, Carmen Montecinos (1995) reminds us that just because a teacher of color is bicultural (her own home culture and white, dominant culture) we cannot make assumptions about her multicultural understandings. Indeed, some students of color even identify most strongly with white cultural frames, given their own class and educational backgrounds. (This does not mean, of course, that they have not encountered racism.)

Prospective teachers come to teacher education programs having been well educated by their culture(s). They have been studying teaching, schooling, and education in their many years spent in their apprenticeships of observation (Lortie 1975): That is, in their 13+ years of formal schooling they have been inducted into how schools are organized, what counts as knowledge, and the differentiated roles and responsibilities of students and teachers. Most people who become teachers were good students in/of school—otherwise, they would not graduate from high school and do well enough in college to be attending a university-based teacher education program. Part of doing well in school is based on compliance to authority and authoritative knowledge; this involves following teacher directions, memorizing the correct information that appears on the quizzes and tests, completing the homework on time, and getting along reasonably well with one's peers.

Education by one's culture(s) also takes place in out-of-school settings, including recreational sports, religious and community institutions, and popular culture media such as television, the arts, literature, film, magazines, and newspapers. Such cultural sites and artifacts are coded with explicit and implicit assumptions and expectations regarding identity, human relationships, power, status, and behavior. These assumptions and expectations are, of course, continuously contested, negotiated, and shifting. They are also multiple, rather than singular, and are offered and taken up (or rejected) in different time periods and different geographical places.

Finally, prospective teachers' cultural immersions also take place in their homes and local communities. These families and communities enact different cultural practices and logic from other families and other communities, even within shared ethnic, religious, national, linguistic, and class groups. Prospective teachers in their home communities may experience a great range of cross-cultural interactions, thus developing differential cross-cultural capital that they can bring to bear in their future classroom teaching. Yet no matter what the similarities and differences among prospective teachers may be, or what they may accrue from, all teachers arrive at their teacher education programs *speaking their culture*(s).

Practices for Social Justice Teacher Education

Given the limited amount of time teacher educators have with our students, we engage in sustained reflection on what practices are most powerful, most productive, and thus most important to prioritize in our teacher education programs. In this section, I outline two broad pedagogical approaches we use in our program: inquiry and multilevel–multicultural instructional planning.

Inquiry

Many teacher education programs assume an inquiry stance toward learning to teach; this means we view teachers' work as complex problem-solving, involving ongoing collection of assessment information that is used to bridge teachers' instructional decision making about the child, the curriculum, and the world of the future. Such an orientation toward teaching means that as teacher educators, we are less interested in providing a list of "best practices" than we are in helping teachers learn to carefully study children's strengths and needs, the requirements of curriculum mandates, and the knowledge and skills needed in our complex and rapidly changing diverse world.

Critical autobiographical analysis. We begin the year-long course that accompanies student teaching by asking each prospective teacher to write a critical autobiographical analysis paper (Genor and Goodwin 2005). This assignment is predicated on the assumption that "we teach who we are." We tell the students that the purpose of the paper is to look reflectively at their life experiences and see how they will impact their practices as teachers. Specifically, we ask them to deeply analyze their assumptions, values, perspectives, positions, cultural locations, biases, and limitations. They have various levels of support for this project, including various book-length accounts related to disability, inclusion, diversity, social class, and multiculturalism. One of the graduates of our program (Barbara Wang) explained the purpose of the assignment in this way:

> [Our] past experiences are often inescapable, regardless of how often we try to avoid or suppress them. They have shaped who we are and in some cases, who we *do not* want to become. Consciously or unconsciously, how, and in what environment we were raised affects who we are today. And as teachers, this translates into the way we teach and respond to children. (Oyler and the Preservice Inclusion Study Group 2006, p. 33)

As a support for student teachers to start examining their own lives and social locations as a powerful influence on their pedagogy, we lead them through the creation of a genogram (Bahr 1990). In our version of this psychology-derived tool for self-understanding, we ask students to portray their family tree with an emphasis on the messages they received about human difference and diversity. In small and then larger groups, they share these various messages and are asked to pay close attention to not only what was said, but also what was left out of their genogram all together. Where are the silences and gaps? What were on your classmates' genograms that were never mentioned in your own life? What are you prepared to talk about and examine, versus what will be new territory for you here in this program, this year?

Unpacking one's implicit expectations for schooling is central to our process. Taking up the matter of social class for example, we want our students to see how their own social class location affects many of their assumptions and then helps structure their subsequent instructional plans. In this instance, teachers must understand how classroom curriculum can privilege children from a higher social class. It often begins insidiously on the first day of school when supply lists are sent home. In her autobiographical analysis one student teacher made this important link between her own experience and a common classroom routine:

> At the school where I am student teaching all the parents were asked to bring in a long list of supplies. As I read the list I could not help but imagine how my mother would have reacted if I had brought a similar list home. I could not have imagined any other reaction except tears. I grew up poor and a list like that would have caused my mother who already worked two jobs, to feel very isolated in our community. She would have felt pressure and been extremely embarrassed. I would never want to put parents in that position.

For this student teacher, who can use her own childhood experience to critically evaluate the effects of this type of "parental involvement," it is easy to see that she will not expect all families to be able to support the classrooms' school supply needs. However, for teacher educators working from a social justice orientation, we have more work to do on this topic: Next, we need for all the students (many of whom come from privileged backgrounds in my university's case) to understand the impossibility for many poor families to devote even a small portion of their incomes to classroom supplies. A very common middle-class teacher analysis of many poor and working-class parents is, "They don't care about their children." In this case, caring would be demonstrated by sending in a bag full of school supplies, using the list that the teacher sent home on the first day of school.

We must make this student teacher's knowledge and feelings, common knowledge, but not at her expense. Thus, we need pedagogical strategies for the teacher education classroom that protect this woman's dignity and do not position her as the one who has to teach all her classmates to feel poverty. I often write Readers' Theater scripts using many student teachers' writings to accomplish this; I also frequently use anonymous free writes that are put in a pile, reshuffled and read out loud by students sitting in a large circle. This collective sharing of knowledge, life experiences, and perspectives is critical as part of social justice-oriented teacher education.

Child inquiry project. The inquiry process next turns from a self-focus to a child-focus. Over the course of an entire semester, student teachers learn a variety of ways to collect data on children's learning and behavior. We draw upon the work of Almy and Genishi (1979) in *Ways of Studying Children*, and also on the Prospect School Descriptive Review of the Child process (Himley 2000). Throughout the semester student teachers bring in their data (children's work samples, anecdotal records, sociograms, transcriptions of classroom talk, behavior tallies, inventories, etc.) As a class, we work together to note where the student teacher may be making assumptions that may not be supported by the data. Student teachers come to realize how many understandings we make as teachers are filtered through our own lenses, which sometimes tint our vision (Goodwin 2002). We challenge the student teachers to brainstorm other possible conclusions they may draw from the data; a process that is much easier when done with colleagues who have a fresh set of eyes on the child.

When all the data have been collected, the culminating project is for student teachers to engage in a collaborative Descriptive Review in which they present their child to their colleagues and discuss instructional implications. This process is supported by having teachers from schools that formally engage in the Descriptive Review process come and talk with our student teachers about how their schools use this approach. Thus, the data collection processes and the collaborative review of the child are tools that teachers can use throughout their careers if they decide to be teachers who base their instructional decision-making on student assessment data. A recent email from a first-year teacher illustrates these points quite well. Suzanne Budesa—in a much longer email to program faculty—wrote:

> I have pages of typed notes on each child so far. I am constantly taking notes on the things they say and do. I am constantly re-evaluating every move I make, thinking of how I can do better for them, how I can better support them. Who needs putty in the meeting area? Who needs to sit on the bench? What about the kid who is not comfortable on the floor, bench or chair? How do I get around the school rule of no gum so that a child can chew that instead of random pieces of plastic he finds I don't even know where? How do I fit into the schedule families coming in to read stories in their native language when I can't even fit math in every day?… The questions I have for myself and the items on my to do list are endless…. I like that I am striving for a better understanding rather than a simple answer…. Every time I write what I observe and make a guess about what may be going on, yet acknowledge that I could be completely off, I think … of the child inquiry study. I think about the language that is used to describe children and how language is so loaded.

Multilevel–Multicultural Curriculum Planning

Even if all students in all social justice-oriented teacher education programs were to develop nuanced, complex understandings of their biases and assumptions and then carefully study children's learning while taking these cultural understandings and misunderstandings into account, it still would not be sufficient to say they would be prepared to actually *teach* for social justice. Not only do teacher education programs have to help preservice teachers unpack their own social locations and identities, we simultaneously have to help them learn specific and general pedagogical practices. Such practices are themselves quite complex, involving equity pedagogy, a wide range of multicultural resources, and oftentimes sophisticated content knowledge. For early childhood and elementary level teachers, this development has to be conducted not only across categories of diversity (religion, gender, sexual orientation and gender expression, race, class, disability and ability, language and dialect, culture, and national origin), but also across all disciplines and content (including science, mathematics, reading, writing, speaking, the social studies, and in many states art, music, and physical education). At entirely the same time, student teachers must learn to interface with students' families: foster families, adoptive parents, grandparents, stepparents, gay and lesbian parents, siblings acting as parents, homeless parents, and parents incarcerated. We also have to prepare preservice teachers to collaborate with other educators: in co-teaching teams between special education and general education, in grade level curriculum development teams, and with special service providers ranging from social workers to speech pathologists, occupational therapists, and physical therapists.

In our program, having successfully completed the critical autobiographical analysis and child inquiry projects, the second semester of student teaching turns to a focus on curriculum development. Although current forms of teacher-proof curriculum often call for scripted lesson plans, we argue that teachers are curriculum designers, who are responsive to external mandates, but who add to and challenge traditional curriculum that is often devoid of critical multicultural content.

As curriculum is the roadmap of knowledge, it automatically carries with it undercurrents of power. Whose knowledge will be included in the curriculum? Indeed, what knowledge is of most worth (Schubert 1985)? What ways of knowing are privileged? What ways of knowing are termed, "folklore" and "myth" and which stories are rendered as "history"? Of equal importance is learning to teach in ways that equalize status interactions (Cohen and Lotan 1996) in the classroom. But if children are to grow up to be citizens who care about and act to promote the common good—and not just their own personal gain—classroom pedagogy must account for, and seek to undermine, social inequalities.

A significant aspect of preparing teachers to be teachers of all children is helping them learn to teach for the heterogeneity of skill level that exists in all classrooms. An old-fashioned concept was that teachers should "teach to the middle," which of course results in many children being bored and many others being frustrated. Both boredom and frustration can easily lead to classroom management problems, to say nothing of learners' time being wasted. To design multilevel curriculum or accessible pedagogy (Oyler 2001), students must draw upon the learner assessment strategies they learned in the child inquiry process. That is, creating classroom instruction that is accessible begins with strong information on what all children know, what their interests are, and most importantly, how they learn.

To engage in such sophisticated multilevel, critical multicultural curriculum planning requires that teachers draw upon multiple sources, ranging from mandated curriculum guides and standards, to published teacher resource materials, to the collection of alternative sources for multiculturally rich artifacts. In our teacher education program, we help student teachers engage in collaborative curriculum framework design, working in small groups throughout the course of one semester. It is their task to design a multiyear, multilevel curriculum framework that includes the following components: a rationale; the organizational principles related to time and coherence and continuity; goals; subject matter overview; a learning experiences bank; and a plan for assessment of student learning. These curriculum frameworks are then housed electronically and can be utilized by the teachers throughout their years in the classroom.

This experience in collaborative curriculum design is a key piece in preparing to be a social justice-oriented teacher. Underlying this assignment is the understanding that no matter what the mandated curriculum in any one school may be, teachers are always making decisions about what to include, what to emphasize, and what to pass over more lightly. They need to understand that the books and materials they select for units of study and the learning experiences in which they ask children to engage, offer children a window into the world and a mirror into their own lives (Style 1988). These choices are cumulative and can foster knowledge that supports the development of multicultural citizenry or limits it. Likewise, if children are carefully taught to work together across their academic and social skill differences, they will emerge from their schooling experiences more competent to assume the role of democratic participation.

Looking Forward: Sharpening Understanding of Teaching for Social Justice

The work of social justice-oriented teacher education is a time-consuming practice that requires ongoing inquiry and also multilevel and multicultural curriculum design. As a scholar of teacher education, I am also eager to engage in research that investigates the relationship between teacher education and classroom-based practice. Specifically, when teachers leave our programs and express the commitment to teach for social justice, what happens to them? What does their curriculum and instruction look and sound like? What happens to their early commitments once they gain experience in the field?

Accordingly, I organized a doctoral research seminar around the task of studying our elementary preservice graduates' enactments of social justice curriculum in their beginning years of teaching. Fifteen doctoral students enrolled in the course. Each doctoral student conducted a small case-study of a beginning teacher. Our idea was to study the teachers' conceptions and understandings and try to trace with the teachers (through interviews) how they came to hold these understandings. Then, we looked at lessons the teachers taught and examined them for evidence of their conceptions of social justice.

As the course unfolded, it became apparent to me both through the data we collected on the beginning teachers, as well as through our own seminar conversations as researchers, that many of the doctoral students and participating teachers talked about their social justice commitments and knowledge in reference to prior experiences (or lack of experiences) with oppression, marginality, and/or resistance. I began to call this "presenting one's social justice credentials." For many of the beginning teachers, they apologized for not having more well-developed credentials, and frequently expressed tentativeness about what social justice actually meant to them. Others of the doctoral students seemed initially interested in determining if the beginning teachers had "correct" interpretations of social justice. They argued that the research team needed to draw up a definition of social justice curriculum and then use those standards to evaluate how closely these beginning teachers matched our criteria.

As anyone who has engaged in this work could predict, the overall findings from our combined case studies demonstrated a wide range of understandings among the teachers about the meanings and implementations of social justice teaching. Although all the teachers were volunteers who invited us into their classrooms to observe social justice curriculum enactments, and were all graduates of the same program, significant differences in interpretation emerged. Approaches compiled across teachers included definitions of curriculum for social justice as: Teaching children to treat others with respect; building democratic classroom communities; helping children learn about different social identities and cultures; teaching children to believe in themselves and stand up for themselves and others; using equity pedagogy in the classroom; and holding high expectations for academic achievement. Other approaches evidenced a stronger degree of analysis of power and structure; these included: helping students learn about power structures in society and deal with the realities of injustice and fight for justice; engaging in community social action projects; teaching with multiple perspectives on knowledge, society and curriculum; and organizing most instruction around social justice goals.

Thinking theoretically across these distinctions and across the literature on teaching for social justice, leads to an analysis of three distinct orientations toward social justice. This analysis also holds implications on how one works for social change. The first approach is personal, fairly individualistic, and tied to what Sleeter and Grant (2003) term a Human Relations approach to multicultural education. This individual, humanist perspective is expressed by students as "hearing, respecting and celebrating differences." Here, differences accrue to individuals, rather than stem from systematic societal oppression. Material conditions are not recognized or accounted for. This understanding of social justice, then, is fairly optimistic in that if we just all work to understand each other, the world will be a better place.

The second main grouping of social justice definitions that teachers expressed fall into what is known as a "distributive justice" orientation (Gale and Densmore 2000). Stemming from a Rawlsian notion of justice as fairness (Rawls 1971), this position is understood as equality of educational opportunity. From this perspective, people should have equal access to the goods of the society, and distribution of these goods should be proportional. Teachers from this perspective speak of access to knowledge, equity, and inclusivity. From this understanding of social justice, everyone deserves an equal share at the table, but the table itself is not critiqued. That is, the cultural and social norms that have created unjust conditions are not questioned. Instead, efforts to achieve justice are centered on everyone getting what is fair for them personally.

The third, and most rare, orientation that teachers expressed in their definitions of social justice can be understood as evidencing "recognitive justice" (Gale and Densmore 2000). From this perspective, inequities are understood not only as occurring to individuals, but because the individuals are constituted by their membership in marginalized or privileged cultural, socio-economic, racial, ethnic, gendered, and ability groups (Fraser 1997; Gale and Densmore 2000; Makler and Hubbard 2000; Young 1990). From this perspective, teachers must act to change not only who is at the table, and how much each individual is given, but question the table and the food itself. It includes determination to challenge essential power structures and demand that groups of people from the margins (and their allies) displace the center so that it no longer holds (Collins 1990).

We must acknowledge that preparing teachers with a social justice orientation does not in any way guarantee that the graduates themselves will take up the agendas of the teacher educators. (Nor would we really want education to function in such a way as it smacks of indoctrination, rather than transformation of knowledge.) Our preservice teachers may never share our passion and urgency: For school to be a place where justice is both learned and practiced, where racism and economic inequality are confronted, and where children are free of other forms of oppression such as gender conformity and ableism. Yet these matters of oppression and marginality, of identity and solidarity, circulate at all times through the curriculum and through classrooms. We must prepare teachers to know that even if they choose *not* to take up these struggles, they are still teaching political and moral values; that silence supports the status quo. There is no place of neutrality.

References

Adams, M., Bell, L. A., & Griffin, P. (2007). *Teaching for diversity and social justice* (2nd ed.). New York: Routledge.

Almy, M. C., & Genishi, C. (1979). *Ways of studying children: An observation manual for early childhood teachers.* New York: Teachers College Press.

Bahr, K. S. (1990). Student responses to genogram and family chronology. *Family Relations, 39*(3), 243–249.

Banks, C. A., & Banks, J. A. (1995). Equity pedagogy: An essential component of multicultural education. *Theory into Practice, 43*(3), 152–158.

Berlak, A., & Moyenda, S. (2001). *Taking it personally: Racism in the classroom from kindergarten to college*. Philadelphia: Temple University Press.

Charlton, J. I. (1998). *Nothing about us without us: Disability oppression and empowerment.* Berkeley: University of California Press.

Cochran-Smith, M. (2004). *Walking the road: Race, diversity and social justice in teacher education.* New York: Teachers College Press.

Cohen, E. G., & Lotan, R. A. (1996). *Working for equity in heterogeneous classrooms: Sociological theory in practice.* New York: Teachers College Press.

Collins, P. H. (1990). *Black feminist thought: Knowledge, consciousness and the politics of empowerment.* Boston: Unwin Hyman.

Comber, B. (2001). Critical literacies and local action: Teacher knowledge and a "new" research agenda. In B. Comber & A. Simpson (Eds.), *Negotiating critical literacies in classrooms* (pp. 271–282). Mahwah: Erlbaum.

Darling-Hammond, L., French, J., & Garcia-Lopez, S. P. (Eds.). (2002). *Learning to teach for social justice.* New York: Teachers College Press.

Delpit, L. (1995). *Other people's children: Cultural conflict in the classroom.* New York: The New Press.

Derman-Sparks, L., & Ramsey, P. R. (2006). *What if all the kids are white?: Anti-bias, multicultural education with young children and families.* New York: Teachers College Press.

Dozier, C., Johnston, P., & Rogers, R. (2005). *Critical literacy/critical teaching: Tools for preparing responsive teachers.* New York: Teachers College Press.

Feinberg, W. (1997). Educational manifestos and the new fundamentalism. (Review of the book. *The schools we need and why we don't have them*). *Educational Researcher, 26*(8), 27–35.

Fennimore, B. S. (2000). *Talk matters*. New York: Teachers College Press.

Fraser, N. (1997). *Justice interruptus: Critical reflections on the "postsocialist" condition.* New York: Routledge.

French, J., & Garcia-Lopez, S. P. (2002). Preface: We wish we could teach like our eyes can see. In L. Darling-Hammond, J. French, & S. P. Garcia-Lopez (Eds.), *Learning to teach for social justice*. New York: Teachers College Press.

Gale, T., & Densmore, K. (2000). *Just schooling*. Philadephia: Open University Press.

Genor, M., & Goodwin, A. L. (2005). Confronting ourselves: Using autobiographical analysis in teacher education. *The New Educator, 1*(4), 311–331.

Goodwin, A. L. (2002). The case of one child: Making the shift from personal knowledge to professionally informed practice. *Teaching Education, 13*(2), 137–154.

Heath, S. B. (1983). *Ways with words: Language, life, and work in communities and classrooms.* New York: Cambridge University Press.

Hehir, T. (2002). Eliminating ableism in education. *Harvard Educational Review, 72*(1), 1–32.

Himley, M. [with Carini, P.] (2000). *From another angle: Children's strengths and school standards*. New York: Teachers College Press.

Irvine, J. J. (2003). *Educating teachers for diversity: Seeing with a cultural eye.* New York: Teachers College Press.

Irvine, J. J., & Armento, B. A. (2001). *Culturally responsive lesson planning for elementary and middle grades.* Boston: McGraw Hill.

Jones, S. (2006). *Girls, social class & literacy: What teachers can do to make a difference.* Portsmouth: Heinemann.

Kliewer, C. (1998). *Schooling children with Down syndrome: Toward an understanding of possibility.* New York: Teachers College Press.

Kluth, P., Straut, D., & Biklen, D. (2003). *Access to academics for all students: Critical approaches to inclusive curriculum, instruction, and policy.* Mahwah: Erlbaum.

Knight, M. (2002). The intersections of race, class, and gender in the teacher preparation of an African-American social justice educator. *Equity & Excellence in Education, 35*(3), 212–224.

Kumashiro, K. K. (2004). *Against common sense: Teaching and learning toward social justice.* New York: Routledge Falmer.
Ladson-Billings, G. (1994). *The dreamkeepers: Successful teachers of African American children.* San Francisco: Jossey-Bass.
Lareau, A. (2003). *Unequal childhood: Class, race, and family life.* Los Angeles: University of California Press.
Linton, S. (1998). *Claiming disability: Knowledge and identity.* New York: New York University Press.
Lortie, D. (1975). *Schoolteacher: A sociological study.* Chicago: University of Chicago Press.
Makler, A., & Hubbard, R. S. (2000). *Teaching for social justice in the social studies classroom: Millions of intricate moves.* Portsmouth: Heinemann.
Moll, L. C., Amanti, C., Neff, D., & Gonzalez, N. (1992). Funds of knowledge for teaching: Using a qualitative approach to connect homes and classrooms. *Theory Into Practice, 31*(2), 132–141.
Montecinos, C. (1995). Multicultural teacher education for a culturally diverse teaching force. In R. Martin (Ed.), *Practicing what we teach: Confronting diversity in teacher education* (pp. 97–116). Albany: State University of New York Press.
Nieto, S. (2000). *Affirming diversity: The sociopolitical context of multicultural education* (3rd ed.). White Plains: Longman.
Oakes, J., & Lipton, M. (2006). *Teaching to change the world* (3rd ed.). New York: McGraw-Hill.
Oliver, M. (1996). *Understanding disability: From theory to practice.* New York: St. Martin's Press.
Oyler, C. (2001, Spring). Democratic classrooms and accessible instruction. *Democracy and Education, 14*(1), 28–31.
Oyler, C., and the Preservice Inclusion Study Group (2006). *Learning to teach inclusively: Student teachers' classroom inquiries.* Mawah: Erlbaum.
Ramsey, P. G. (2004). *Teaching and learning in a diverse world* (3rd ed.). New York: Teachers College Press.
Rawls, J. (1971). *A theory of justice.* Oxford: Oxford University Press.
Sapon-Shevin, M. (1999). *Because we can change the world: A practical guide to building cooperative, inclusive, classroom communities.* Needham Heights: Allyn & Bacon.
Sapon-Shevin, M. (2007). *Widening the circle: The power of inclusive classrooms.* Boston: Beacon Press.
Schniedewind, N., & Davidson, E. (2006). *Open minds to equality: A sourcebook of activities to affirm diversity and promote equity* (3rd ed.). Milwaukee: Rethinking Schools.
Schubert, W. H. (1985). *Curriculum: Perspective, paradigm, and possibility.* New York: Macmillan.
Sleeter, C. E. (2005). *Unstandardizing curriculum: Multicultural teaching in the standards-based classroom.* New York: Teachers College Press.
Sleeter, C. E., & Grant, C. A. (2003). *Making choices for multicultural education: Five approaches to race, class, and gender.* New York: Wiley.
Soohoo, S. (2006). *Falling leaves: Narratives of otherness.* Cresskill: Hampton.
Style, E. (1988). Curriculum as window and mirror. In *Listening for all voices: Gender balancing the school curriculum.* Proceedings of a conference held at Oak Knoll School, Summit, NJ, pp. 6–12.
Swadener, B. B., & Lubeck, S. (Eds.). (1995). *Children and families at promise: Deconstructing the discourse of risk.* Albany: SUNY University Press.
Vasquez, V. M. (2004). *Negotiating critical literacies with young children.* Mahwah: Erlbaum.
Whitson, T. (1991). Poststructuralist pedagogy as counter-hegemonic practice (Can we find the baby in the bath water?). *Education and Society, 9*(1), 73–86.
Young, I. M. (1990). *Justice and the politics of difference.* Princeton: Princeton University Press.

Chapter 14
Protecting the Rights of All Children: Using What We Know

A. Lin Goodwin

> *Our children are our future decision-makers and leaders. They will set public policy and implement laws. In essence, they will shape the future of not only American society and culture, but that of the world. Thus, we need to raise resilient children who will make good citizens, who care about others, who share our values, and who will make excellent parents.* ***In order for children to thrive, childhood needs to be made a national as well as global priority*** *(emphasis in original).*
>
> (The Campaign for U.S. Ratification of the Convention on the Rights of the Child 2010)

The unanimous adoption of the Convention on the Rights of the Child (CRC) by the U.N. General Assembly on November 1989, followed by its entry into force on September 2, 1990 (Office of the United Nations Commissioner for Human Rights 1996–2007), marked "the beginning of a new way of dealing with children, enshrined now in hard law by the international community" (Verhellen 2006, p. 9). Ratified by 194 nations—the United States alone continues to withhold its endorsement (The Campaign for U.S. Ratification of CRC 2010)—CRC "is the first legally binding international treaty to give universally-recognized norms and standards for the protection and promotion of children's rights in a single text" (United Nations cyberschoolbus 1996–2010). Rather than being perceived "as creatures who are 'not yet' human beings…children are now formally recognized as bearers of human rights" (Verhellen 2006, p. 9, 10).

We began this conversation by invoking the Convention on the Rights of the Child, so it seems fitting to close this set of thoughtful and critical narratives that have laid out pathways to social justice for young children by revisiting this historical decision. As we near the 20th anniversary of the almost wholesale international ratification of CRC, we can see that writing a commitment into law and upholding and enacting law are not always synonymous. The care and protection of children

A. L. Goodwin (✉)
Teachers College, Columbia University, New York, NY, USA
e-mail: goodwin@exchange.tc.columbia.edu

B. S. Fennimore, A. L. Goodwin (eds.), *Promoting Social Justice for Young Children*, Educating the Young Child 3, DOI 10.1007/978-94-007-0570-8_14,

remains a global imperative and their welfare is, if anything, more precarious than ever, as evidenced by the U.N. General Assembly's adoption in 2000 of "two Optional Protocols to the Convention to increase the protection of children from involvement in armed conflicts and from sexual exploitation" (UNICEF 2009).

Each of the chapters in this book has spoken to this global imperative and offered a particular perspective on the rights of young people to a life that is safe, healthy, physically and emotionally secure, inclusive, and meaningful. Each author has also carefully explicated the vulnerabilities children experience, the ways in which youth are put, borrowing Van Hoorn and Levin's (in this volume) poignant use of the phrase, "in harm's way," often *by the very adults* who are supposed to keep them from harm. Each has pointed to actions and inquiries that we all can pursue to protect the youngest among us and advocate for social justice. Collectively, this series of writings is unified by their insistence that children *deserve* and are *worthy* of attention—that they think about, fully experience, and are deeply affected by the "world stew" in which they live and daily observe (Smith and Goodwin 1997). Indeed, rather than being too innocent for the world, children stand witness to and are affected by the world. Lastly, each essay also speaks to the four key principles of CRC that emphasize:

- Non-discrimination
- Best interests of the child
- Right to life, survival, and development
- Views of the child

These "four general principles…express [CRC] philosophy and offer guidance to national programs for putting that philosophy into effect" (United Nations cyberschoolbus 1996–2010). They emerge as relevant themes interwoven throughout this anthology that render visible the multiple meanings, as well as the power, of each principle in the lives of children, and illuminate possible actions adults—parents, families, teachers, educators, citizens—might take to uphold these principles in their struggle to preserve children's rights. Exploring these themes through the various texts and the very words penned by the contributors themselves seems like a fitting way to bookend this volume.

Non-discrimination

So much of the history of non-discrimination in this country is grounded in a deficit perspective that then calls for compensatory actions (Carter and Goodwin 1994). Thus, those seen as "different" are afforded a leg-up, a handout, some special dispensation, so they can become more "normal" or *more like us*. This perspective of non-discrimination leaves the norm undisturbed; those who are privileged by the system continue to enjoy unfair, and unearned, advantages (McIntosh 1988), even while they receive praise for their charity work with the poor "misfits and unfortunates."

Non-discrimination must move beyond simplistic notions of fairness or equal access, or the mere absence of bias. Non-discrimination fundamentally means that "all rights apply to all children without exception" (Amnesty International USA 2010). Within this definition, non-discrimination is much more than missionary work or isolated acts of kindness, more than well-intentioned, but ultimately passive decisions to condemn or refrain from engaging in exclusionary or intolerant acts. Rather, it requires a firm and deliberate resolution to actively resist discriminatory and oppressive behavior and to consciously strive to seek and uphold justice for all children.

Resistance to discriminatory practices could take the form of teachers and other adults who work with children assuming a "capacity—rather than a deficit—orientation to young children, their families, and their communities" (Oyler), or "moving beyond inclusion toward honoring disability identity, culture, and politics" (Ferri and Bacon). Non-discrimination also "conceptualizes multiple cultural practices and legacies as equally worthy and valid…by embracing the humanity of each student and valuing their cultural, social, and linguistic backgrounds" (Souto-Manning), and is embodied in "the core belief that every child [comes] to school owning a language he or she can share with others" (Hong).

Adopting a capacity orientation that embraces and *assumes* everyone's humanity means that we each need to develop "the skills to recognize how these forms of oppression are commonly expressed in the curriculum and in day-to-day school (and everyday living) practices" (Oyler). Otherwise, "the quiet erosion of multicultural education" (DeGaetano) will inevitably continue, spurred on by growing anti-immigrant sentiment, educational policies that prize standardized test achievement over learning, and the pathologizing of difference.

The active and deliberate stances adopted by the authors reveal the subtle, yet immeasurable, distance between *Not Doing* and *Doing*. "Not Doing" may "seek to ignore or homogenize difference," but "Doing" embraces difference "as an essential aspect of what it means to be human" (Ferri and Bacon). "Not Doing" may "create programs and services for children…in need" by assigning them "negative labels and terminology" (DeGaetano); "Doing" requires educators to "advocate for equal educational opportunity for all children…regardless of their personal beliefs" (Rong, Dávila, and Hilburn). "Doing" is the energy, commitment, and choice "to take positive action to promote children's rights" (Amnesty International USA 2010).

Right to Life, Survival, and Development

While the language of CRC highlights the responsibilities of parents and families to care for children, it is clearly the State that has "an obligation to ensure the child's survival and development" (Amnesty International USA 2010). Perhaps it is no surprise then that the U.S. stands alone in the world as the one nation that has failed to ratify CRC, given the conditions under which too many children in this country exist (versus live).

First, there are "damaging disparities in access…to healthcare and nutrition… often based on race, ethnicity, religion, class, and other pretexts for discrimination, oppression, and exploitation" (Sparrow), while "the number of children and youth experiencing episodic and chronic homelessness has risen to 1.35 million" (Polakow). "The poorest segment" of the U.S. population includes "the children of America's most invisible and lowest paid workers"—recent immigrants (Rong, Davila, and Hilburn), who have minimal (or no) access to safe, quality, and affordable child care, a problem that is "particularly acute for single mothers with very young children" (Polakow).

As a consequence of the "social toxicity" (Polakow) that characterizes the communities of America's homeless, poor, and working class poor, the country's youngest citizens are exposed to numerous "structural vulnerabilities" (Rong, Davila, and Hilburn) and "aggressions" (Sparrow), including the "structural violence of war" (Van Hoorn and Levin). With few choices due to severe economic challenges, poor families and their children "tend to live in crime-ridden neighborhoods, and in multi-family living arrangements, and…must also move frequently from place to place" (Rong, Davila, and Hilburn). In the midst of a national war-time context where "parents' multiple deployments is taking a toll on their healthy development, learning, and behavior," children are constantly exposed to "pretend and real violence and war coverage throughout their lifetimes" (Van Hoorn and Levin). The media not only feeds children a steady diet of aggressive behavior perpetrated by adults, leaders, and nations, but also exposes them "to an unprecedented amount of sex, violence, and other messages about social behavior and relationships" (Levin). Children's immersion in and vulnerability to all these "environmental toxins" (Sparrow)—both physical and social—"produces long-lasting damage to social, emotional, cognitive, and physiological health" (Polakow), and teaches "both girls and boys…harmful lessons about femaleness and sexuality…lessons that limit the development of their full potential" (Levin).

In a country as wealthy as the United States, with all manner of technological and scientific advances, excellent health and medical facilities, and world-class educational institutions, it is our national disgrace that so many of our children endure lives of desperate want, despair, and violence, struggle for survival on a daily basis, and experience development that is impeded at best, but more often permanently damaged. There is much public rhetoric about the preciousness of our children, but these lofty platitudes quickly fall away in the face of public and political moralizing of "(poor) adults who are presumed to be lacking in moral value, personal competence, and willingness to work" (Fennimore), deficit views that demonize the poor and "[locate] the 'cause' of poverty within the child" (Sparrow), and sheer unbridled greed. Shamefully, amidst the current financial crisis and contentious quarrels about who *deserves* assistance and who does not, those who occupy "the Other America" (Polakow 2007) are more invisible than ever, excluded from ongoing discussions about government bailouts, tax breaks, and mortgage assistance.

"Every child has the inherent right to life" (Amnesty International USA 2010). To ensure this, or to even move towards this goal, requires "a comprehensive paradigm shift on the way we think about child entitlements" (Fennimore). Children's right to life, survival, and development can be supported by a "peace and social justice perspective [that] leads us to ask why children's welfare ranks so low in the United States compared to children in comparable nations" (Van Hoorn and Levin). Each one of us can agitate against injustice by asking such critical questions, educating ourselves and raising public consciousness, and partnering with "organizations that have been successful at organizing the public to work for change" (Levin). In one voice, the authors all encourage us to use what we already know, to pool our collective power, and press our country, politicians, educators, social systems, and neighbors to follow the example of international peers who have "invested wisely in the well-being of children, integrating early care and pedagogy into national systems that are consistently rated as high quality" (Polakow). There are no easy answers; there certainly are no cheap ones. However, if for nothing but selfish reasons alone, we/the United States must ensure entitlements for poor children and their families because "[all] children's well-being affects all aspects of our lives at the present time and for years to come" (Rong, Davila, and Hilburn).

Best Interests of the Child and Views of the Child

The concept of childhood as a state separate from adulthood is a fairly recent phenomenon, brought about by social changes, advancements in psychology, and shifts in cultural norms (Verhellen 2006).

> Thus gradually children became a *separate* group with *separate* characteristics, of whom *specific* behaviour (sic) was expected.... In this way children were gradually put in the *position of not yet being*, not yet knowing, not yet able to therefore not yet able to express themselves, not yet responsible.... Children ended up in limbo, they were put on hold. (Verhellen 2006, p. 13, 16)

Without political or economic power and therefore the ability to affect society or social decisions, children must rely upon the care and sponsorship of adults. They have come to be seen as incapable of complex or critical thinking, too innocent for the harsh ways of the world, and lacking the sophistication to make thoughtful and rational choices. In keeping with these perceptions, children's views are easily and typically "put on hold," while decisions are made on their behalf, by more knowledgeable elders, presumably with their interests in mind. Inevitably, the norm is for children's best interests to be forwarded by (more powerful) others, and for their views to be heard in the context of adult indulgence or permission. Children's interests and children's views seem inextricably tied, making it prudent to examine them together.

According to the articles of CRC, "all actions concerning the child shall take full account of his or her best interests," and each child's "right to express his or her opinion freely and to have that opinion taken into account" or to "obtain information, and make ideas or information known," are guaranteed (Amnesty International USA 2010). Yet, these rights are consistently violated, oftentimes with the best of intentions. Children are seldom consulted about events and actions that affect them deeply, shape their realities and world view, and can harm them indelibly. Yet, whether adults either persist in the mythology of children's innocence that requires shielding them from the world, or persistently exploit children's "innocence" as a saleable commodity or an opportunistic avenue for the sale of commodities, children stand fully present in the world, reading and "enact[ing] the world" (Genishi, Dyson, and Russo), listening, watching, and learning in ways that can sometimes have detrimental consequences, for them, and ultimately for all of us.

The authors describe many adult decisions that make little sense for children and certainly cannot have their best interests in mind. Special mention must be reserved for No Child Left Behind (NCLB), "federal legislation designed to promote equity and accountability" that has perversely "inundated [children] with assessments and scripted curricula" (Hong), "narrowed the curriculum and diminished instructional time in the arts and humanities, especially for children living in poverty" (Purnell). While "children's voices carry echoes of their sociocultural histories, [and] their family circumstances" (Genishi, Dyson, and Russo), "mass-produced curriculum materials and assessments threatens to depersonalize education, and to devalue the role of local culture and community in the lives of young children" (Purnell). Instead of "offering choices that make sense to them," young children find themselves in classrooms "so filled with academic lessons" (Genishi, Dyson, and Russo), that the very essence of each child, their very identity, is suppressed.

Embedded within the idea of honoring children's views and interests is the issue of identity and naming. Adults ignore children's views and interests when they label and categorize children, assigning them to static conditions that identify them as broken. Immigrant children are defined as deficient because of their lack of fluency in English, but there is minimal attempt to learn about or value "what the child may *already* know about language and literacy" in English or her home language (Hong). Learners who do not meet "so-called universal parameters of normal development" come to be labeled "as abnormal or at risk" (Ferri and Bacon), even while definitions of "normal" are socially constructed notions that are arbitrarily created and invariably favor the dominant group in society. Even the very name, "heavily laden with cultural ideals and norms," bestowed by culturally and linguistically diverse families or parents on their children, is frequently devalued by "institutional discourses" that support "assimilationist practices" (Souto-Manning) which result in children being re-named as "Anglo" for/at the convenience of their teacher.

What would it mean for children's interests and views to be at the center of curriculum and instruction, social services, and government policy? "A very simple, yet critical step is to first presume that each and every child is competent…[to] recognize every child as becoming, growing, and learning" (Ferri and Bacon). We would follow children's lead by "expanding curricular spaces to incorporate the many forms of play that children embrace without instruction" (Genishi, Dyson, and Russo), and ensure that all children can "feel empowered to make choices that make sense to [them], that will help [them] reach learning and mastery in ways that are purposeful and connected to who [they] are" (Hong). Adults, whether teachers, caregivers, doctors, social workers, or politicians, would "recognize children's unique gifts and strengths and build upon them" (Souto-Manning), and every child would enjoy—come to expect—"a threshold of social care under which no child in the nation will ever be permitted to fall" (Fennimore).

Conclusions

The authors in this volume have eloquently laid out the issues, the barriers that get in the way of protecting children's rights and achieving social justice for children. They have offered ideas, strategies to adopt, programs to access, and they have each pointed to the future, the possibilities of a brighter, more positive, and inclusive tomorrow. We have a lot of work to do to meet the goals of the Convention on the Rights of the Child; we have a lot we must do before every child in our rich and resource-full country can be *entitled* to a basic level of care and social support. That is, care and support that are not simply adequate but comprehensive, coordinated, and automatically available and generously provided. This is necessary to achieve because we are concerned about our own survival, because it is the humane thing to do, because it is the right thing to do by all children—ours and other people's.

References

Amnesty International USA. (2010). http://www.amnestyusa.org/children/crn_crc.html. Accessed 25 Feb 2010.

Carter, R., & Goodwin, A. L. (1994). Racial identity and education. In L. Darling-Hammond (Ed.), *Review of research in education* (Vol. 20, pp. 291–336). Washington: American Educational Research Association.

McIntosh, P. (1988). *White privilege: Unpacking the invisible knapsack.* Wellesley: Wellesley College Center for Research on Women.

Office of the United Nations Commissioner for Human Rights. (1996–2007). Convention on the Rights of the Child. http://www2.ohchr.org/english/law/crc.html. Accessed 20 Feb 2010.

Polakow, V. (2007). *Who cares for our children? The child care crisis in the other America.* New York: Teachers College Press.

Smith, Y., & Goodwin, A. L. (1997). The democratic, child-centered classroom: Provisioning for a vision. In A. L. Goodwin (Ed.), *Assessment for equity and inclusion: Embracing all our children* (pp. 101–120). New York: Routledge.

The Campaign for U.S. Ratification of the Convention on the Rights of the Child (CRC). (2010). http://childrightscampaign.org/crcindex.php. Accessed 20 Feb 2010.

UNICEF. (2009). Optional protocols to the Convention on the Rights of the Child (23 Nov 2009). http://www.unicef.org/crc/index_protocols.html. Accessed 2 March 2010.

United Nations cyberschoolbus. (1996–2010). http://www.cyberschoolbus.un.org/treaties/child.asp. Accessed 20 Feb 2010.

Verhellen, E. (2006). *Convention of the Rights of the Child* (4th ed.). Antwerp: Garant.

Author Index

B. S. Fennimore, A. L. Goodwin (eds.), *Promoting Social Justice for Young Children*,
Educating the Young Child 3, DOI 10.1007/978-94-007-0570-8,

Subject Index

B. S. Fennimore, A. L. Goodwin (eds.), *Promoting Social Justice for Young Children*, Educating the Young Child 3, DOI 10.1007/978-94-007-0570-8,

Kolibri 360 GmbH
Ferdinand-Jühlke-Straße 7
99095 Erfurt, Deutschland
produktsicherheit@kolibri360.de